Plin[...]
Lette[...]

| DATE DUE | | | |
|---|---|---|---|
| | | | |
| | | | |
| | | | |
| | | | |
| | | | |
| | | | |

# PLINY

## LETTERS

## II

# PLINY

## LETTERS

WITH AN ENGLISH TRANSLATION BY
### WILLIAM MELMOTH

REVISED BY
### W. M. L. HUTCHINSON

IN TWO VOLUMES
## II

CAMBRIDGE, MASSACHUSETTS
## HARVARD UNIVERSITY PRESS
LONDON
## WILLIAM HEINEMANN LTD
MCMLVIII

*First printed 1915*
*Reprinted 1924, 1927, 1935, 1947, 1953, 1958*

*Printed in Great Britain*

# CONTENTS

# THE LETTERS OF PLINY

## BOOK VII

# C. PLINII CAECILII SECUNDI EPISTULARUM

## LIBER SEPTIMUS

### I

#### C. Plinius Gemino Suo S.

Terret me haec tua tam pertinax valetudo et quamquam te temperantissimum noverim, vereor tamen, ne quid illi etiam in mores tuos liceat. Proinde moneo, patienter resistas; hoc laudabile, hoc salutare. Admittit humana natura, quod suadeo. Ipse certe sic agere sanus cum meis soleo: 'Spero quidem, si forte in adversam valetudinem incidero, nihil me desideraturum vel pudore vel paenitentia dignum; si tamen superaverit morbus, denuntio, ne quid mihi detur, nisi permittentibus medicis, sciatisque, si dederitis, ita vindicaturum, ut solent alii, quae negantur.'

Quin etiam, cum perustus ardentissima febre tandem remissus unctusque acciperem a medico

# THE LETTERS OF PLINY

## BOOK VII

### I

#### To Geminus

THIS obstinate distemper which hangs upon you,
greatly alarms me ; and though I know how extremely
temperate you are, yet I am afraid your disease
should get the better of your habits. Let me
counsel you then to offer a steady resistance ; this
is the praiseworthy, this is the salutary course.
There is nothing beyond the power of human
nature in what I recommend. I myself, at least,
while in ordinary health, make a practice of giving
my household the following directions. "I hope,
that should I be attacked with any disorder, I shall
desire nothing of which I either ought to be
ashamed, or have reason to repent ; however, if my
distemper should get the upper hand, give me
nothing, I charge you, but by the consent of my
physicians ; be assured that if you do, I shall punish
your compliance, as much as another man would
your refusal."

I had once, in fact, a most violent fever ; when
the fit was a little abated, and I had been anointed,

3

potionem, porrexi manum, utque tangeret, dixi
admotumque iam labris poculum reddidi. Postea
cum vicesimo valetudinis die balineo praepararer
mussantesque medicos repente vidissem, causam
requisivi. Responderunt posse me tuto lavari,
non tamen omnino sine aliqua suspicione. 'Quid'
inquam 'necesse est?' atque ita spe balinei, cui
iam videbar inferri, placide leniterque dimissa ad
abstinentiam rursus non secus ac modo ad balineum
animum vultumque composui. Quae tibi scripsi,
primum ut te non sine exemplo monerem, deinde ut
in posterum ipse ad eandem temperantiam adstrin-
gerer, cum me hac epistula quasi pignore obligassem.
Vale.

## II

### C. Plinius Iusto Suo S.

Quem ad modum congruit, ut simul et adfirmes te
adsiduis occupationibus impediri et scripta nostra
desideres, quae vix ab otiosis impetrare aliquid
perituri temporis possunt? Patiar ergo aestatem
inquietam vobis exercitamque transcurrere et hieme
demum, cum credibile erit noctibus saltem vacare
te posse, quaeram, quid potissimum ex nugis meis
tibi exhibeam. Interim abunde est, si epistulae non
sunt molestae; sunt autem et ideo breviores erunt.
Vale.

my physician offered me something to drink; I put
out my hand, bade him feel my pulse, and returned
the cup, though it was just at my lips. Afterwards,
when I was preparing to go into the bath, twenty
days from the first attack of my illness, perceiving
on a sudden the physicians whispering together, I
inquired what they were saying. They replied, I
might possibly bathe with safety, however, they were
not without some suspicion of hazard. "What
need," said I, "of doing it at all?" And thus,
with great complacency, I gave up the expected
pleasure of bathing, and abstained from the bath
with the same inward and outward composure I was
going to enter it. I mention this, not only in order
to enforce my advice by example, but also that this
letter may be a sort of pledge binding me to
persevere in the same abstinence for the future.
Farewell.

## II

### To Justus

Are you not inconsistent with yourself, when you
assure me you have no intermission from business,
and yet at the same time express an earnest desire
to see my works; upon which even the idle will
scarce bestow some of their useless hours? I will
not then break in upon your affairs during this busy
summer season; but when the return of winter shall
make it reasonable to suppose that your evenings,
at least, may be disengaged, I will look over my
trifles for something worth showing you. In the
meanwhile, I shall be well satisfied, if my letters are
not troublesome, as I suspect they are, and therefore
shorten them. Farewell.

## III

### C. Plinius Praesenti Suo S.

Tantane perseverantia tu modo in Lucania, modo
in Campania? 'Ipse enim' inquis 'Lucanus, uxor
Campana.' Iusta causa longioris absentiae, non
perpetuae tamen. Quin ergo aliquando in urbem
redis? ubi dignitas, honor, amicitiae tam superiores
quam minores. Quousque regnabis? quousque
vigilabis, cum voles? dormies, quamdiu voles?
quousque calcei nusquam, toga feriata, liber totus
dies?

Tempus est te revisere molestias nostras vel ob
hoc solum, ne voluptates istae satietate languescant.
Saluta paulisper, quo sit tibi iucundius salutari, terere
in hac turba, ut te solitudo delectet. Sed quid
imprudens, quem evocare[1] conor, retardo? Fortasse
enim his ipsis admoneris, ut te magis ac magis otio
involvas; quod ego non abrumpi, sed intermitti volo.
Ut enim si cenam tibi facerem, dulcibus cibis acres
acutosque miscerem, ut obtusus illis et oblitus stoma-

---

[1] evocare *Bipons, Müller,* revocare *K.*

6

## III

### To Praesens

ARE you determined then to pass your whole
time between Lucania and Campania? Your answer,
I suppose, will be, that the former is your native
country; and the latter that of your wife. This, I
admit, may justify a long absence, but I cannot
allow it as a reason for a perpetual one. Why not
then at last return to Rome, that theatre of dignities,
preferment, and friendships alike of the superior
and lower sort? Are you obstinately bent to live
despotically, and sleep and rise when you think
proper? Will you for ever go unshod, wear full
dress only on holy days, and spend your whole day
as you please?

It is time, however, you should revisit our troubled
scene, were it only that your rural pleasures may
not grow languid from a surfeit. Make your bow
at one or two levees of the great, that you may
enjoy the return of the compliment with more
satisfaction; and mix in our crowd, that you may
have a stronger relish for the charms of solitude.
But am I not inadvertently retarding the friend I
would rouse? It is these very circumstances,
perhaps, that counsel you every day more and more
to wrap yourself up in retirement. All however I
mean to persuade you to, is only to intermit, not
renounce your repose. As, if I were giving you
a dinner, I would blend dishes of a sharper taste
with those of a luscious kind, in order to raise the
edge of your palate by the one, which had been

7

chus his excitaretur, ita nunc hortor, ut iucundissimum genus vitae non nullis interdum quasi acrioribus
condias. Vale.

## IV

### C. Plinius Pontio Allifano[1] Suo S.

Ais legisse te hendecasyllabos meos ; requiris etiam,
quem ad modum coeperim scribere, homo, ut tibi
videor, severus, ut ipse fateor, non ineptus. Numquam a poëtice (altius enim repetam) alienus fui ;
quin etiam quattuordecim natus annos Graecam
tragoediam scripsi. ' Qualem ? ' inquis. Nescio ; tra-
goedia vocabatur. Mox, cum e militia rediens in
Icaria insula ventis detinerer, Latinos elegos in illud
ipsum mare ipsamque insulam feci. Expertus sum
me aliquando et heroo, hendecasyllabis nunc primum,
quorum hic natalis, haec causa est.

Legebantur in Laurentino mihi libri Asini Galli de
comparatione patris et Ciceronis. Incidit epigramma
Ciceronis in Tironem suum. Dein, cum meridie (erat
enim aestas) dormiturus me recepissem, nec obreperet
somnus, coepi reputare, maximos oratores hoc studii

[1] Allifano *add. Müller.*

---

[a] See iv. 14, note.

[b] Not Pliny's correspondent (ii. 17, iv. 17, viii. 20), but the
son of the famous orator Pollio, and possibly the child whose
birth Virgil celebrated in his Fourth Eclogue.

[c] Cicero's well-known character makes it certain that this
epigram is spurious. Tiro was his freedman and trusted
friend.

flattened and overloaded by the other; so I now advise you to season your agreeable mode of living from time to time with some condiments of a sharper relish. Farewell.

## IV

### To Pontius Allifanus

You have read, you tell me, my hendecasyllabic [a] poems, and are desirous to know how it happened that a man of my gravity (as you are pleased to call me, as I will say for myself, not a trifler) could fall into this way of composition. To take the account then a good way backwards, I must acquaint you that I had always an inclination to poetry, insomuch that, when I was fourteen years of age, I composed a Tragedy in Greek. If you should ask me what sort of one, I protest I don't know; all I can say is, that it was called a Tragedy. Some time afterwards, on my return from the army, being detained in the Island of Icaria by contrary winds, I composed some Latin elegiac verses upon that island and its sea. I have sometimes tried my hand at Epic poetry; but these are the first hendecasyllabic poems I ever composed; to which the following accident gave birth.

The treatise of Asinius Gallus [b] was read to me one day at my Laurentine villa, wherein he draws a comparison between his father and Cicero; and there I met with an epigram of Tully's on his favourite Tiro. [c] Upon retiring to take my afternoon's nap (for it was summer time), and not being visited by sleep, I began to reflect that the greatest orators have been fond of this kind of composition, and

genus et in oblectationibus habuisse et in laude
posuisse. Intendi animum contraque opinionem
meam post longam desuetudinem perquam exiguo
temporis momento id ipsum, quod me ad scribendum
sollicitaverat, his versibus exaravi:

Cum libros Galli legerem, quibus ille parenti
ausus de Cicerone dare est palmamque decusque,
lascivum inveni lusum Ciceronis et illo
spectandum ingenio, quo seria condidit et quo
humanis salibus multo varioque lepore
magnorum ostendit mentes gaudere virorum.
Nam queritur, quod fraude mala frustratus amantem
paucula cenato sibi debita savia Tiro
tempore nocturno subtraxerit. His ego lectis
'cur post haec,' inquam, 'nostros celamus amores
nullumque in medium timidi damus atque fatemur
Tironisque dolos, Tironis nosse fugaces
blanditias et furta novas addentia flammas?'

Transii ad elegos; hos quoque non minus celeriter
explicui; addidi alios facilitate corruptus. Deinde
in urbem reversus sodalibus legi. Probaverunt.
Deinde plura metra, si quid otii, maxime in itinere
temptavi. Postremo placuit exemplo multorum unum
separatim hendecasyllaborum volumen absolvere, nec
paenitet. Legitur, describitur, cantatur etiam et a

valued themselves upon it. I tried therefore what
I could do in this way; and though I had long disused
myself to things of this nature, I jotted down in
almost no time the following lines upon the subject
which had prompted me to compose :—

" When Gallus I read, who pretends that his sire
  Had far more than Tully poetical fire,
  The wisest of men, I perceived, held it fit
  To temper his wisdom with love and with wit ;
  For Tully, grave Tully, in amorous strains,
  Of the frauds of his paramour Tiro complains,
  That faithless to love, and to pleasure untrue,
  From his promis'd embrace the arch wanton with-
    drew.
  Then said I to my heart, Why shouldst thou
    conceal
  The sweetest of passions, the love which you feel ?
  Yes, fly wanton Muse, and proclaim it around,
  Thy Pliny has lov'd, and his Tiro has found ;
  The coy one so artful, who sweetly denies,
  And from the soft flame, but to heighten it, flies."

From this I turned to an elegiac poem, which I
finished as rapidly ; and yielding to the temptation
of facility, I added other verses. At my return to
Rome I read my performances to some of my friends,
who were pleased to approve of them. Afterwards
whenever I had leisure, and particularly when I
travelled, I made attempts in several metres. At
length I determined, after the example of many
others, to complete for publication a separate volume
of erotic poems ; and I have no reason to repent of
my resolution. They are much the mode, copies are in
everybody's hands ; they are even sung to harp or lyre

Graecis quoque, quos Latine huius libelli amor docuit,
nunc cithara, nunc lyra personatur.

Sed quid ego tam gloriose? Quamquam poëtis
furere concessum est; et tamen non de meo, sed
de aliorum iudicio loquor; qui sive iudicant sive
errant, me delectat.[1] Unum precor, ut posteri
quoque aut errent similiter aut iudicent. Vale.

## V

### C. PLINIUS CALPURNIAE SUAE S.

INCREDIBILE est, quanto desiderio tui tenear. In
causa amor primum, deinde quod non consuevimus
abesse. Inde est, quod magnam partem noctium in
imagine tua vigil exigo, inde, quod interdiu, quibus
horis te visere solebam, ad diaetam tuam ipsi me, ut
verissime dicitur, pedes ducunt; quod denique aeger
et maestus ac similis excluso, vacuo limine recedo.
Unum tempus his tormentis caret, quo in foro et
amicorum litibus conteror. Aestima tu, quae vita
mea sit, cui requies in labore, in miseria curisque
solacium. Vale.

## VI

### C. PLINIUS MACRINO SUO S.

RARA et notabilis res Vareno contigit, sit licet adhuc
dubia. Bithyni accusationem eius ut temere inchoa-

---

[1] delectat *M, Müller,* delectant *rell.*

accompaniments, and by the Greeks, too, who have been learning Latin out of fondness for my little book.

But what will you think of this boasting? Remember, however, poets have the privilege of raving. Still, I am not giving you my own judgement, but that of others, which, be it just or mistaken I am much pleased with. My one prayer is, that posterity may endorse their judgement, or their mistake, whichever it be. Farewell.

## V

### To Calpurnia

It is incredible how I miss you; such is the tenderness of my affection for you, and so unaccustomed are we to a separation! I lie awake the greatest part of the night in conjuring up your image, and by day (to use a very common, but very true expression) my feet carry me of their own accord to your apartment, at those hours I used to visit you; but not finding you there, I return with as much sorrow and disappointment as an excluded lover. The only intermission my torment knows, is when I am engaged at the bar, and in the causes of my friends. Judge how wretched must *his* life be, who finds no repose but in toil, no consolation but in dealing with distress and anxieties. Farewell.

## VI

### To Macrinus

A very singular and remarkable accident has happened to Varenus,[a] the consequence of which is yet in suspense. The Bithynians, it is reported,

[a] v. 20.

tam omisisse narrantur. Narrantur dico? adest provinciae legatus, attulit decretum concilii ad Caesarem,
attulit ad multos principes viros, attulit etiam ad nos
Vareni advocatos.  Perstat tamen idem ille Magnus:
quin etiam Nigrinum, optimum virum, pertinacissime
exercet.  Per hunc a consulibus postulabat, ut Varenus exhibere rationes cogeretur.

Adsistebam Vareno iam tantum ut amicus et tacere
decreveram.  Nihil enim tam contrarium, quam si
advocatus a senatu datus defenderem ut reum, cui
opus esset, ne reus videretur.  Cum tamen finita
postulatione Nigrini consules ad me oculos retulissent,
'Scietis,' inquam, 'constare nobis silentii nostri
rationem, cum veros legatos provinciae audieritis.'
Contra Nigrinus: 'Ad quem missi sunt?' Ego: 'Ad
me quoque; habeo decretum provinciae.' Rursus ille:
'Potest tibi liquere.' Ad hoc ego: 'Si tibi ex
diverso liquet, potest et mihi, quod est melius,
liquere.' [1]  Tum legatus Polyaenus causas abolitae
accusationis exposuit postulavitque, ne cognitioni

---

[1] quod est melius liquere *Bipons*, *K* (*ex Mα*), q. e. mel.
causa liqueret (loquetur) legatus *Dpr*, q. e. mel. †causa
liquere *Müller*, (q. e. mei iuris) causa liquere *Kukula*.

have dropped their prosecution of him, as an ill-advised proceeding. *Reported*, I said; but 'tis no matter of hearsay. A delegate from that province is arrived, who has brought with him a decree of their assembly; copies of which he has delivered to Caesar, to several of the principal persons in Rome, and to us the advocates for Varenus. Magnus, however, whom I mentioned in my last letter to you, persists in his prosecution; and, moreover, is incessantly teasing the worthy Nigrinus. This excellent person, acting as his counsel, was making application to the consuls, that Varenus might be compelled to produce his accounts.

As at this stage I attended Varenus merely as a friend, I had determined to be silent. I thought it highly prejudicial for me, who was appointed his counsel by the senate, to attempt to defend him as a person accused, when it was his business to make it appear that there was actually no charge subsisting against him. However, when Nigrinus had finished his application, the consuls turning their eyes upon me, I rose up, and, when they should hear, I said, what the real delegates from the province had to say, they would be sensible that my silence was not without just reason. Upon this Nigrinus asked me to whom these deputies were sent? I replied, "To me, amongst others; the decree of the province is in my hands." "*You* may be clear on that point," says he. To which I retorted, "If it is clear to *you* who are our opponent, it may well be clear to *me*, and so much the better." Then Polyaenus, the delegate from the province, stated their grounds for abandoning the prosecution, and desired it might be without prejudice to Caesar's holding an inquiry

Caesaris praeiudicium fieret. Respondit Magnus iterumque Polyaenus. Ipse raro et breviter interlocutus multum me intra silentium tenui. Accepi enim non minus interdum oratorium esse tacere quam dicere atque adeo repeto quibusdam me capitis reis vel magis silentio quam oratione accuratissima profuisse.

Mater amisso filio (quid enim prohibet, quamquam alia ratio scribendae epistulae fuerit, de studiis disputare?) libertos eius eosdemque coheredes suos falsi et veneficii reos detulerat ad principem iudicemque impetraverat Iulium Servianum. Defenderam reos ingenti quidem coetu. Erat enim causa notissima; praeterea utrimque ingenia clarissima. Finem cognitioni quaestio imposuit; quae secundum reos dedit. Postea mater adiit principem, adfirmavit se novas probationes invenisse. Praeceptum est Suburano, ut vacaret finitam causam retractanti, si quid novi adferret. Aderat matri Iulius Africanus, nepos illius oratoris, quo audito Passienus Crispus dixit: 'Bene mehercule, bene; sed quo tam bene?' Huius nepos, iuvenis ingeniosus, sed parum callidus, cum multa dixisset adsignatumque tempus implesset, 'Rogo,' inquit, 'Suburane, permittas mihi unum versum[1]

[1] versum *Dpa, Müller,* verbum *Mr, Bipons, K.*

on the case. Magnus answered him; Polyaenus
replied; as for myself, I only now and then threw in a
word, observing in general a profound silence. For
I have learned, that upon some occasions there is as
much eloquence in taciturnity, as in speech; nay, I
remember, in some criminal cases, to have done
even more service to my clients by holding my
tongue, than I could have by the most artful
pleading.

To enter into the subject of eloquence is indeed
very foreign to the intent of my letter, yet allow me
to give you one instance. A certain lady having
lost her son, suspected that his freedmen, whom he
had appointed coheirs with her, were guilty of
forging the will and poisoning him. Accordingly
she charged them with the fact before the Emperor,
who directed Julius Servianus to try the cause. I
was counsel for the defendants, and the case being
notorious, and the advocates concerned on both sides
of high reputation, it drew together a very numerous
audience. The event was, the slaves being examined
under torture, my clients were acquitted. But the
mother applied a second time to the Emperor,
asserting she had discovered some new evidence.
Suburanus was directed to hear her application for a
new trial, and see if she could produce any fresh proofs.
Her counsel was Julius Africanus, grandson to the
famous orator of that name, of whom it is reported
that Passienus Crispus hearing him one day plead,
archly said, " Very fine, upon my word, very fine;
but what is the point of it?" This Africanus, who
is a young man of good parts but not much experience,
having harangued a great deal and exhausted the
time allotted to him, entreated Suburanus to allow

adicere.' Tum ego, cum omnes me ut diu respon-
surum intuerentur, 'Respondissem,' inquam, 'si unum
illud versum [1] Africanus adiecisset, in quo non dubito
omnia nova fuisse.' Non facile me repeto tantum
consecutum adsensum agendo quantum tunc non
agendo.

Similiter nunc et probatum et exceptum est, quod
pro Vareno hactenus <tantum >[2] non tacui. Consules,
ut Polyaenus postulabat, omnia integra principi
servaverunt; cuius cognitionem suspensus exspecto.
Nam dies ille nobis pro Vareno aut securitatem et
otium dabit aut intermissum laborem renovata solli-
tudine iniunget. Vale.

# VII

## C. PLINIUS SATURNINO SUO S.

ET proxime Prisco nostro et rursus, quia ita
iussisti, gratias egi, libentissime quidem. Est enim
mihi periucundum, quod viri optimi mihique ami-
cissimi adeo cohaesistis, ut invicem vos obligari
putetis. Nam ille quoque praecipuam se voluptatem
ex amicitia tua capere profitetur certatque tecum
honestissimo certamine mutuae caritatis, quam ipsum
tempus augebit.

[1] versum *Dpa, Müller*, verbum *Mr, Bipons, K.*
[2] tantum non *Stangl*, hactenus tacui *Sichardus*, h. non
tacui *codd. et edd. (cum cruce Müller).*

him to add one line more. [Suburanus refused.[a]]
Then, seeing the eyes of the whole assembly fixed
upon me in expectation of a lengthy reply, " I should
have answered Africanus," said I, " if he had added
that one line he begged leave to do, which I doubt
not would have contained all the new proofs we were
to hear." I do not remember to have gained so much
applause by any speech that I ever made, as I did
here upon making none.

On the present occasion the little that I said for
Varenus was received with the same general approbation. The consuls, agreeably to the request of
Polyaenus, reserved the case for the judgement of
the Emperor, whose inquiry I anxiously await; for
the day it is held will decide whether I may sit
down in full security with respect to Varenus, or
must again renew all my toil and solicitude upon his
account. Farewell.

## VII

### To Saturninus

Though I had very lately made my acknowledgements to our friend Priscus, yet, since it was your
desire, I willingly repeated them again. It is with
great pleasure I see so much harmony subsist between
two such worthy men, whom I tenderly esteem,
that you consider your obligations as mutual. For he
professes also on his part to receive much happiness
from your friendship, and, with a very generous
contention, endeavours to rival you in that reciprocal
affection, which time, I am persuaded, will augment.

[a] *Negavit ille*, or the like, has fallen out after *adicere*.
(Mommsen.)

Te negotiis distineri ob hoc moleste fero, quod
deservire studiis non potes ; si tamen alteram litem
per iudicem, alteram, ut ais, ipse finieris, incipies
primum istic otio frui, deinde satiatus ad nos reverti.
Vale.

## VIII

### C. Plinius Prisco Suo S.

Exprimere non possum, quam iucundum sit mihi,
quod Saturninus noster summas tibi apud me gratias
aliis super alias epistulis agit. Perge, ut coepisti,
virumque optimum quam familiarissime dilige magnam
voluptatem ex amicitia eius percepturus nec ad breve
tempus. Nam cum omnibus virtutibus abundat tum
hac praecipue, quod habet maximam in amore constantiam. Vale.

## IX

### C. Plinius Fusco Suo S.

Quaeris, quem ad modum in secessu, quo iamdiu
frueris, putem te studere oportere. Utile in primis,
et multi praecipiunt,[1] vel ex Graeco in Latinum, vel
ex Latino vertere in Graecum ; quo genere exerci-
tationis proprietas splendorque verborum, copia figu-
rarum, vis explicandi, praeterea imitatione opti-
morum similia inveniendi facultas paratur ; simul,

[1] praecipiunt *Ma, Bipons,* praeceperunt *D, Müller.*

I regret your immersion in business, as it prevents your devoting yourself to letters; however, when you have settled one of your two law-suits by arbitration, and the other out of court (as you say you expect to do), you will begin to enjoy the sweets of leisure down yonder; and when you are satiated with that, we may hope for your return hither.   Farewell.

## VIII

### To Priscus

THE warm acknowledgements of your favours which our friend Saturninus repeatedly makes in his letters to me, afford me inexpressible satisfaction.   Do you go on as you began, and cherish intimacy with so worthy a man, from whose friendship you will receive a strong and lasting pleasure.   For as he is rich in every virtue, so particularly, in that of constancy towards those he loves.   Farewell.

## IX

### To Fuscus

You desire my sentiments concerning the method of study you should pursue, in that retirement which you have long enjoyed.   It is a very advantageous practice (and what many recommend) to translate either from Greek into Latin, or from Latin into Greek.   By this sort of exercise one acquires noble and proper expressions, variety of figures, and a forcible turn of exposition.   Besides, to imitate the most approved authors, gives one aptitude to invent

quae legentem fefellissent, transferentem fugere non possunt. Intellegentia ex hoc et iudicium adquiritur.

Nihil offuerit, quae legeris hactenus, ut rem argumentumque teneas, quasi aemulum scribere lectisque conferre ac sedulo pensitare, quid tu, quid ille commodius. Magna gratulatio, si non nulla tu, magnus pudor, si cuncta ille melius.

Licebit interdum et notissima eligere et certare cum electis. Audax haec, non tamen improba, quia secreta contentio; quamquam multos videmus eius modi certamina sibi cum multa laude sumpsisse, quosque subsequi satis habebant, dum non desperant, antecessisse.

Poteris, et quae dixeris, post oblivionem retractare, multa retinere, plura transire, alia interscribere, alia rescribere. Laboriosum istud et taedio plenum, sed difficultate ipsa fructuosum, recalescere ex integro et resumere impetum fractum omissumque, postremo nova velut membra peracto corpori intexere nec tamen priora turbare.

after their manner, and at the same time, things which you might have overlooked in reading cannot escape you in translating : and this method will open your understanding and improve your judgement.

It may not be amiss when you have read only so much of an author at once, as to carry in your head his subject and argument, to turn, as it were, his rival, and write something on the same topic ; then compare your performance and his, and minutely examine in what points either you or he most happily succeeded. It will be a matter of very pleasing congratulation to yourself, if you shall find that in some things you have the advantage of him, as it will be a great mortification if he should rise above you in all.

You may sometimes venture to pick out and try to emulate the most shining passages of an author. Such a contest is, indeed, something bold ; but as it passes in secret, it cannot be taxed with presumption. Not but that we see many persons enter this sort of lists with great applause, and because they do not despair of themselves, advance before those whom they thought it sufficient honour to follow.

Again, after laying aside a composition until it is no longer fresh in your memory, you may revise it ; retaining several things but rejecting still more ; inserting a passage here, and re-writing one there. It is a laborious and tedious task, I own, thus to re-enflame the mind after the first heat is over, to recover an impulse when its force has been checked and spent, in a word, to interweave new parts into the texture of a composition without disturbing or confounding the original plan ; but the very difficulty of this method renders it a profitable one.

Scio nunc tibi esse praecipuum studium orandi ;
sed non ideo semper pugnacem hunc et quasi bella-
torium stilum suaserim.  Ut enim terrae variis
mutatisque seminibus ita ingenia nostra nunc hac,
nunc illa meditatione recoluntur.  Volo interdum
aliquem ex historia locum adprehendas, volo epistulam diligentius scribas.  Nam saepe in orationes [1]
quoque non historica modo, sed prope poëtica
descriptionum necessitas incidit, et pressus sermo
purusque ex epistulis petitur.  Fas est et carmine
remitti, non dico continuo et longo (id enim perfici
nisi in otio non potest) sed hoc arguto et brevi, quod
apte quantas libet occupationes curasque distinguit.
Lusus vocantur ; sed hi lusus non minorem interdum
gloriam quam seria consecuntur ; atque adeo (cur
enim te ad versus non versibus adhorter ?)

Ut laus est cerae, mollis cedensque sequatur
  si doctos digitos iussaque fiat opus
et nunc informet Martem castamque Minervam,
  nunc Venerem effingat, nunc Veneris puerum,
utque sacri fontes non sola incendia sistunt,
  saepe etiam flores vernaque prata iuvant,[2]
sic hominum ingenium flecti ducique per artes
  non rigidas docta mobilitate decet.

Itaque summi oratores, summi etiam viri sic se aut
exercebant aut delectabant, immo delectabant exer-

---

[1] orationes *M D a, Bipons, K I.*, oratione *r, K II.*
[2] iuvant *M r, Bipons, K,* lavant *D p a, Müller.*

I know your main bent at present is towards
forensic oratory; but I would not for that reason
advise you always to wield the controversial and, so
to say, militant pen. As land is improved by sowing
it with various crops in rotation so is the mind by
exercising it with different studies. I would have
you, therefore, sometimes single out a fine passage of
history, and practise epistolary composition. For in
pleading one has frequently occasion to use not only
the historical, but an almost poetical style for
descriptions; while a succinct and chaste style is
cultivated by letter-writing. It is well also to unbend
your mind with poetry; I do not mean of the long
and sustained order (for that can only be achieved
by men of leisure), but those little witty pieces
which serve as proper reliefs to every degree of care
and occupation. They commonly go under the title
of *amusements*; but these amusements have sometimes
gained as much fame as works of a more serious
nature; and indeed (for while I am exhorting you to
poetry, why should I not be poetical myself?)

"As wax by pliancy our praise commands,
    Submissive shap'd beneath the Artist's hands;
Now Mars' or chaste Minerva's form puts on,
Now moulds the charms of Venus, or her son;
As not alone to quench the raging flame
The sacred fountain pours her friendly stream;
But sweetly gliding through the flow'ry green,
Spreads glad refreshment o'er the smiling scene:
So, wisely ductile, should man's reasoning part
Receive the impress of each various art."

In this manner the greatest orators, and the greatest
men as well, used either to exercise or amuse them-

cebantque. Nam mirum est, ut his opusculis animus intendatur remittaturque. Recipiunt enim amores, odia, iras, misericordiam, urbanitatem, omnia denique, quae in vita atque etiam in foro causisqu versantur. Inest his quoque eadem quae aliis carminibus utilitas, quod metri necessitate devincti[1] soluta oratione laetamur et, quod facilius esse comparatio ostendit, libentius scribimus.

Habes plura etiam fortasse, quam requirebas, unum tamen omisi. Non enim dixi, quae legenda arbitrarer; quamquam dixi, cum dicerem, quae scribenda. Tu memineris sui cuiusque generis auctores diligenter eligere. Aiunt enim multum legendum esse, non multa. Qui sint hi, adeo notum probatumque[2] est, ut demonstratione non egeat; et alioqui tam immodice epistulam extendi, ut, dum tibi, quem ad modum studere debeas, suadeo, studendi tempus abstulerim. Quin ergo pugillares resumis et aliquid ex his vel istud ipsum, quod coeperas, scribis? Vale.

[1] devincti *Dpra, Bipons, Müller,* devinctis *M,* defuncti *K II. (auct. Barth., Gesner).*
[2] probatumque *M, Bipons, K,* pervagatumque *Otto, Müller,* provocatumque *Dpra,* pervulgatumque *Schaefer.*

selves, **or rather** did both. The mind is surprisingly
entertained and enlivened by these little compositions, for they turn upon subjects of gallantry,
antipathies, quarrels, pity, politeness, and everything,
in short, that concerns daily life and even the forensic
sphere. Besides, the same advantage attends these
as every other sort of poems; that **we** delight in
prose after being fettered by numbers, and more
willingly employ what comparison shows to be the
easier form of composition.

And now, perhaps, I have more than satisfied your
demands; however, there is one thing which I have
omitted: I have not told you what books I think
you should read, though indeed, that was implied by
my telling you what you should write. Pray remember to select with care the standard authors on each
subject; for, as the saying is, "though we should
read much, we should not read many books." Who
those authors are is so clearly settled, and so
generally known, that I need not point them out to
you; besides, I have already extended this letter to
such an immoderate length, that I have curtailed the
time, by recommending the course, of your studies.
Back, then, to your writing-tablets, and either write
something from the hints I have now given you,
or continue the composition on which you were
already engaged. Farewell.

# THE LETTERS OF PLINY

## X

### C. PLINIUS MACRINO SUO S.

QUIA ipse, cum prima cognovi, iungere extrema quasi avulsa cupio, te quoque existimo velle de Vareno et Bithynis reliqua cognoscere. Acta causa hinc a Polyaeno, inde a Magno. Finitis actionibus Caesar 'Neutra' inquit, 'pars de mora quereretur; erit mihi curae explorare provinciae voluntatem.' Multum interim Varenus tulit. Etenim quam dubium est, an merito accusetur, qui an omnino accusetur, incertum est! Superest, ne rursus provinciae, quod damnasse dicitur, placeat, agatque paenitentiam paenitentiae suae. Vale.

## XI

### C. PLINIUS FABATO PROSOCERO SUO S.

MIRARIS, quod Hermes libertus meus, hereditarios agros, quos ego iusseram proscribi, non exspectata auctione pro meo quincunce ex septingentis milibus Corelliae addixerit. Adicis posse eos nongentis milibus venire ac tanto magis quaeris, an, quod gessit, ratum servem. Ego vero servo; quibus ex causis

---

<sup>a</sup> See vii. 6.

## X

### To Macrinus

Since, for my part, when I have learned the beginning of a story I long to join on the sequel, as if it were a severed fragment, I think you will likewise wish to know the event of the cause between the Bithynians and Varenus.[a] Polyaenus pleaded on one side, and Magnus on the other. When Caesar had heard both, "Neither party," said he, "shall have reason to complain of delay; I will undertake to sound the sentiments of the province." In the meanwhile, Varenus has gained a very considerable point; for how doubtful is the justness of an accusation against a person while it remains uncertain whether he is accused at all? We have only to wish that the province may not again approve of what it is said she has condemned, and repent of her repentance. Farewell.

## XI

### To Fabatus, His Wife's Grandfather

You are surprised, I find, that my recent legacy of five-twelfths of an estate, which I had directed to be sold to the best bidder, should have been disposed of, by my freedman Hermes, to Corellia (without putting it up to auction) at the rate of seven hundred thousand sesterces. And as you think it might have produced nine hundred thousand, you are so much the more desirous to know whether I am inclined to ratify what he has done. I am; and will now

accipe. Cupio enim et tibi probatum et coheredibus meis excusatum esse, quod me ab illis maiore officio iubente secerno.

Corelliam cum summa reverentia diligo primum ut sororem Corelli Rufi, cuius mihi memoria sacrosancta est, deinde ut matri meae familiarissimam. Sunt mihi et cum marito eius, Minicio Iusto, optimo viro, vetera iura : fuerunt et cum filio maxima, adeo quidem, ut praetore me ludis meis praesederit. Haec, cum proxime istic fui, indicavit mihi cupere se aliquid circa Larium nostrum possidere. Ego illi ex praediis meis, quod vellet et quanti vellet, obtuli exceptis paternis maternisque ; his enim cedere ne Corelliae quidem possum. Igitur cum obvenisset mihi hereditas, in qua praedia ista, scripsi ei venalia futura. Has epistulas Hermes tulit exigentique, ut statim portionem meam sibi addiceret, paruit.

Vides, quam ratum habere debeam, quod libertus meus meis moribus gessit. Superest, ut coheredes aequo animo ferant separatim me vendidisse, quod mihi licuit omnino non vendere. Nec vero coguntur imitari meum exemplum; non enim illis eadem cum Corellia iura. Possunt ergo intueri utilitatem suam, pro qua mihi fuit amicitia. Vale.

state upon what grounds. For I wish not only that you may approve, but that my fellow coheirs may excuse me, for having in obedience to a higher duty, separated my interest from theirs.

I have the highest esteem for Corellia, both as the sister of Corellius Rufus, whose memory is most sacred to me, and as she was an intimate friend of my mother's. Besides, I am bound by a long-standing friendship to her husband, the excellent Minicius Iustus; as I was by a very close one to her son; so much so, that I fixed upon him to preside at the games which I exhibited as Praetor. This lady, when I was last in your vicinity, expressed a wish to possess something upon our lake of Comum; I made her an offer, at her own price, of any part of my estate there, except what came to me from my father and mother; for that I could not resign, even to Corellia. So, when the inheritance which comprised farms in that district fell to me, I wrote to acquaint her it was to be sold. This letter I sent by Hermes, who upon her requesting him that he would immediately let her have my proportion of the estate, consented to do so.

You see how fully I ought to confirm what my freedman has done agreeably to my inclinations. It only remains to wish my fellow-coheirs may not take it amiss, that I sold what I was at liberty not to sell at all. They are under no necessity of following my example, since they have not the same connexions with Corellia that I have. They are free, therefore, to be guided by self-interest, a motive in my own case supplanted by friendship. Farewell.

# THE LETTERS OF PLINY

## XII

### C. PLINIUS MINICIO SUO S.

LIBELLUM formatum a me, sicut exegeras, quo
amicus tuus, immo noster (quid enim non commune
nobis?), si res posceret, uteretur, misi tibi ideo
tardius, ne tempus emendandi eum, id est, disperdendi, haberes. Habebis tamen, an emendandi,
nescio, utique disperdendi. Ὑμεῖς γὰρ οἱ εὔζηλοι
optima quaeque detrahitis. Quod si feceris, boni
consulam. Postea enim illis ex aliqua occasione ut
meis utar et beneficio fastidii tui ipse laudabor, ut in
eo, quod adnotatum invenies et superscripto aliter [1]
explicitum. Nam cum suspicarer futurum ut tibi
tumidius videretur, quod est sonantius et elatius,
non alienum existimavi, ne te torqueres, addere
statim pressius quiddam et exilius vel potius humilius
et peius, vestro tamen iudicio rectius. Cur enim non
usquequaque tenuitatem vestram insequar et exa-
gitem? Haec, ut inter istas occupationes aliquid
aliquando rideres; illud serio; vide, ut mihi viaticum
reddas, quod impendi data opera cursore dimisso.
Ne tu, cum hoc legeris, non partes libelli, sed totum
libellum improbabis negabisque ullius pretii esse,
cuius pretium reposceris. Vale.

---

[1] superscripto aliter *Kukula*, suprascr. aliter *codd.*, *K I.*,
superscr. alio *K II.*

## XII

### To Minicius

I HAVE been so much the longer in sending you
the petition which I have drawn up at your request
for your, or rather I should say *our*, friend (for what
is there that we do not possess in common?) to use
if necessary, in order that you might have no time to
correct, that is, to spoil it. You will have time, all
the same, perhaps not to correct, but at any rate to
spoil it; for you hypercritical people throw out the
most shining parts of every composition. But you
are welcome to do so; for I shall upon some future
occasion use these fine passages myself, and win
applause from what you fastidiously reject; as for
instance in the passage you will find interlined with
a differently expressed version. For I suspected
you would call every thing bombast which is elevated
and sounding; I thought proper therefore for your
ease, to subjoin a more concise and dry, or rather, a
flatter and inferior, rendering; though you, I know
(for why should I not rally your refined taste?)
will esteem it an improvement. Thus far in
order to make you smile in the midst of your
serious occupations I have been jocose; but without
doubt, I am wondrous serious in what I am going to
add: I expect to be reimbursed the charges I have
been at in sending a messenger express with this.
Now are you not disposed to condemn this petition,
not only in part, but in the whole, and insist upon it
that you ought not to pay for a thing which is
absolutely of no value? Farewell.

## XIII

### C. Plinius Feroci Suo S.

Eadem epistula et non studere te et studere
significat. Aenigmata loquor? Ita plane, donec
distinctius, quod sentio, enuntiem. Negat enim te
studere, sed est tam polita, quam nisi a studente non
potest scribi; aut es tu super omnes beatus, si talia
per desidiam et otium perficis. Vale.

## XIV

### C. Plinius Corelliae Suae S.

Tu quidem honestissime, quod tam impense et
rogas et exigis, ut accipi iubeam a te pretium agrorum
non ex septingentis milibus, quanti illos a liberto
meo, sed ex nongentis, quanti a publicanis partem
vicesimam emisti. Invicem ego et rogo et exigo,
ut, non solum quid te, verum etiam quid me deceat,
aspicias patiarisque me in hoc uno tibi eodem animo
repugnare, quo in omnibus obsequi soleo. Vale.

---

<sup>a</sup> Letter 11 of this book.
<sup>b</sup> Augustus imposed a tax of a twentieth on all legacies
and inheritances. It seems that Corellia, on acquiring this

## XIII

### To Ferox

You inform me in the same letter, that you do and do not study. I speak in riddles? Yes, to be sure, till I express my meaning more clearly. Well, then, you say that you have bid adieu to study; but such an air of elegance runs through your letter, that it is impossible it should have been written by anyone but a student; or else you are blest beyond the rest of mankind, since you can compose such a finished work in your hours of idleness. Farewell.

## XIV

### To Corellia

'Tis extremely noble in you to desire and insist so vehemently that I should fix the price you are to pay for my estate, not at seven hundred thousand sesterces (for which sum you bought it of my freedman),[a] but at nine hundred thousand, being the rateable value on which you paid the farmers of the revenues for their twentieth part.[b] But I must desire and insist in my turn, that you will consider not only what befits your character, but also what befits mine; and will suffer me to oppose your inclination in this single instance, with the same warmth that I obey it in all others. Farewell.

property, had to pay the legacy-duty; the literal expression is, "you bought the twentieth part from the tax-farmers."

## XV

### C. Plinius Saturnino Suo S.

Requiris, quid agam. Quae nosti; distringor officio, amicis deservio, studeo interdum, quod non interdum, sed solum semperque facere non audeo dicere rectius, certe beatius erat. Te alia omnia, quam quae velis, agere moleste ferrem, nisi ea, quae agis, essent honestissima. Nam et reipublicae suae negotia curare et disceptare inter amicos laude dignissimum est.

Prisci nostri contubernium iucundum tibi futurum sciebam. Noveram simplicitatem eius, noveram comitatem; eundem esse, quod minus noram, gra-tissimum experior, cum tam iucunde officiorum nos-trorum meminisse eum scribas. Vale.

## XVI

### C. Plinius Fabato Prosocero Suo S.

Calestrium Tironem familiarissime diligo et privatis mihi et publicis necessitudinibus implicitum. Simul militavimus, simul quaestores Caesaris fuimus. Ille me in tribunatu liberorum iure praecessit, ego illum

---

<sup>a</sup> The charge of the public treasury.    <sup>b</sup> See vii. 8.

## XV

### To Saturninus

You ask me, what I am doing? Just the things you are familiar with. I am immersed in the business of my post;[a] I devote myself to the service of my friends; now and then I study; if the latter were not my occasional, but my sole and constant occupation, I should certainly be more happily (I do not venture to say, more virtuously) employed. It would distress me that your own activities are the reverse of agreeable to you, were it not that they are extremely noble. For nothing can be more worthy of applause, than to be at the same time administering public business and settling disputes between one's private friends.

I was well persuaded you would find our friend Priscus[b] a congenial companion, for I knew the simplicity and politeness of his manners: but I had yet to learn (what I had the pleasure to be informed of by your letter) that he so obligingly remembers the services I had done him. Farewell.

## XVI

### To Fabatus

Calestrius Tiro, to whom I am bound alike by private and public ties, is one of my most cherished intimates. We served together in the army, and were both Quaestors at the same time to Caesar. He got the start of me, indeed, in the Tribunate, by the privilege which the law gives to those who

in praetura sum consecutus, cum mihi Caesar annum remisisset. Ego in villas eius saepe secessi, ille in domo mea saepe convaluit.

Hic nunc pro consule provinciam Baeticam per Ticinum est petiturus. Spero, immo confido facile me impetraturum, ut ex itinere deflectat ad te, si voles vindicta liberare, quos proxime inter amicos manumisisti. Nihil est, quod verearis, ne sit hoc illi molestum, cui orbem terrarum circumire non erit longum mea causa. Proinde nimiam istam verecundiam pone teque, quid velis, consule. Illi tam iucundum, quod ego, quam mihi, quod tu iubes. Vale.

## XVII

### C. PLINIUS CELERI SUO S.

SUA cuique ratio recitandi; mihi, quod saepe iam dixi, ut, si quid me fugit, ut certe fugit, admonear.

---

<sup>a</sup> By a law at first proposed by Augustus, but which on passing with several alterations in 9 A.D. was known as the *Lex Julia et Papia Poppaea*, it was enacted, amongst other things, "that any person might stand sooner than ordinary for an office, if he had as many children as he wanted years to be capable of bearing such a dignity." (Melm.) See ii. 13, x. 2.

have children; *a* but I overtook him in the Praetorship by the indulgence of the Emperor, who dispensed with my wanting a year of the legal age for that office. I have frequently gone for a holiday to his country villas; he has often recruited his health under my roof.

Tiro is now setting out for Baetica, having been appointed proconsul of that province, and will pass through Ticinum on his way. I hope, nay, I am confident, I can easily prevail with him to turn out of his road to your house, if you should wish to emancipate formally *b* those slaves to whom you have already given their liberty in the presence of your friends. You need be under no apprehension that he will look upon this as a trouble, who would make nothing of travelling round the world for my sake. I beg therefore you would lay aside your excessive delicacy in such matters, and only consider your own convenience. For my commands are as welcome to Tiro, as yours are to me. Farewell.

## XVII

### To Celer

EVERY author has his particular reasons for reciting his works; mine, I have often said, is, that if I have overlooked any errors (which I am certain to do), they may be brought to my notice. I am the more

*b* Lit. "by the staff" (*vindicta*). The ceremony of touching a slave with a staff in presence of a magistrate was necessary to admit the freedman to full citizenship. Cf. vii 32. To pronounce a slave free in the presence of five friends was one of the informal methods of manumission which only admitted him to the "Latin" franchise. See x. 104, n.

Quo magis miror, quod scribis fuisse quosdam, qui
reprehenderent, quod orationes omnino recitarem;
nisi vero has solas non putant emendandas.    A
quibus libenter requisierim, cur concedant, si concedant tamen, historiam debere recitari, quae non
ostentationi, sed fidei veritatique componitur, cur
tragoediam, quae non auditorium, sed scaenam et
actores, cur lyrica, quae non lectorem, sed chorum et
lyram poscunt.

At horum recitatio usu iam recepta est.  Num
ergo culpandus est ille, qui coepit?  Quamquam
orationes quoque et nostri quidam et Graeci
lectitaverunt.  Supervacuum tamen est recitare, quae
dixeris.  Etiam, si eadem omnia, si iisdem omnibus,
si statim recites; si vero multa inseras, multa
commutes, si quosdam novos, quosdam eosdem, sed
post tempus adsumas, cur minus probabilis sit causa
recitandi, quae dixeris, quam edendi?  Sed difficile
est, ut oratio, dum recitatur, satisfaciat.  Iam hoc
ad laborem recitantis pertinet, non ad rationem non
recitandi.

Nec vero ego, dum recito, laudari, sed dum legor,
cupio.  Itaque nullum emendandi genus omitto.
Ac primum, quae scripsi, mecum ipse pertracto;

surprised to find from your letter that there are
some who disapprove of my reciting *speeches* at all;
I cannot guess why, unless, indeed, they think a
speech the one form of composition that ought not
to be corrected. I would willingly ask them why
they allow (if indeed they do allow) that History
may be recited, since it is written in the interests
of truth and honesty, not for display? Or why
Tragedy, when it requires a stage and actors, not an
audience-hall? Or Lyric Poetry, which requires not
a reader, but a chorus and a harp-accompaniment?

They will rejoin that in the instances mentioned,
recitation has become established by custom. Well,
we are not therefore, I suppose, to condemn the
person who first introduced the practice? However,
I need not labour this point, for certain of our own
orators, and the Greeks generally, have been in
the habit of reciting their speeches. "But it is
superfluous," says someone, "to recite a speech
which has already been delivered." Yes, if you
recite it exactly as delivered, to the very same
audience, and immediately; but if you make several
additions and alterations; if you collect an audience
composed partly of the same, and partly of different
persons, and after an interval, why is it less plausible
to recite your speech than to publish it? As to the
difficulty they may allege of giving satisfaction by
the mere recital of a speech, *that* is simply a question
of how much trouble the reciter takes, and no
argument against reciting in general.

For my part, it is not whilst I am reciting but
whilst I am read, that I would be applauded;
accordingly I omit no method of correction. In the
first place, I revise my composition in private, next I

deinde duobus aut tribus lego; mox aliis trado
adnotanda notasque eorum, si dubito, cum uno
rursus aut altero pensito; novissime pluribus recito
ac, si quid mihi credis, tunc acerrime emendo. Nam
tanto diligentius quanto sollicitius intendo. Optime
autem reverentia, pudor, metus iudicant; idque
adeo sic habe: nonne, si locuturus es cum aliquo
quamlibet docto, uno tamen, minus commoveris,
quam si cum multis vel indoctis? Nonne, cum
surgis ad agendum, tunc maxime tibi ipse diffidis,
tunc commutata, non dico plurima, sed omnia
cupis? Utique si latior scaena et corona diffusior;
nam illos quoque sordidos pullatosque reveremur.
Nonne, si prima quaeque improbari putas, debilitaris
et concidis? Opinor, quia in numero ipso est
quoddam magnum collatumque consilium, quibusque
singulis iudicii parum, omnibus plurimum.

Itaque Pomponius Secundus, hic scriptor tragoe-
diarum, si quid forte familiarior amicus tollendum,
ipse retinendum arbitraretur, dicere solebat: ' Ad
populum provoco ' atque ita ex populi vel silentio
vel adsensu aut suam aut amici sententiam sequebatur.

---

*a* There is a kind of witticism in this expression, which
will be lost to the mere English reader, unless he be informed
that the Romans had a privilege confirmed to them by
several laws which passed in the earlier ages of the republic,
of appealing from the decisions of the magistrates to the
general assembly of the people: and they did so in the form
of words which Pomponius here applies to a different
purpose. (Melm.)

read it to two or three friends, and then give it to
others to annotate; if I doubt the justness of their
corrections, I carefully weigh them again with a
friend or two.    Last of all, I recite the piece to a
numerous assembly, and this is the time, if you can
believe me, when I exercise the most rigid criticism;
for my attention rises in proportion to my solicitude.
Again nothing so much awakens the judgement as
that reverence, and modest timidity, which one feels
upon those occasions.    For do but reflect and tell me
whether you would not be infinitely less affected if
you were to speak before a single person only, though
ever so learned, than before a numerous assembly,
even though it were composed of none but illiterate
people?    Is it not when you rise up to plead, that
you are most diffident of yourself, and wish you could
alter not merely a great deal, but the whole of your
plea? especially if you are to speak in a good-sized
court and before a largish attendance of the public;
for even the most low and ragamuffin audience inspires
one with awe.    And if you fancy your exordium
meets with disapproval, do you not feel your powers
weakened and your resolution sink under you?    The
reason I imagine to be, that a certain large collective
wisdom resides in a crowd, as such; and men whose
individual judgement is defective are excellent judges
when grouped together.

Agreeably to this notion, Pomponius Secundus
(the tragic poet), whenever some particular friend
and he differed about retaining or rejecting anything
in his plays, used to say, "I appeal $^a$ to the
people"; and followed either his own or his friend's
judgement in accordance with that expressed by their
silence or applause in the theatre.    So highly did he

Tantum ille populo dabat. Recte an secus, nihil ad me. Ego enim non populum advocare, sed certos electosque soleo, quos intuear, quibus credam, quos denique et tamquam singulos observem et tamquam non singulos timeam. Nam, quod M. Cicero de stilo, ego de metu sentio. 'Timor est, timor emendator asperrimus.'[1] Hoc ipsum, quod nos recitaturos cogitamus, emendat, quod auditorium ingredimur, emendat, quod pallemus, horrescimus, circumspicimus, emendat.

Proinde non paenitet me consuetudinis meae, quam utilissimam experior, adeoque non deterreor sermunculis istorum, ut ultro te rogem, monstres aliquid, quod his addam. Nihil enim curae meae satis est. Cogito, quam sit magnum dare aliquid in manus hominum, nec persuadere mihi possum non et cum multis et saepe tractandum, quod placere et semper et omnibus cupias. Vale.


## XVIII

### C. PLINIUS CANINIO SUO S.

DELIBERAS mecum, quem ad modum pecunia, quam municipibus nostris in epulum obtulisti, post

[1] Cic. *de Orat.* i. 33, 150.

rate public opinion! Whether rightly or not, it does not concern me to determine; I do not invite the public to my recitals but only a limited and select audience consisting of persons whom I respect and trust, in fine, to whom I pay the attention due to each as an individual, while I stand in awe of them as a collective body. What Cicero says of composing, in my opinion, applies to this awe: "Fear is the most rigid critic imaginable." The mere thought of reciting, the entering an assembly, the fact that we turn pale, shudder, and look about us there—all these are so many aids to emendation.

I cannot, therefore, repent of a practice which I have found exceedingly beneficial; and am so far from being discouraged by the tittle-tattle of yonder criticasters, that I beg you would point out some method of correction, which I may add to those I have described. For nothing can satisfy my zeal for perfection. I reflect what a serious thing it is to place a work in the hands of the public; and I cannot but be persuaded that you should revise repeatedly, and in consultation with numerous advisers, a piece that you wish to be universally and for ever admired. Farewell.

# XVIII

## To CANINIUS

You ask my advice in what manner you shall settle the sum of money, which you have presented to our fellow townsmen for an annual feast, so as to secure the just application of it after your death.

te quoque salva sit. Honesta consultatio, non expedita sententia. Numeres reipublicae summam? Verendum est, ne dilabatur. Des agros? ut publici, neglegentur. Equidem nihil commodius invenio, quam quod ipse feci. Nam pro quingentis milibus nummum, quae in alimenta ingenuorum ingenuarumque promiseram, agrum ex meis longe pluris actori publico mancipavi; eundem vectigali imposito recepi tricena milia annua daturus. Per hoc enim et reipublicae sors in tuto nec reditus incertus, et ager ipse propter id, quod vectigal large supercurrit, semper dominum, a quo exerceatur, inveniet.

Nec ignoro me plus aliquanto, quam donasse videor, erogavisse, cum pulcherrimi agri pretium necessitas vectigalis infregerit. Sed oportet privatis utilitatibus publicas, mortalibus aeternas anteferre multoque diligentius muneri suo consulere quam facultatibus. Vale.

## XIX

### C. Plinius Prisco Suo S

Angit me Fanniae valetudo. Contraxit hanc, dum adsidet Iuniae virgini, sponte primum (est enim

Your question proceeds from a truly generous principle, but the answer to it is not very easy. Should you pay down the money to the community, there is a risk that it will be squandered away. Should you settle lands for that purpose, they will probably be neglected, as those of the public usually are. For my part, I can think of no better plan than what I adopted myself. Having undertaken to give five hundred thousand sesterces for the maintenance of well-born boys and girls, I sold at that price to the public agent some land of mine which was worth considerably more ; he reconveyed it back to me, charged with a yearly rent of 30,000 sesterces. By this means the principal was secured to the community, at the same time the interest was certain, and the estate itself (as it was of much greater value than the rent charged upon it) was always sure of finding a tenant.

I am well aware that I have disbursed considerably more than the nominal amount of my gift, since the value of this fine estate has been diminished by the encumbrance with which it is charged. But a man must rate public and permanent, above private and fleeting advantages and study how to render his benefaction most useful, rather than how he may bestow it with least expense. Farewell.

## XIX

### To Priscus

I AM deeply afflicted at the ill state of health of my friend Fannia, which she contracted during her attendance on Junia, one of the Vestal virgins. She

adfinis), deinde etiam ex auctoritate pontificum. Nam
virgines, cum vi morbi atrio Vestae coguntur excedere, matronarum curae custodiaeque mandantur.
Quo munere Fannia dum sedulo fungitur, hoc discrimine implicita est.  Insident febres, tussis incres-
cit, summa macies, summa defectio : animus tantum
et spiritus viget Helvidio marito, Thrasea patre
dignissimus, reliqua labuntur meque non metu
tantum, verum etiam dolore conficiunt.  Doleo enim
maximam feminam eripi oculis civitatis nescio an
aliquid simile visuris.

Quae castitas illi, quae sanctitas, quanta gravitas,
quanta constantia !  Bis maritum secuta in exsilium
est, tertio ipsa propter maritum relegata.  Nam, cum
Senecio reus esset, quod de vita Helvidi libros com-
posuisset, rogatumque se a Fannia in defensione
dixisset, quaerente minaciter Mettio Caro, an rogasset,
respondit, ' Rogavi ' ; an commentarios scripturo de-
disset : ' Dedi ' ; an sciente matre : ' Nesciente ' ;
postremo nullam vocem cedentem periculo emisit.
Quin etiam illos ipsos libros, quamquam ex necessi-

---

engaged in this good office at first voluntarily, Junia
being her relation; afterwards also by order of the
Pontiffs; for these virgins, when severe illness
obliges them to remove from the hall of Vesta,[a] are
delivered to the care and custody of some matron.
It was Fannia's assiduity in the execution of this
charge that occasioned her present disorder, which is
a continual fever, attended with a cough that
increases daily. She is extremely emaciated, and
seems in a total decay of everything but spirits:
those indeed she preserves in their full vigour; and
in a manner worthy the wife of Helvidius and the
daughter of Thrasea. In all the rest she is so
greatly impaired, that I am more than apprehensive
upon her account; I am deeply afflicted. I grieve,
my friend, that so excellent a woman is going to be
removed from the eyes of the world, which will
never, perhaps, again behold her equal.

How consummate is her virtue, her sanctity, her
sobriety, her courage! She twice followed her
husband into exile, and once was banished herself
upon his account. For Senecio, when he was tried
for writing the life of Helvidius, having said in his
defence that he composed that work at the request
of Fannia, Mettius Carus, with a stern and threatening air, asked her whether it was true? She
acknowledged it was; and when he further questioned
her whether she supplied him likewise with private
memoirs for that purpose, and whether her mother
was privy to this transaction? she admitted the
former, but absolutely denied the latter. In short,
she uttered not a single word calculated to lessen
her peril. She even had the courage when her
effects were confiscated, to preserve a copy of those

tate et metu temporum abolitos senatus consulto, publicatis bonis servavit, habuit tulitque in exsilium exsilii causam.

Eadem quam iucunda, quam comis, quam denique, quod paucis datum est, non minus amabilis quam veneranda! Erit sane, quam postea uxoribus ostentare possimus; erit, a qua viri quoque fortitudinis exempla sumamus, quam sic cernentes audientesque miramur ut illas, quae leguntur. Ac mihi domus ipsa nutare convulsaque sedibus suis ruitura supra videtur, licet adhuc posteros habeat. Quantis enim virtutibus quantisque factis adsequentur, ut haec non novissima occiderit?

Me quidem illud etiam adfligit et torquet, quod matrem eius, illam (nihil possum illustrius dicere) tantae feminae matrem, rursus videor amittere, quam haec, ut reddit ac refert nobis, sic auferet secum meque et novo pariter et rescisso vulnere adficiet. Utramque colui, utramque dilexi; utram magis, nescio, nec discerni volebant. Habuerunt officia mea in secundis, habuerunt in adversis. Ego solacium relegatarum, ego ultor reversarum. Non feci tamen paria atque eo magis hanc cupio servari, ut mihi

---

[a] Pliny's hyperbolical way of saying "We shall not look upon her like again." Cf. Tennyson on the death of the Duke of Wellington—"The last great Englishman is low."

very memoirs which the Senate, over-awed by the tyranny of the times, had ordered to be suppressed; and took with her as the companion of her exile, what had been the cause of it.

How pleasing is her conversation, how polite her address, and (which seldom unites in the same character) how venerable is she as well as amiable! She is indeed a woman whom, when she is gone, we may hold up as a model to our wives; from whose fortitude even our own sex may take example; and whom, while yet we have the pleasure of seeing and conversing with her, we may contemplate with the same admiration as those heroines who are celebrated in ancient story. To me, this illustrious house seems shaken to its very foundations, and ready to fall into ruins with her: for though she leaves descendants behind her, yet what must be their virtues and their exploits, if they are to ensure against this excellent woman dying the last of her race ! *a*

It aggravates my affliction that by her death I seem to lose a second time her mother, that worthy mother (and what can I say higher in her praise?) of so amiable a person! who, as she is restored to us in her daughter, so she will now again be taken from us, and the loss of Fannia will thus pierce my heart at once with a fresh stab, and at the same time tear open a former wound. I loved and honoured them both, and know not which I loved and honoured more; nor did they wish this point decided. Alike in their prosperity and their adversity, my services were at their command; I was their comforter in exile, and their avenger on their return. But I have done less for them, than they for me; and am all the more solicitous for the preservation of this lady,

solvendi tempora supersint.  In his eram curis, cum
scriberem ad te; quas si deus aliquis in gaudium
verterit, de metu non querar.  Vale.


## XX

### C. Plinius Tacito Suo S.

Librum tuum legi et, quam diligentissime potui,
adnotavi, quae commutanda, quae eximenda arbitrarer.  Nam et ego verum dicere adsuevi et tu
libenter audire.  Neque enim ulli patientius repre-
henduntur, quam qui maxime laudari merentur.

Nunc a te librum meum cum adnotationibus tuis
exspecto.  O iucundas, o pulchras vices!  quam me
delectat, quod, si qua posteris cura nostri, usquequaque narrabitur, qua concordia, simplicitate, fide
viximus!  Erit rarum et insigne duos homines
aetate, dignitate propemodum aequales, non nullius
in litteris nominis (cogor enim de te quoque parcius
dicere, quia de me simul dico), alterum alterius
studia fovisse.  Equidem adulescentulus, cum iam
tu fama gloriaque floreres, te sequi, tibi 'longo
sed proximus intervallo[1]' et esse et haberi con-
cupiscebam.

Et erant multa clarissima ingenia; sed tu mihi
(ita similitudo naturae ferebat) maxime imitabilis,

[1] *Aeneid* v. 320.

as it will give me time to repay my obligations.   Such
is the anxiety under which I write this letter ; should
some deity transmute it into joy, I shall not complain
of the alarms I now suffer.    Farewell.


## XX

### To Tacitus

I HAVE perused your oration, and with all the
attention   I   was   master   of   have   marked   the
passages where I think alteration or excision advisable.
For 'tis my habit to speak truth, and yours to hear
it gladly—very naturally, since none are more patient
of censure than those who have the best claim to
applause.

I now expect in return, your observations upon
the speech of mine which I sent you.   How agreeable,
how  noble  is  such  a  commerce !  and  how  am  I
pleased with the thought, that posterity, if it shall at
all concern itself with us, will not cease to recount
in   what   harmony,   what   openness,   what   mutual
confidence we lived together !   It will be an instance
as remarkable as it is uncommon, that two persons
nearly of the same age and official rank, and of some
literary reputation (for since I join myself with you,
I am obliged to speak of your merit with reserve)
should thus foster each other's studies.   When I was
a very young man, and you already in the prime of
your glory and renown, I longed to follow your
steps, and to be both really and reputedly " next,
but with many a length between," to yourself.

There were at that time many celebrated geniuses
in Rome ; but you of all others (owing to a similarity in

maxime imitandus videbaris. Quo magis gaudeo,
quod, si quis de studiis sermo, una nomina-
mur, quod de te loquentibus statim occurro. Nec
desunt, qui utrique nostrum praeferantur. Sed nos,
nihil interest mea quo loco, iungimur; nam mihi
primus, qui a te proximus. Quin etiam in testamen-
tis debes adnotasse; nisi quis forte alterutri nostrum
amicissimus, eadem legata et quidem pariter accipi-
mus. Quae omnia huc spectant, ut invicem
ardentius diligamus, cum tot vinculis nos studia,
mores, fama, suprema denique hominum iudicia
constringant. Vale.

## XXI

### C. Plinius Cornuto Suo S

Pareo, collega carissime, et infirmitati oculorum,
ut iubes, consulo. Nam et huc tecto vehiculo
undique inclusus quasi in cubiculo perveni et hic
non stilo modo, verum etiam lectionibus difficulter,
sed abstineo solisque auribus studeo. Cubicula
obductis velis opaca nec tamen obscura facio.
Cryptoporticus quoque adopertis inferioribus fenestris

our dispositions) appeared to me the easiest and the most worthy object of my imitation. I am the more rejoiced to find that whenever oratory is the topic of conversation, we are always mentioned together, and that my name comes up as soon as anyone talks of you. There are some who prefer you to me, as others, on the contrary, give me the advantage; but I care not in what order we are placed, so that we are united; for in my estimation, whoever is next to you stands before everybody else. You cannot but have remarked that in wills (unless in the case of particular friendship to either of us), we are named side by side, and the legacies bequeathed to us are the same in value. Since therefore we are thus closely linked together by our pursuits, manners, reputation, and even by those last instances of human judgment,[a] should all this not tend to enflame us mutually with the most ardent affection? Farewell.

## XXI

### To Cornutus.

I obey, my dear Colleague, your obliging commands to favour the weakness of my eyes, and accordingly I came hither in a covered litter, in which I was as much sheltered as if I had been in my chamber. I forbear too (with difficulty indeed, however, I do forbear) not only writing but reading, and study only with my ears. By drawing the curtains of my chamber, I make it gloomy, yet not dark, and when in my covered portico, I close the shutters of the lower windows, and by that means enjoy as much

* See vii. 31, n. c.

tantum umbrae quantum luminis habet. Sic paulatim lucem ferre condisco. Balineum adsumo, quia
prodest, vinum, quia non nocet, parcissime tamen.
Ita adsuevi, et nunc custos adest.

Gallinam ut a te missam libenter accepi; quam
satis acribus oculis, quamquam adhuc lippus, pinguis-
simam vidi. Vale.

## XXII

### C. Plinius Falconi Suo S.

Minus miraberis me tam instanter petisse, ut in
amicum meum conferres tribunatum, cum scieris, quis
ille qualisque. Possum autem iam tibi et nomen
indicare et describere ipsum, postquam polliceris.
Est Cornelius Minicianus, ornamentum regionis meae
seu dignitate seu moribus. Natus splendide abundat
facultatibus, amat studia, ut solent pauperes. Idem
rectissimus iudex, fortissimus advocatus, fidelissimus
amicus. Accepisse te beneficium credes, cum propius inspexeris hominem omnibus honoribus, omnibus
titulis (nihil volo elatius de modestissimo viro dicere)
parem. Vale.

shade as light. Thus I endeavour to accustom
myself to the light by degrees. The bath being
of service in this case, I allow myself the use of it,
as I do of wine, because it is not judged prejudicial;
but I take it with great moderation. I do so, you
know, at all times, but particularly now that I have
one who narrowly observes me.[a]

I received the pullet with great pleasure, as
coming from you; weak as my eyes still are, they
are strong enough, however, to discern that it is
extremely fat. Farewell.

## XXII

### To FALCO

You will not wonder I so strongly pressed you to
confer the Tribunate upon my friend, when you
shall be informed who and what he is; and as you
have complied with my request, I may now acquaint
you with his name and character. It is Cornelius
Minicianus, who both in rank and character is the
ornament of that province to which I owe my birth.
His family and fortune are noble, and yet he
pursues his profession with all the ardour of a poor
man. He is a most upright juror, a most strenuous
advocate, a most faithful friend. You will look upon
the favour as conferred on yourself, when you shall
have taken a nearer view of this excellent person,
who (not to speak in too lofty terms of so modest a
man) is equal to all honours and titles that can be
conferred upon him. Farewell.

[a] Meaning his wife, perhaps, or his physician. (Melm.)

# THE LETTERS OF PLINY

## XXIII

### C. Plinius Fabato Prosocero Suo S.

Gaudeo quidem esse te tam fortem, ut Mediolani
occurrere Tironi possis, sed ut perseveres esse tam
fortis, rogo, ne tibi contra rationem aetatis tantum
laboris iniungas. Quin immo denuntio, ut illum et
domi et intra domum atque etiam intra cubiculi limen
exspectes. Etenim, cum a me ut frater diligatur,
non debet ab eo, quem ego parentis loco observo,
exigere officium, quod parenti suo remisisset. Vale.

## XXIV

### C. Plinius Gemino Suo S.

Ummidia Quadratilla paulo minus octogesimo
aetatis anno decessit usque ad novissimam valetudinem viridis atque etiam ultra matronalem modum
compacto corpore et robusto. Decessit honestissimo
testamento; reliquit heredes ex besse nepotem, ex
tertia parte neptem.

Neptem parum novi; nepotem familiarissime diligo,
adulescentem singularem nec iis tantum, quos san-
guine attingit, inter propinquos amandum. Ac primum
conspicuus forma omnes sermones malignorum et

## XXIII

### To Fabatus, His Wife's Grandfather

I GREATLY rejoice that your strength permits of your journeying to meet Tiro at Milan; but that you may continue to enjoy that vigour, I beg you will spare yourself a fatigue so improper for a man of your years. Nay, I must insist that you wait for him at home, and that you do not stir out of your own house, nor even out of your chamber to receive him. As I love him like a brother, it would be unreasonable he should exact from one whom I honour as my parent, an attention which he would not require from his own. Farewell.

## XXIV

### To Geminus

UMMIDIA QUADRATILLA is dead, having lived almost to her eightieth year. She enjoyed till her last sickness an uninterrupted state of health, with a strength and firmness of body unusual even to matrons in their prime. She has left a will that does her great credit, having disposed of two-thirds of her estate to her grandson, and the rest to her granddaughter.

The young lady I know little of, but the grandson is one of my most intimate friends. He is a young man of singular worth, for whom others than his own kin may well feel the affection due to a kinsman. Though he is extremely beautiful, he escaped every malicious imputation both whilst a

59

puer et iuvenis evasit intra quartum et vicesimum annum maritus et, si deus adnuisset, pater.

**Vixit** in contubernio aviae delicatae severissime et tamen obsequentissime. Habebat illa pantomimos fovebatque effusius, quam principi feminae convenit.[1] Hos Quadratus non in theatro, non domi spectabat; nec illa exigebat. Audivi ipsam, cum mihi commendaret nepotis sui studia, solere se ut feminam in illo otio sexus laxare animum lusu calculorum, solere spectare pantomimos suos; sed, cum factura esset alterutrum, semper se nepoti suo praecepisse, abiret studeretque; quod mihi non amore eius magis facere quam reverentia videbatur.

Miraberis, et ego miratus sum. Proximis sacerdo talibus ludis productis in commissione pantomimis, cum simul theatro ego et Quadratus egrederemur, ait mihi : ' Scis me hodie primum vidisse saltantem aviae meae libertum?' Hoc nepos. At hercule alienissimi homines in honorem Quadratillae (pudet me dixisse honorem) per adulationis officium in theatrum

---

[1] convenit *M, Bipons, K,* conveniret *Dpra, Otto, Müller.*

[a] See vi. 11.

[b] The *ludi* (a term which included horse-races, theatricals, and athletic games) exhibited at certain religious festivals were severally organised by the various priestly colleges. What especial *ludi* Pliny here refers to, is unknown.

boy and when a youth; he was a husband at
four and twenty, and would have been a father if
providence had not disappointed his hopes.

He lived in the family of his grandmother, who
was exceedingly devoted to the pleasures of the
town, with great severity of conduct, yet at the
same time with the utmost compliance. She
retained a sett of pantomimes, whom she encouraged
more than becomes a lady of quality. But
Quadratus never witnessed their performances, either
when she exhibited them in the theatre, or in her
own house; nor did she exact his attendance. I
once heard her say, when she was commending her
grandson's oratorical studies to my care,[a] that it was
her habit, being a woman and as such debarred from
active life, to amuse herself with playing at chess
or backgammon, and to look on at the mimicry of
her pantomimes; but that before engaging in either
diversion, she constantly sent away her grandson to
his studies: a custom, I imagine, which she observed
as much out of a certain reverence, as affection, to
the youth.

I was a good deal surprised, as I am persuaded
you will be, at what he told me the last time the
Sacerdotal Games [b] were exhibited. As we were
coming out of the theatre together, where we had
been entertained with a contest of these pantomimes,
"Do you know," said he, "this is the first time I
ever saw one of my grandmother's freedmen
dance?" Such was the conduct of the grandson;
while a set of men of a far different stamp, in order
to do honour to Quadratilla (I am ashamed to
employ that word to what, in truth, was but the
lowest and grossest flattery) used to flock to the

cursitabant, exsultabant, plaudebant, mirabantur ac deinde singulos gestus dominae cum canticis reddebant ; qui nunc exiguissima legata, theatralis operae corollarium, accipient ab herede, qui non spectabat.

Haec, quia soles, si quid incidit novi, non invitus audire, deinde quia iucundum est mihi, quod ceperam, gaudium scribendo retractare. Gaudeo enim pietate defunctae, honore optimi iuvenis ; laetor etiam, quod domus aliquando C. Cassi, huius qui Cassianae scholae princeps et parens fuit, serviet domino non minori. Implebit enim illam Quadratus meus et decebit rursusque ei pristinam dignitatem, celebritatem, gloriam reddet, cum tantus orator inde procedet, quantus iuris ille consultus. Vale

## XXV

### C. PLINIUS RUFO SUO S

O QUANTUM eruditorum aut modestia ipsorum aut quies operit ac subtrahit famae ! At nos eos tantum

---

ª This great lawyer, descended from the Cassius who

68

theatre, where they would rise up and clap in an excess of admiration at the performances of those pantomimes, slavishly copying all the while, with shrieks of applause, every sign of approbation given by the lady patroness of this *Company*. But now all that these *claqueurs* have got in pay is only a few trifling legacies, which they have the mortification to receive from an heir who was never so much as present at Quadratilla's shows.

I send you this account, as knowing it is not disagreeable to you to hear the news of the town, and because I love to renew a pleasure by relating it. And indeed this instance of family affection in Quadratilla, and the honour done therein to that excellent youth her grandson, has afforded me a very sensible satisfaction; I rejoice also that the house which once belonged to Cassius,[a] the founder and chief of the Cassian school of jurists, is to have a master no wise inferior to him. For be assured, my friend, Quadratus will fill and adorn it with his presence, and revive its pristine dignity, fame, and glory, by making it the home of as eminent an advocate as Cassius was a jurisconsult. Farewell.

## XXV

### To Rufus

WHAT numbers of learned men does their own modesty or love of repose conceal and withdraw from the notice of the world! And yet when we

murdered Julius Caesar, lived under Nero and Vespasian. He was an ancestor of Quadratus.

dicturi aliquid aut lecturi timemus, qui studia sua proferunt; cum illi, qui tacent, hoc amplius praestent, quod maximum opus silentio reverentur. Expertus scribo, quod scribo.

Terentius Iunior equestribus militiis atque etiam procuratione Narbonensis provinciae integerrime functus recepit se in agros suos paratisque honoribus tranquillissimum otium praetulit. Hunc ego invitatus hospitio ut bonum patrem familiae, ut diligentem agricolam intuebar de his locuturus, in quibus illum versari putabam; et coeperam, cum ille me doctissimo sermone revocavit ad studia. Quam tersa omnia, quam Latina, quam Graeca! Nam tantum utraque lingua valet, ut ea magis videatur excellere, qua cum maxime loquitur. Quantum ille legit, quantum tenet! Athenis vivere hominem, non in villa putes.

Quid multa? auxit sollicitudinem meam effecitque, ut illis, quos doctissimos novi, non minus hos seductos et quasi rusticos verear. Idem suadeo tibi. Sunt enim, ut in castris sic etiam in litteris nostris plures cultu pagano, quos cinctos et armatos et quidem ardentissimo ingenio diligentius [1] scrutatus invenies. Vale.

[1] diligentius *Dpa, Bipons, Otto, Müller,* diligenter *Mr, K.*

---

[a] On joining the army, members of the Equestrian order entered, without passing through the rank of centurion, on what was called the *equestres militiae*, of which the successive grades were (1) *praefectura cohortis,* (2) *praefectura alae, tribunatus legionis.* (Hardy.)

are going to speak or recite in public, it is only the men who parade their studies that we are afraid of; whereas in truth, those who say nothing about them have so much a higher claim to regard, as they pay the homage of silence to the noblest of employments. These observations I give you upon experience.

Terentius Junior, having blamelessly passed through the military posts belonging to the Equestrian order[a] and held that of Procurator in Narbonensian Gaul, retired to his estates, preferring an uninterrupted leisure to the offices that awaited him. He invited me lately to his house; looking upon him only as a worthy father of a family and an industrious farmer, I meditated such topics as I imagined him versed in; but I no sooner began, than he led me back to professional subjects by his cultured conversation. How pithy his every remark! How pure his Latin and his Greek! For he is so perfectly master of both languages that whichever he uses at the moment seems to be the one wherein he particularly excels. How extensive is his reading! how tenacious his memory! You would think the man lived in Athens, instead of at a farm-house.

To be short with you, Terentius has augmented my solicitude and taught me to fear these retired and so to speak rustic gentry, no less than the most cultivated men I know. I advise you to do the same, for, believe me, upon a careful observation, you will often find in the literary as well as military world, most formidable abilities concealed under a very rustical appearance. Farewell.

# THE LETTERS OF PLINY

## XXVI

### C. Plinius Maximo Suo S.

Nuper me cuiusdam amici languor admonuit optimos esse nos, dum infirmi sumus. Quem enim infirmum aut avaritia aut libido sollicitat? Non amoribus servit, non adpetit honores, opes neglegit et quantulumcunque ut relicturus satis habet. Tunc deos, tunc hominem esse se meminit, invidet nemini, neminem miratur, neminem despicit ac ne sermonibus quidem malignis aut attendit aut alitur; balinea imaginatur et fontes. Haec summa curarum, summa votorum, mollemque in posterum et pinguem, si contingat evadere, hoc est innoxiam beatamque, destinat vitam.

Possum ergo, quod plurimis verbis, plurimis etiam voluminibus philosophi docere conantur, ipse breviter tibi mihique praecipere, ut tales esse sani perseveremus, quales nos futuros profitemur infirmi. Vale.

## XXVII

### C. Plinius Surae Suo S.

Et mihi discendi et tibi docendi facultatem otium praebet. Igitur perquam velim scire, esse phantas-

## XXVI

### To Maximus

THE lingering disorder of a friend lately reminded me that we are never so virtuous as when we are in sickness. For where is the invalid who is troubled by the promptings of avarice or of lust? Such an one is neither a slave of love, nor covetous of office; he disregards wealth, and is contented with ever so small a portion of it, as being upon the point of leaving even that little. It is then he recollects there are Gods, and that he himself is but a man; no mortal is then the object of his envy, his admiration, or his contempt; and the slanderous reports neither raise his attention nor feed his curiosity; his imagination dwells upon baths and medicinal springs. These form the sum of his cares and prayers; and he resolves that if he has the luck to recover, his life shall be passed in luxurious ease, that is, in harmless happiness.

I may therefore briefly lay down to you and myself a maxim which philosophers endeavour to inculcate at the expense of many words, and even many volumes; namely, that we should be as virtuous in health as we resolve to be in sickness. Farewell.

## XXVII

### To Sura

THE present recess from business affords you leisure to give, and me to receive, instruction. I am extremely desirous therefore to know your senti-

mata et habere propriam figuram numenque aliquod
putes an inania et vana ex metu nostro imaginem
accipere.

Ego ut esse credam, in primis eo ducor, quod
audio accidisse Curtio Rufo. Tenuis adhuc et obscu-
rus obtinenti Africam comes haeserat. Inclinato die
spatiabatur in porticu ; offertur ei mulieris figura
humana grandior pulchriorque : perterrito Africam
se futurorum praenuntiam dixit ; iturum enim Romam
honoresque gesturum atque etiam cum summo
imperio in eandem provinciam reversurum ibique
moriturum. Facta sunt omnia. Praeterea accedenti
Carthaginem egredientique nave eadem figura in
litore occurrisse narratur. Ipse certe implicitus morbo
futura praeteritis, adversa secundis auguratus spem
salutis nullo suorum desperante proiecit.

Iam illud nonne et magis terribile et non minus
mirum est, quod exponam, ut accepi ? Erat Athenis

---

<sup>a</sup> This story is likewise related by Tacitus *Ann.* xi. 21.
(Melm.)
<sup>b</sup> Lucian (*Philopseud.* 29) ridicules a story pretty much
resembling this, but lays the scene of it in Corinth. (Melm.)

ments concerning spectres, whether you believe they actually exist and have their own proper shapes and a measure of divinity, or are only the false impressions of a terrified imagination?

What particularly inclines me to give credit to their existence, is a story[a] which I heard of Curtius Rufus. When he was in low circumstances and unknown in the world, he attended the newly-made governor of Africa into that province. One afternoon as he was walking in the public portico he was extremely daunted with the figure of a woman which appeared to him, of a size and beauty more than human. She told him she was the tutelar Genius that presided over Africa, and was come to inform him of the future events of his life:—that he should go back to Rome, where he should hold office, and return to that province invested with the proconsular dignity, and there should die. Every circumstance of this prophecy was actually accomplished. It is said farther, that upon his arrival at Carthage, as he was coming out of the ship, the same figure accosted him upon the shore. It is certain, at least, that being seized with a fit of illness, though there were no symptoms in his case that led his attendants to despair, he instantly gave up all hope of recovery; judging, it should seem, of the truth of the future part of the prediction, by that which had already been fulfilled; and of the misfortune which threatened him, by the success which he had experienced.

To this story, let me add another as remarkable as the former, but attended with circumstances of greater horror; which I will give you exactly as it was related to me.[b] There was at Athens a large

spatiosa et capax domus, sed infamis et pestilens.
Per silentium noctis sonus ferri et, si attenderes
acrius, strepitus vinculorum longius primo, deinde e
proximo reddebatur.   Mox apparebat idolon, senex
macie et squalore confectus, promissa barba, horrenti
capillo ; cruribus compedes, manibus catenas gerebat
quatiebatque.   Inde inhabitantibus tristes diraeque
noctes per metum vigilabantur ; vigiliam morbus et
crescente formidine mors sequebatur.   Nam interdiu
quoque, quamquam abscesserat imago, memoria ima-
ginis oculis inerrabat, longiorque causis timoris timor
erat.   Deserta inde et damnata solitudine domus
totaque illi monstro relicta ; proscribebatur tamen, seu
quis emere seu quis conducere ignarus tanti mali
vellet.

Venit Athenas philosophus Athenodorus, legit
titulum auditoque pretio quia suspecta vilitas, per-
cunctatus omnia docetur ac nihilo minus, immo tanto
magis conducit.   Ubi coepit advesperascere, iubet

---

<sup>a</sup> There were two Stoic philosophers of this name, both
natives of Tarsus or its vicinity.  One was long domiciled
with Cato, the other taught Augustus.  Which of the two is
meant here remains unknown.

and spacious, but ill-reputed and pestilential house. In the dead of the night a noise, resembling the clashing of iron, was frequently heard, which, if you listened more attentively, sounded like the rattling of fetters; at first it seemed at a distance, but approached nearer by degrees; immediately afterward a phantom appeared in the form of an old man, extremely meagre and squalid, with a long beard and bristling hair, rattling the gyves on his feet and hands. The poor inhabitants consequently passed sleepless nights under the most dismal terrors imaginable. This, as it broke their rest, threw them into distempers, which, as their horrors of mind increased, proved in the end fatal to their lives. For even in the day time, though the spectre did not appear, yet the remembrance of it made such a strong impression upon their imaginations that it still seemed before their eyes, and their terror remained when the cause of it was gone. By this means the house was at last deserted, as being judged by everybody to be absolutely uninhabitable; so that it was now entirely abandoned to the ghost. However, in hopes that some tenant might be found who was ignorant of this great calamity which attended it, a bill was put up, giving notice that it was either to be let or sold.

It happened that Athenodorus the philosopher [a] came to Athens at this time, and reading the bill ascertained the price. The extraordinary cheapness raised his suspicion; nevertheless, when he heard the whole story, he was so far from being discouraged, that he was more strongly inclined to hire it, and, in short, actually did so. When it grew towards evening, he ordered a couch to be prepared

sterni sibi in [1] prima domus parte, poscit pugillares, stilum, lumen ; suos omnes in interiora dimittit, ipse ad scribendum animum, oculos, manum intendit, ne vacua mens audita simulacra et inanes sibi metus fingeret. Initio, quale ubique, silentium noctis ; deinde [2] concuti ferrum, vincula moveri ; ille non tollere oculos, non remittere stilum, sed obfirmare animum auribusque praetendere. Tum crebrescere fragor, adventare et iam ut in limine, iam ut intra limen audiri ; respicit, videt agnoscitque narratam sibi effigiem. Stabat innuebatque digito similis vocanti. Hic contra, ut paulum exspectaret, manu significat rursusque ceris et stilo incumbit. Illa scribentis capiti catenis insonabat. Respicit rursus idem quod prius innuentem nec moratus tollit lumen et sequitur. Ibat illa lento gradu quasi gravis vinculis. Postquam deflexit in aream domus, repente dilapsa deserit comitem. Desertus herbas et folia concerpta signum loco ponit. Postero die adit magistratus, monet, ut illum locum effodi iubeant. Inveniuntur ossa inserta catenis et implicita, quae corpus aevo terraque putrefactum nuda et exesa reliquerat vinculis. Collecta publice sepeliuntur. Domus postea rite conditis manibus caruit.

[1] in *K, om. M, Bipons, K¹.*
[2] deinde *pra, Bipons,* dein *K.*

for him in the fore-part of the house, and after calling for a light, together with his pen and tablets, he directed all his people to retire within. But that his mind might not, for want of employment, be open to the vain terrors of imaginary noises and apparitions, he applied himself to writing with all his faculties. The first part of the night passed with usual silence, then began the clanking of iron fetters; however, he neither lifted up his eyes, nor laid down his pen, but closed his ears by concentrating his attention. The noise increased and advanced nearer, till it seemed at the door, and at last in the chamber. He looked round and saw the apparition exactly as it had been described to him: it stood before him, beckoning with the finger. Athenodorus made a sign with his hand that it should wait a little, and bent again to his writing, but the ghost rattling its chains over his head as he wrote, he looked round and saw it beckoning as before. Upon this he immediately took up his lamp and followed it. The ghost slowly stalked along, as if encumbered with its chains; and having turned into the courtyard of the house, suddenly vanished. Athenodorus being thus deserted, marked the spot with a handful of grass and leaves. The next day he went to the magistrates, and advised them to order that spot to be dug up. There they found bones commingled and intertwined with chains; for the body had mouldered away by long lying in the ground, leaving them bare, and corroded by the fetters. The bones were collected, and buried at the public expense; and after the ghost was thus duly laid the house was haunted no more.

Et haec quidem adfirmantibus credo; illud adfirmare
aliis possum. Est libertus mihi Marcus[1] non
illiteratus. Cum hoc minor frater eodem lecto
quiescebat. Is visus est sibi cernere quendam in
toro residentem admoventemque capiti suo cultros
atque etiam ex ipso vertice amputantem capillos.
Ubi illuxit, ipse circa verticem tonsus, capilli iacentes
reperiuntur. Exiguum temporis medium, et rursus
simile aliud priori fidem fecit. Puer in paedagogio
mixtus pluribus dormiebat; venerunt per fenestras
(ita narrat) in tunicis albis duo cubantemque
detonderunt et, qua venerant, recesserunt. Hunc
quoque tonsum sparsosque circa capillos dies ostendit.
Nihil notabile secutum, nisi forte quod non fui reus;
futurus, si Domitianus, sub quo haec acciderunt,
diutius vixisset. Nam in scrinio eius datus a Caro
de me libellus inventus est; ex quo coniectari potest,
quia reis moris est submittere capillum, recisos meorum capillos depulsi, quod imminebat, periculi signum
fuisse.

Proinde rogo eruditionem tuam intendas. Digna
res est, quam diu multumque consideres, ne ego
quidem indignus, cui copiam scientiae tuae facias.
Licet etiam utramque in partem, ut soles, disputes,

---

[1] Marcus *Catan.*, *Müller*, *inclus. Bipons post* illit. *D p*, om.
*K*, *Merrill*.

This story I believe upon the affirmation of others; I can myself affirm to others what I now relate. I have a freed-man named Marcus, who has some tincture of letters. One night, his younger brother, who was sleeping in the same bed with him, saw, as he thought, somebody sitting on the couch, who put a pair of shears to his head, and actually cut off the hair from the very crown of it. When morning came, they found the boy's crown was shorn, and the hair lay scattered about on the floor. After a short interval, a similar occurrence gave credit to the former. A slave-boy of mine was sleeping amidst several others in their quarters, when two persons clad in white came in (as he tells the story) through the windows, cut off his hair as he lay, and withdrew the same way they entered. Daylight revealed that this boy too had been shorn, and that his hair was likewise spread about the room. Nothing remarkable followed, unless it were that I escaped prosecution; prosecuted I should have been, if Domitian (in whose reign these things happened) had lived longer. For an information lodged by Carus[a] against me was found in his scrutore. Hence it may be conjectured, since it is customary for accused persons to let their hair grow, that this cutting of my servants' hair was a sign I should defeat the peril that hung over me.

I beg, then, you will apply learning to this question. It merits your prolonged and profound consideration; and I am not myself an unworthy recipient of your abounding knowledge. And though you should, after your manner, argue on both sides;

[a] See i. 5.

ex altera tamen fortius, ne me suspensum incertumque
dimittas, cum mihi consulendi causa fuerit, ut dubitare
desinerem.   Vale.


## XXVIII

### C. Plinius Septicio Suo S.

Ais, quosdam apud te reprehendisse, tamquam
amicos meos ex omni occasione ultra modum laudem.
Agnosco crimen, amplector etiam.   Quid enim
honestius culpa benignitatis?  Qui sunt tamen isti,
qui amicos meos me[1] melius norint?   Sed, ut
norint, quid invident mihi felicissimo errore?   Ut
enim non sint tales, quales a me praedicantur, ego
tamen beatus, quod mihi videntur.   Igitur ad alios
hanc sinistram diligentiam conferant; nec sunt
parum multi, qui carpere amicos suos iudicium vocant;
mihi numquam persuadebunt, ut meos amari a me
nimium putem.[2]   Vale.


## XXIX

### C. Plinius Montano Suo S.

Ridebis, deinde indignaberis, deinde ridebis, si
legeris, quod nisi legeris, non potes credere.   Est via
Tiburtina intra primum lapidem (proxime adnotavi)

[1] me *add. Bipons, Mommsen, Müller.*
[2] nimium putem *a, Bipons, K,* nimium autem *M,* nimis
unquam *Dp, Müller.*

yet I hope you will throw your weightiest reasons into one scale, lest you should dismiss me in suspense and uncertainty, whereas I consult you on purpose to determine my doubts. Farewell.

## XXVIII

### To Septicius

There are, you say, who have condemned me to you, as being upon all occasions too lavish in commendation of my friends. I own, nay, welcome the impeachment; for can there be a nobler error than an excess of benevolence? Yet, who are these that know my friends better than I do myself? However, grant there are any such, why will they grudge me the happiest of mistakes? For supposing my friends are not what I proclaim them, nevertheless I am happy in believing they are. Then let these critics transfer their inauspicious attentions to others; there lack not people who call it *sound judgement* to disparage their friends; but never will they persuade *me* into thinking I love mine too well. Farewell.

## XXIX

### To Montanus

It will raise your laughter first, and then your indignation, and then your laughter again, when you read a fact you could not credit without reading. In the Tiburtine road, before you come to the first mile-stone, stands (as I lately observed) the monu-

# THE LETTERS OF PLINY

monumentum **Pallantis** ita inscriptum: 'Huic senatus
ob fidem pietatemque erga patronos ornamenta
praetoria decrevit et sestertium centies quinquagies,
cuius honore contentus fuit.'

Equidem numquam sum miratus, quae saepius a
fortuna quam a iudicio proficiscerentur; maxime
tamen hic me titulus admonuit, quam essent mimica
et inepta, quae interdum in hoc caenum, in[1] has
sordes abicerentur, quae denique ille furcifer et
recipere ausus est et recusare atque etiam ut
moderationis exemplum posteris prodere. Sed quid
indignor? Ridere satius, ne se magnum aliquid
adeptos putent, qui huc felicitate perveniunt, ut
rideantur. Vale.


## XXX

### C. Plinius Genitori Suo S.

Torqueor, quod discipulum, ut scribis, optimae
spei amisisti, cuius et valetudine et morte impedita
studia tua quidni sciam, cum sis omnium officiorum
observantissimus, cumque omnes, quos probas,
effusissime diligas!

Me huc quoque urbana negotia persecuntur. Non

---

[1] in *add. Dpra, Bipons, Müller, om. M, K.*

a Freedman and favourite of the Emperor Claudius. The
special insignia worn by triumphing generals, consuls,

ment of Pallas,[a] with the following inscription: " The Senate decreed to him, as a reward for his fidelity and affection to his patrons, the insignia of a praetor, together with the sum of fifteen million sesterces; but he was contented with accepting only the honour."

I am not indeed apt to wonder at distinctions of this sort, which oftener proceed from Fortune than judgement; but I was forcibly reminded by this inscription, how farcical and ridiculous are those honours, which are thus sometimes thrown away upon dirt and infamy; which such a rascal in short, had the assurance both to accept and to refuse, and then set himself forth to posterity as an example of moderation! Yet why should it raise my indignation? rather let me laugh at it, that those persons may not flatter themselves they have obtained any thing very considerable, whose success procures them nothing more than ridicule. Farewell.

## XXX

### To Genitor

I am extremely concerned that, as your letter informs me, you have lost a most promising pupil. Can I want to be informed that his sickness and death must have interrupted your studies, knowing as I do, with what exactness you fill up every duty of life, and how unlimited your affection is to all those whom you esteem?

As for myself, the busy cares of town-life follow me even hither; for I am not out of the reach of

and praetors were freely bestowed *honoris causa* under the Empire.

desunt enim, qui me iudicem aut arbitrum faciant. Accedunt querellae rusticorum, qui auribus meis post longum tempus suo iure abutuntur. Instat et necessitas agrorum locandorum perquam molesta; adeo rarum est invenire idoneos conductores.

Quibus ex causis precario studeo, studeo tamen; nam et scribo aliquid et lego; sed, cum lego, ex comparatione sentio, quam male scribam, licet tu mihi bonum animum facias, qui libellos meos de ultione Helvidi orationi Demosthenis κατὰ Μειδίου confers; quam sane, cum componerem illos, habui in manibus, non ut aemularer (improbum enim ac paene furiosum), sed tamen imitarer et sequerer, quantum aut diversitas ingeniorum, maximi et minimi, aut causae dissimilitudo pateretur. Vale.


## XXXI

### C. PLINIUS CORNUTO SUO S.

CLAUDIUS POLLIO amari a te cupit dignus hoc ipso, quod cupit, deinde, quod ipse te diligit. Neque enim fere quisquam exigit istud, nisi qui facit. Vir alioqui rectus, integer, quietus ac paene ultra modum, si quis tamen ultra modum, verecundus.

people who oblige me to act either as their judge, or their arbitrator. To this I must add, not only the complaints of the rustics, who claim to weary my ears in virtue of my having been so long absent, but the necessity of letting out my farms; an affair which gives me much trouble, as it is exceedingly difficult to find proper tenants.

For these reasons I can only study by snatches; still, however, I study. For I both read and compose; but my reading teaches me, by comparison, with what ill success I attempt to be an author myself. Though indeed you give me great encouragement, when you compare the piece I wrote *on the avenging of Helvidius,*[a] to the oration of Demosthenes against Midias. I confess I had that speech in my hands when I composed mine; not that I pretend to rival it (that would be an excessive and mad attempt indeed), but I endeavoured, I own, to imitate it, as far as the difference of our subjects would admit, and as nearly as a genius of the lowest rank can copy one of the highest. Farewell.

## XXXI

### To Cornutus

Claudius Pollio is desirous of your affection, and he deserves it not only for that reason, but because he gives you *his* ! (few, you know, ever demand that boon without bestowing it). Apart from this, he is an upright, honest, good-natured man, and modest almost beyond measure; if indeed it is possible to be so.

a See ix. 13.

Hunc, cum simul militaremus, non solum ut commilito inspexi. Praeerat alae militari; ego iussus a legato consulari rationes alarum et cohortium excutere ut magnam quorundam foedamque avaritiam et neglegentiam paremita huius summam integritatem, sollicitam diligentiam inveni. Postea promotus ad amplissimas procurationes nulla occasione corruptus ab insito abstinentiae amore deflexit; numquam secundis rebus intumuit, numquam officiorum varietate continuam laudem humanitatis infregit eademque firmitate animi laboribus suffecit, qua nunc otium patitur. Quod quidem paulisper cum magna sua laude intermisit et posuit a Corellio nostro ex liberalitate imperatoris Nervae emendis dividendisque agris adiutor adsumptus. Etenim qua gloria dignum est summo viro in tanta eligendi facultate praecipue placuisse!

Idem quam reverenter, quam fideliter amicos colat, multorum supremis iudiciis, in his Anni Bassi, gravissimi civis, credere potes, cuius memoriam tam grata praedicatione prorogat et extendit, ut librum de vita eius (nam studia quoque sicut alias artes bonas veneratur) ediderit. Pulchrum istud et raritate ipsa probandum, cum plerique hactenus defunctorum meminerint, ut querantur.

---

*a* *Alae*, the cavalry divisions (lit. *wings*) of a Roman army; *cohortes*, the auxiliary troops, both horse and foot.

*b* Nerva restored to the Romans all that Domitian had plundered them of, and gave a very large sum to be laid out in the purchase of lands for the support of decayed families. (Melm.)

*c* *i.e.* from their leaving him legacies. Such complimentary bequests are several times cited by Cicero as a testimonial to the recipient's character; *cf.* vii. 20.

We served in the army together, and I had a
nearer view of his character, than merely what his
being my comrade gave me. He commanded a
division of horse, when I was appointed by the
consular Legate to examine the accounts of the
cavalry and the cohorts; [a] and as I found disgusting
rapacity and corresponding neglect in some officers,
so I found the highest integrity and exactest care in
him. He was afterwards promoted to high adminis-
trative offices; yet no temptations could turn
aside the innate bias of his soul from honesty,
no prosperity swell his breast; he preserved in all
the variety of posts through which he passed, an
unbroken reputation of humanity; and discharged
his toilsome duties in the same resolved spirit as he
now supports his want of occupation. He once
indeed quitted his retirement for a short interval,
with great applause, being chosen by our friend
Corellius as his coadjutor in purchasing and allotting
lands under the benefaction of the Emperor Nerva.[b]
And could there be a greater honour than to be
selected by so eminent a man, who had, moreover,
such an extensive range of choice?

You may believe how faithfully he reveres the ties
of friendship, from the dying testimony of many
persons,[c] including that most respectable citizen,
Annius Bassus. Pollio (who venerates letters as
well as every other valuable art) keeps alive, and
spreads, the memory of Bassus by the most grateful
eulogy, insomuch that he has published a memoir of
him. A fine action, and the more commendable
from its very uncommonness, since men in general
confine their recollection of the dead to what they
can complain about.

Hunc hominem adpetentissimum tui, mihi crede, complectere, adprehende, immo et invita ac sic ama, tamquam gratiam referas.  Neque enim obligandus, sed remunerandus est in amoris officio, qui prior coepit.  Vale.

## XXXII

### C. Plinius Fabato Prosocero Suo S.

Delector iucundum tibi fuisse Tironis mei adventum; quod vero scribis oblata occasione proconsulis plurimos manumissos, unice laetor.  Cupio enim patriam nostram omnibus quidem rebus augeri, maxime tamen civium numero; id enim oppidis firmissimum ornamentum.  Illud etiam me non ut ambitiosum, sed tamen iuvat, quod adicis te meque et gratiarum actione et laude celebratos.  Est enim, ut Xenophon ait, ἥδιστον ἄκουσμα ἔπαινος,[1] utique si te mereri putes.  Vale.

## XXXIII

### C. Plinius Tacito Suo S.

Auguror nec me fallit augurium historias tuas immortales futuras; quo magis illis (ingenue fatebor)

[1] Xen. *Mem.* ii. 1, 31.

Receive then this worthy man, greatly desirous (believe me) of your friendship, with the embraces of the warmest affection; nay, court and love him as though you were returning a favour; for he who makes the first amicable advances, is not to be obliged, but repaid.   Farewell.

## XXXII

### To Fabatus

I AM charmed that the advent of my friend Tiro was agreeable to you.   But I especially rejoice that (as your letter informs me) you took the opportunity of a proconsul's presence to manumit a large number of slaves.[a]   For as I wish to see our country improved by every possible method, so particularly by an increase of citizens, as that is the strongest ornament her townships can receive.   I am pleased too (not out of a spirit of vanity, however, I confess I am pleased) with what you add, that you and I were extolled both in the speech of thanks and in the encomiums which were delivered upon this occasion; for as Xenophon observes *"praise is the sweetest hearing,"* especially when we think we deserve it.   Farewell.

## XXXIII

### To Tacitus

I STRONGLY presage (and I am persuaded not falsely) that your histories will be immortal. I ingenuously own therefore, I so much the more covet

***

a See vii. 16.

inseri cupio. Nam si esse nobis curae solet, ut facies nostra ab optimo quoque artifice exprimatur, nonne debemus optare, ut operibus nostris similis tui scriptor praedicatorque contingat? Demonstro ergo, quamquam diligentiam tuam fugere non possit, cum sit in publicis actis, demonstro tamen, quo magis credas, iucundum mihi futurum, si factum meum, cuius gratia periculo crevit, tuo ingenio, tuo testimonio ornaveris.

Dederat me senatus cum Herennio Senecione advocatum provinciae Baeticae contra Baebium Massam damnatoque Massa censuerat, ut bona eius publice custodirentur. Senecio, cum explorasset consules postulationibus vacaturos, convenit me et 'Qua concordia' inquit 'iniunctam nobis accusationem exsecuti sumus, hac adeamus consules petamusque, ne bona dissipari sinant, quorum esse in custodia debent.' Respondi: 'Cum simus advocati a senatu dati, dispice, num peractas putes partes nostras senatus cognitione finita.' Et ille: 'Tu, quem voles, tibi terminum statues, cui nulla cum provincia necessitudo nisi ex beneficio tuo et hoc recenti; ipse et natus ibi et quaestor in ea fui.' Tum ego: 'Si fixum tibi istud ac deliberatum,

---

ᵃ Pending restitution to the provincials of the moneys extorted by Massa in his governorship.

a place in them. If we are generally careful to
have our faces taken by the best artists, ought we
not to desire that our actions may be celebrated by
an author like yourself? In view to this, I acquaint
you with the following affair, which though it cannot
have escaped your attention, as it is mentioned in
the journals of the public, still I acquaint you with
it, that you may be the more sensible how agreeable
it will be to me, that my action, greatly heightened
by the hazard which attended it, should receive an
additional lustre from the testimony of so bright
a genius.

The Senate had appointed Herennius Senecio
and myself as counsel for the province of Baetica,
in their prosecution of Baebius Massa. He was
convicted; and the House ordered his effects to be
placed under official custody.[a] Senecio, having learnt
that the consuls were about to sit to hear complaints,
came to me, and proposed that with the same unanimity with which we had conducted the prosecution
enjoined us, we should lodge an application with the
consuls, that they would not suffer Massa's effects to
be dissipated by those whose duty it was to guard
them. I answered, " As we were appointed counsel
in this cause by the Senate, you had better consider
whether we have not done our part, now the Senate's
inquiry is over." " You are at liberty," said he, " to
prescribe what bounds you please to yourself, who
have no particular connections with the province,
except what arise from your late services to them ;
but it is not so with me, who was born there, and
enjoyed the post of Quaestor among them." If
such, I told him, was his determined resolution, I
was ready to attend him, that whatever resentment

sequar te, ut, si qua ex hoc invidia, non tua tantum sit.'

Venimus ad consules; dicit Senecio, quae res ferebat, aliqua subiungo. Vixdum conticueramus, et Massa questus Senecionem non advocati fidem, sed inimici amaritudinem implesse impietatis reum postulat. Horror omnium; ego autem 'Vereor' inquam 'clarissimi consules, ne mihi Massa silentio suo praevaricationem obiecerit, quod non et me reum postulavit.' Quae vox et statim excepta et postea multo sermone celebrata est. Divus quidem Nerva (nam privatus quoque attendebat his, quae recte in publico fierent) missis ad me gravissimis litteris non mihi solum, verum etiam saeculo est gratulatus, cui exemplum (sic enim scripsit) simile antiquis contigisset.

Haec, utcunque se habent, notiora, clariora, maiora tu facies; quamquam non exigo, ut excedas actae rei modum. Nam nec historia debet egredi veritatem, et honeste factis veritas sufficit. Vale.

should be the consequence of this affair, it might not
fall singly upon himself.

We went to the consuls; Senecio spoke what
was proper to the occasion, to which I subjoined
some remarks. We had scarce ended, when Massa,
complaining that Senecio had not acted from
loyalty to his clients but bitter animosity against
himself, desired leave to prosecute him for high
treason.[a] The whole assembly was struck with
consternation. I immediately rose up; " Most noble
consuls," said I, " I am afraid that Massa has tacitly
charged me with betrayal of my client's interests,
since he has not asked leave to prosecute me
likewise." This speech was instantly caught up,
and soon afterwards was the talk of the town. The
late Emperor Nerva (who while still a subject
remarked every worthy action which passed in
public) wrote a most impressive letter to me,
congratulating not only me, but the age, which had
been vouchsafed an example so much in the spirit
(as he was pleased to call it) of the ancients.

But be my action what it may, 'tis yours to heighten
and spread the lustre of it; not that I require you to
exceed the bounds of reality. For History ought not
to depart from the truth, and the truth is all the
praise that virtuous actions need. Farewell.

[a] Under Domitian's reign of terror, such a charge was
often brought on the most frivolous pretexts.

# BOOK VIII

# LIBER OCTAVUS

## I

### C. Plinius Septicio Suo S.

Iter commode explicui, excepto quod quidam ex meis adversam valetudinem ferventissimis aestibus contraxerunt. Encolpius quidem lector, ille seria nostra, ille deliciae, exasperatis faucibus pulvere sanguinem reiecit. Quam triste hoc ipsi, quam acerbum mihi, si is, cui omnis ex studiis gratia, inhabilis studiis fuerit! Quis deinde libellos meos sic leget, sic amabit? quem aures meae sic sequentur? Sed di laetiora promittunt. Stetit sanguis, resedit dolor. Praeterea continens ipse, nos solliciti, medici diligentes. Ad hoc salubritas caeli, secessus, quies tantum salutis quantum otii pollicentur. Vale.

## II

### C. Plinius Calvisio Suo S.

Alii in praedia sua proficiscuntur, ut locupletiores revertantur, ego, ut pauperior. Vendideram vinde-

# BOOK VIII

## I

### To Septicius

I HAD a good journey hither, excepting only that some of my servants were disordered by the violent heats. Poor Encolpius, my reader, who is the soul of my studies and amusements, had his throat so much irritated by the dust as to spit blood; an accident that will prove as grievous to me, as to himself, should he be thereby rendered unfit for those literary services which are his prime recommendation. Where, in that event, shall I find one to read, and love, my works as he does; or whose voice will be so grateful to my ears? But the gods seem to favour our better hopes, as his bleeding is stopped and his pain abated. Moreover, he is a temperate man; no solicitude is wanting on my part; no care on that of his physicians. This, with a wholesome air, change to the country, and complete quiet, promises to contribute as much to his health as to his repose. Farewell.

## II

### To Calvisius

OTHER people visit their estates in order to recruit their purses; whilst I go to mine only to return so much the poorer. I had sold my vintage to the

mias certatim negotiatoribus ementibus. Invitabat
pretium, et quod tunc et quod fore videbatur. Spes
fefellit. Erat expeditum omnibus remittere aequa-
liter, sed non satis aequum. Mihi autem egregium
in primis videtur ut foris ita domi, ut in magnis ita in
parvis, ut in alienis ita in suis agitare iustitiam. Nam
si paria peccata, pares etiam laudes.

Itaque omnibus quidem, ne quis ' Mihi non
donatus abiret,'[1] partem octavam pretii, quo quis
emerat, concessi; deinde his, qui amplissimas summas emptionibus occupaverant, separatim consului.
Nam et me magis iuverant et maius ipsi fecerant
damnum. Igitur his, qui pluris quam decem milibus
emerant, ad illam communem et quasi publicam
octavam addidi decumam eius summae, qua decem
milia excesserant. Vereor, ne parum expresserim;
apertius calculos ostendam. Si qui forte quindecim
milibus emerant, hi et quindecim milium octavam et
quinque milium decumam tulerunt.

Praeterea, cum reputarem quosdam ex debito
aliquantum, quosdam aliquid, quosdam nihil repo-
suisse; nequaquam verum arbitrabar, quos non
aequasset fides solutionis, hos benignitate remissionis
aequare. Rursus ergo iis, qui solverant, eius, quod

[1] *Aeneid* v. 305.

---

[a] A doctrine maintained by the Stoics.

merchants, who were eager to purchase it, encouraged by the price it then bore, and what it was probable it would rise to; however they were disappointed in their expectations. To have made the same abatement to them all, would have been the easy, but not the equitable, course. Now the noblest part, according to my estimate, is to pursue justice in one's domestic as well as public conduct; in minute as in great affairs; and in our own, as well as in other men's concerns. For if "all sins are equal," [a] so are all meritorious actions.

Accordingly, I remitted to all in general one-eighth part of the price they had agreed to give me, that none "without my largesse might depart"; next, I made separate provision for those who had invested large sums in their purchase; since they had not only contributed more to my profit, but lost more heavily. To those, therefore, who had bought to the value of more than ten thousand sesterces, I remitted (over and beside the general and, so to speak, public eighth) a tenth part of what they had paid above that sum. I don't know whether I express myself clearly enough; so I will set out my reckoning more plainly. Suppose a man had purchased to the value of fifteen thousand sesterces, he got back one-eighth part of that amount, *plus* one-tenth of five thousand sesterces.

Besides, considering that some had paid over either large or small instalments of the purchase-money, whilst others had paid nothing; I thought it would be not at all fair to favour with the same remission those who had discharged their debt in varying proportions. To those therefore who had made any payments, I further returned a tenth part

solverant, decumam remisi. Per hoc enim aptissime
et in praeteritum singulis pro cuiusque merito gratia
referri, et in futurum omnes cum ad emendum tum
etiam ad solvendum allici videbantur.

Magno mihi seu ratio haec seu facilitas stetit ; sed
fuit tanti. Nam regione tota et novitas remissionis
et forma laudatur. Ex ipsis etiam, quos non una, ut
dicitur, pertica, sed distincte gradatimque tractavi,
quanto quis melior et probior, tanto mihi obligatior
abiit expertus non esse apud me, ἐν δὲ ἰῇ τιμῇ ἠμὲν
κακὸν ἠδὲ καὶ ἐσθλόν.[1] Vale.


### III

#### C. Plinius Sparso Suo S.

Librum, quem novissime tibi misi, ex omnibus meis
vel maxime placere significas. Est eadem opinio
cuiusdam eruditissimi. Quo magis adducor, ut
neutrum falli putem, quia non est credibile utrumque
falli, et quia tam blandior mihi. Volo enim proxima
quaeque absolutissima videri et ideo iam nunc contra
istum librum faveo orationi, quam nuper in publicum

[1] *Iliad* ix. 319.

upon each of the sums so paid. This was a neat way of my returning thanks to each of them for their past conduct, according to his respective deserts; and at the same time tempting them as a body, not only to deal with me for the future, but to be forward in their payments.

This instance of my good nature or my judgement (call it which you please) was a very considerable expense to me. However, I found my account in it; for all the country-side extols both this novel rebate, and the method in which I conducted it. Even those whom I did not measure (as they say) by the same ell, but distinguished according to their several degrees, thought themselves obliged to me, in proportion to the integrity of their dispositions; and went away pleased with having experienced, that not with me

" The brave and mean like honour find."

Farewell.

## III

### To Sparsus

You tell me that of all my works, the last I sent you has your decided preference. The same opinion has been expressed by a certain most learned friend; and I am the more persuaded to think you are both in the right, not only as 'tis incredible you should both be in the wrong, but because I am much given to flatter myself. For I always wish my latest performance to be thought the most finished; and so a speech I have just published is already more my

dedi communicaturus tecum, ut primum diligentem
tabellarium invenero. Erexi exspectationem tuam,
quam vereor ne destituat oratio in manus sumpta.
Interim tamen tamquam placituram (et fortasse
placebit) exspecta. Vale.

## IV

### C. Plinius Caninio Suo S.

Optime facis, quod bellum Dacicum scribere paras.
Nam quae tam recens, tam copiosa, tam lata, quae
denique tam poëtica et quamquam in verissimis
rebus tam fabulosa materia? Dices immissa terris
nova flumina, novos pontes fluminibus iniectos,
insessa castris montium abrupta, pulsum regia, pulsum
etiam vita regem nihil desperantem; super haec,
actos bis triumphos, quorum alter ex invicta gente
primus, alter novissimus fuit.

Una, sed maxima difficultas, quod haec aequare
dicendo arduum, immensum etiam tuo ingenio, quamquam altissime adsurgat et amplissimis operibus
increscat. Non nullus et in illo labor, ut barbara et

---

[a] Trajan fought two campaigns in Dacia, which he annexed 105 A.D.

[b] Trajan diverted from its course the river Sargetia, on a
report that the treasures of Decebalus, the Dacian king,
were concealed under its bed; and he built a great bridge
across the Danube.

favourite than the one you have. I will send it you as soon as I can meet with a trustworthy post-carrier. And now I have raised your expectations of this piece I fear you will be disappointed when it comes to your hands. In the meanwhile, however, pray expect it as something that will please you; and who knows but it may? Farewell.

## IV

### To CANINIUS

I GREATLY approve your design of writing a poem upon the Dacian war,[a] for where could you have chosen a subject so new, so full of events, so extensive, and so poetical? a subject which while it has all the marvellous of fiction, has all the solidity of truth. You will sing of rivers turned into new channels, and rivers bridged for the first time,[b] of camps pitched upon craggy mountains, and of a king[c] superior to adversity, though forced to abandon his capital city and even his life. You will describe, too, the victor's double triumph, one of which was the first that was ever gained over that nation,[d] 'till then unsubdued, as the other was the final.

I foresee only one difficulty, but that one is serious; to make the style equal to the grandeur of the subject is a vast and arduous undertaking even for *your* genius, though that is capable of the loftiest flights and grows in proportion to the magnitude of its theme. Something, too, there will be of labour in reconciling those barbarous and uncouth names,

---

[c] Decebalus killed himself to escape falling into the hands of the conqueror.

[d] Domitian celebrated one, 91 A.D., but see iv. 11, note.

fera nomina, in primis regis ipsius, Graecis versibus
non resultent. Sed nihil est, quod non arte curaque,
si non potest vinci, mitigetur. Praeterea, si datur
Homero et mollia vocabula et Graeca ad lenitatem
versus contrahere, extendere, inflectere, cur tibi
similis audentia, praesertim non delicata, sed necessaria, negetur? Proinde iure vatum, invocatis dis et
inter deos ipso, cuius res, opera, consilia dicturus es,
immitte rudentes, pande vela ac, si quando alias, toto
ingenio vehere. Cur enim non ego quoque poëtice
cum poeta?

Illud iam nunc paciscor; prima quaeque, ut
absolveris, mittito, immo etiam ante quam absolvas,
sic ut erunt recentia et rudia et adhuc similia na-
scentibus. Respondebis non posse perinde carptim [1]
ut contexta, perinde inchoata placere ut effecta
Scio. Itaque et a me aestimabuntur ut coepta,
spectabuntur ut membra extremamque limam tuam
opperientur in scrinio nostro. Patere hoc me super
cetera habere amoris tui pignus, ut ea quoque norim,
quae nosse neminem velles. In summa potero
fortasse scripta tua magis probare, laudare, quanto
illa tardius cautiusque sed ipsum te magis amabo
magisque laudabo, quanto celerius et incautius
miseris. Vale.

[1] carptim contexta *Kukula*, carptim < texta > ut contexta
*Ernestius*, carptim < coniecta > ut contexta *Leithaüser*.

especially that of the king himself, to the harmony of Grecian number. There is nothing, however, so hard that art and industry cannot at least mitigate, if not absolutely subdue. Besides, if Homer is allowed to contract or lengthen, or change even Grecian names, and those, too, nothing harsh to the ear, in order to make them run more smoothly in his verse; why should the same licence be forbidden to you, especially since it springs from necessity and not affectation? Come on then, my friend, and after having, in right of your bardship, invoked the gods, and among the rest that divine hero whose deeds, works, and counsels you are going to celebrate, loosen all your cordage, spread every sail, and now, if ever, give free course to your genius—for you must allow me to be poetical too, when I am talking to a poet!

And now I insist that you send me every part, as soon as it has received your last finishing touches; nay before, while it is in its first rough and embryonic state. You will tell me, that excerpts cannot please like one entire piece, nor a sketch like a completed design. I am very sensible of that and therefore shall judge your work as an essay only, and survey it, as so many disjoined members; and shall faithfully lay it up in my scrutoire, to wait your last hand. Indulge me then with this additional pledge of your affection, that you let me into a secret you would wish kept from everybody. In fine I may possibly admire and applaud your poems the more highly, the more tardy and cautious you are in communicating them; but the more quickly and heedlessly you do so, the more I shall love and applaud the poet himself. Farewell.

## V

### C. PLINIUS GEMINO SUO S.

GRAVE vulnus Macrinus noster accepit. Amisit uxorem singularis exempli, etiamsi olim fuisset. Vixit cum hac triginta novem annis sine iurgio, sine offensa. Quam illa reverentiam marito suo praestitit, cum ipsa summam mereretur! quot quantasque virtutes ex diversis aetatibus sumptas collegit et miscuit!

Habet quidem Macrinus grande solacium, quod tantum bonum tam diu tenuit; sed hoc magis exacerbatur, quod amisit. Nam fruendis voluptatibus crescit carendi dolor. Ero ergo suspensus pro homine amicissimo, dum admittere avocamenta et cicatricem pati possit, quam nihil aeque ac necessitas ipsa et dies longa et satietas doloris inducit. Vale.

## VI

### C. PLINIUS MONTANO SUO S.

COGNOVISSE iam ex epistula mea debes adnotasse me nuper monumentum Pallantis sub hac inscriptione: 'Huic senatus ob fidem pietatemque erga patronos ornamenta praetoria decrevit et sestertium

## V

### To Geminus

Our friend Macrinus is pierced with the severest affliction. He has lost his wife; a lady whose virtues would have made her a pattern even to ancient times. He lived with her thirty-nine years in the most uninterrupted harmony. How respectful was her behaviour to him! and how did she herself deserve the highest respect! How she blended and united in her character all those amiable virtues that distinguish the different periods of female life!

It should, methinks, afford great consolation to Macrinus, that he has thus long enjoyed so exquisite a blessing. Yet that reflection the more embitters his loss; for the pain of parting with our happiness, still rises in proportion to the length of its continuance. I shall be in suspense, therefore, for so valuable a friend, until he can bring himself to submit to soothing treatment, and endure having his wound closed—a process best effected by the sheer force of necessity, by lapse of time, and by satiety of grief. Farewell.

## VI

### To Montanus

My last letter [a] should by this time have informed you, that I remarked lately a monument to Pallas, with this inscription: " The Senate decreed to him for his fidelity and affection to his patrons, the praetorian insignia, together with fifteen million

[a] vii. 29.

centies quinquagies cuius honore contentus fuit.'
Postea mihi visum est pretium operae ipsum senatus
consultum quaerere.   Inveni tam copiosum et effu-
sum, ut ille superbissimus titulus modicus atque
etiam demissus videretur.   Conferant se non dico illi
veteres Africani, Achaici, Numantini, sed hi proximi,
Marii, Sullae, Pompeii, nolo progredi longius ; infra
Pallantis laudes iacebunt.

Urbanos, qui illa censuerunt, putem an miseros ?
Dicerem urbanos, si senatum deceret urbanitas,
miseros sed nemo tam miser est, ut illa cogatur.
Ambitio ergo et procedendi libido ?  Sed quis adeo
demens, ut per suum, per publicum dedecus procedere velit in ea civitate, in qua hic esset usus
florentissimae dignitatis, ut primus in senatu laudare
Pallantem posset ?

Omitto, quod Pallanti servo praetoria ornamenta
offeruntur (quippe offeruntur a servis), mitto, quod
censent non exhortandum modo, verum etiam com-
pellendum ad usum aureorum anulorum (erat enim
contra maiestatem senatus, si ferreis praetorius
uteretur) ; levia haec et transeunda, illa memoranda,
quod ' nomine Pallantis senatus ' (nec expiata postea
curia est), ' Pallantis nomine senatus gratias agit
Caesari, quod et ipse cum summo honore mentionem
eius prosecutus esset et senatui facultatem fecisset

<hr>

a The badge of equestrian rank, as an iron one was of servitude.   (Melm.)

sesterces; but he was contented with accepting only the honour." I afterwards thought it worth while to search for this decree, and found it so copious and effusive that this arrogant inscription seems moderate and actually humble in comparison. Our national heroes all put together—I do not speak of such ancient worthies as the Scipios and the Mummii; but take the more modern ones, the Marii, the Syllas, and the Pompeys, to name no more—all these could not come up to the character it gives of Pallas.

Was it the wit, shall I suppose, or the misery, of its authors that inspired this decree? I should say the former, were not raillery unbecoming the dignity to the Senate; the latter, but that no wretchedness could enforce such baseness. Perhaps then, it was ambition and greed of promotion? But who would be madman enough to dishonour himself and the State for the sake of rising in a commonwealth where the highest office carried with it one function only—to lead the Senate in eulogising Pallas?

I pass by their offering to a slave the Praetorian ornaments (they were slaves themselves who did so). I pass by their voting that Pallas should be not only entreated, but compelled, to wear the golden ring *a* (no doubt it was not consistent with the dignity of the Senate, that a person of Praetorian rank should wear an iron one). These are trifles not worth dwelling upon; but here is a truly memorable clause: "The Senate, on behalf of Pallas" (and the senate-house was not purified after so vile a pollution). "The Senate returns thanks to Caesar on behalf of Pallas, not only for the high honour he was pleased to bestow on him at their recommendation, but for

testandi erga eum benevolentiam suam. Quid enim senatui pulchrius, quam ut erga Pallantem satis gratus videretur? Additur: 'Ut Pallas, cui se omnes pro virili parte obligatos fatentur, singularis fidei, singularis industriae fructum meritissimo ferat.' Prolatos imperii fines, redditos exercitus rei publicae credas.

Adstruitur his: 'Cum senatui populoque Romano liberalitatis gratior repraesentari nulla materia possit, quam si abstinentissimi fidelissimique custodis principalium opum facultates adiuvare contigisset.' Hoc tunc votum senatus, hoc praecipuum gaudium populi, haec liberalitatis materia gratissima, si Pallantis facultates adiuvare publicarum opum egestione contingeret. Iam quae sequuntur, 'voluisse quidem senatum censere dandum ex aerario sestertium centies quinquagies, et quanto ab eiusmodi cupiditatibus remotior eius animus esset, tanto impensius petere a publico parente, ut eum compelleret ad cedendum senatui.' Id vero deerat, ut cum Pallante auctoritate publica ageretur, Pallas rogaretur, ut senatui cederet, ut illi superbissimae abstinentiae Caesar ipse advocatus esset, ne sestertium centies quinquagies sperneret. Sprevit, quod solum potuit tantis opibus publice oblatis adrogantius facere, quam si accepisset.

Senatus tamen id quoque similis querenti laudibus tulit his quidem verbis: 'sed cum princeps optimus

the opportunity afforded the House of testifying
their good will towards him." Nothing you see
could more ennoble the Senate, than to appear duly
grateful to Pallas ! It goes on : " That Pallas to
whom we all, as far as in us lies, acknowledge our
several obligations, may reap the just reward of his
singlar fidelity and diligence." One would think he
had extended the bounds of the empire, and then
resigned to the State the command of the legions he
had led !

The next clause is : " Since the Senate and the
Roman People could not have a more agreeable
occasion for their liberality, than the opportunity of
enriching so thrifty and honest a guardian of the
Imperial funds." Such at that time was the aspiration
of the Senate ; such the highest pleasures of the
people ; such the most agreeable occasion of exercising
their liberality—an opportunity to enrich Pallas by
depleting the public funds ! Now mark the conclusion :
" the Senate would have wished to vote him fifteen
million sesterces out of the treasury ; and as he has a
soul far above desires of this kind they the more
urgently request the Father of the State to oblige him
to comply with their wish." 'Twas indeed the one
thing wanting, that public influence should be brought
to bear on Pallas that he should be pressed to yield
to the Senate ; and Caesar himself be called in to
oppose this insolent piece of self denial—all to
prevent Pallas from rejecting the gift of fifteen million
sesterces ! He did reject it—the only way in which
he could treat the State's offer of so vast a sum more
arrogantly than by accepting it.

Yet even this the Senate endured, and while adopting
an injured tone, applauded as follows : " But whereas

parensque publicus rogatus a Pallante eam partem
sententiae, quae pertinebat ad dandum ei ex aerario
centies quinquagies sestertium, remitti voluisset;
testari senatum, etsi[1] libenter ac merito hanc summam inter reliquos honores ob fidem diligentiamque
Pallanti decernere coepisset,[2] voluntati tamen principis sui, cui in nulla re fas putaret repugnare, in hac
quoque re obsequi.'

Imaginare Pallantem velut intercedentem senatus
consulto moderantemque honores suos et sestertium
centies quinquagies ut nimium recusantem, cum
praetoria ornamenta tamquam minus recepisset,
imaginare Caesarem liberti precibus vel potius
imperio coram senatu obtemperantem (imperat enim
libertus patrono, quem in senatu rogat), imaginare
senatum usquequaque testantem merito libenterque
se hanc summam inter reliquos honores Pallanti
coepisse decernere et perseveraturum fuisse, nisi
obsequeretur principis voluntati, cui non esset fas
in ulla re repugnare. Ita, ne sestertium centies
quinquagies Pallas ex aerario ferret, verecundia
ipsius, obsequio senatus opus fuit in hoc praecipue
non obsecuturi, si in ulla re putasset fas esse non
obsequi.

Finem existimas? Mane dum et maiora accipe:
'Utique, cum sit utile principis benignitatem
promptissimam ad laudem praemiaque merentium

---

[1] etsi *r*, *K* ii., et se *M*,*a*.
[2] coepisset *Catan.*, coepisse *M a*.

---

[a] *i.e.* assuming the prerogative of a Tribune of the Plebs.
[b] Because the fiction of the Senate's supreme authority
was still kept up.

our excellent prince and father of his country has
desired, at the instance of Pallas, to have that clause
of the decree rescinded which assigns him fifteen
million sesterces out of the treasury; the Senate
declares that although they had gladly and justly set
about decreeing that sum to Pallas, amongst other
honours, on account of his fidelity and diligence; yet
even in this matter they obey the will of their
sovereign, which they think can never be combated
without impiety."

Figure to yourself Pallas putting his veto,[a] as it
were, on a decree of the Senate; setting limits to
his own honours, and refusing fifteen million sesterces
as above his deserts, after accepting the Praetorian
insignia as below them. Imagine Caesar obeying
the treaties, or rather the commands, of his freedman
in the face of the Senate (for a freedman's request
to his patron becomes a command when he delivers it
from a seat in that House[b]). Imagine the Senate
declaring all the time that it had willingly and
justly designed, among other honours, to vote Pallas
this sum: and that it would have persevered
but for its obedience to the will of the Emperor,
which it was impious to oppose on any point. Did it
need then the obsequiousness of the Senate and his
own modesty to prevent Pallas from carrying off
fifteen millions out of the treasury? And was it in
this case, of all others, that the Senate would have
been disobedient, if they had thought it lawful to
be so in any?

And now, perhaps, you think you are got to the
end? But wait a bit; here is something still grander
for you: "AND WHEREAS IT IS EXPEDIENT, that the
gracious promptitude of the Emperor to commend

illustrari ubique et maxime his locis, quibus incitari
ad imitationem praepositi rerum eius curae possent,
et Pallantis spectatissima fides atque innocentia
exemplo provocare studium tam honestae aemulationis
posset, ea quae IV Kal. Februarias, quae proximae
fuissent, in amplissimo ordine optimus princeps
recitasset, senatusque consulta de iis rebus facta
in aere inciderentur, idque aes figeretur ad statuam
loricatam divi Iulii.' Parum visum tantorum de-
decorum esse curiam testem, delectus est celeber-
rimus locus, in quo legenda praesentibus, legenda
futuris proderentur. Placuit aere signari omnes
honores fastidiosissimi mancipii, quosque repudiasset
quosque, quantum ad decernentis pertinet, gessisset.
Incisa et insculpta sunt publicis aeternisque monu-
mentis praetoria ornamenta Pallantis sic quasi
foedera antiqua, sic quasi sacrae leges. Tanta
principis, tanta senatus, tanta Pallantis ipsius—quid
dicam, nescio, ut vellent in oculis omnium figi Pallas
insolentiam suam, patientiam Caesar, humilitatem
senatus.

Nec puduit rationem turpitudini obtendere, egre-
giam quidem pulchramque rationem, 'ut exemplo
Pallantis praemiorum ad studium aemulationis ceteri
provocarentur.' Ea honorum vilitas erat, illorum
etiam, quos Pallas non dedignabatur. Inveniebantur

---

ª *loricata*, "wearing a cuirass," seems to have been the
regular designation of this statue, which stood in the Forum.

and reward merit should be everywhere made public,
especially in those places where his departmental
officers may be excited to an imitation and the
approved fidelity and integrity of Pallas may call
forth efforts at so laudable an emulation, IT IS
THEREFORE RESOLVED, that the memorial which the
Emperor read to the honourable House on the 29th
of January last, together with their decree upon this
question, shall be engraved on a brazen tablet, and
the said tablet affixed to the mail-clad statue *a* of the
divine Julius Caesar." It was not deemed sufficient
that the senate-house should be witness to this
complicated disgrace ; the most frequented spot in
all Rome was chosen to display the inscription to
that and future ages. It was thought proper that all
the honours of a most insolent slave, both those
which he refused and those which, as much as in the
authors of the decree lay, he had borne, should be
inscribed in bronze. The granting of the Praetorian
insignia to Pallas was deeply engraven, like ancient
treaties or sacred laws, upon public and everlasting
monuments. The Emperor, the Senate, and Pallas
himself behaved—I lack a name for such behaviour—
as if Caesar meant to put up a notice of his weakness,
the Senate of its servility, and Pallas of his insolence,
in the face of all the world !

The Senate was not ashamed to palliate this
turpitude with the show of reason, and a vastly noble
one it was, even "that others might be stimulated
by the rewards conferred upon Pallas, to try to
emulate his example !" Thus cheap were all
honours rendered, even those which Pallas did not
disdain ! And yet there were found men of good

tamen honesto loco nati, qui peterent cuperentque,
quod dari liberto, promitti servis videbant.

Quam iuvat, quod in tempora illa non incidi,
quorum sic me, tamquam illis vixerim, pudet! Non
dubito, similiter adfici te. Scio, quam sit tibi vivus
et ingenuus animus; ideoque facilius est, ut me,
quamquam indignatione quibusdam in locis fortasse
ultra epistulae modum extulerim, parum doluisse
quam nimis credas. Vale.

## VII

### C. Plinius Tacito Suo S.

Neque ut magistro magister neque ut discipulo
discipulus (sic enim scribis), sed ut discipulo magister
(nam tu magister, ego contra; atque adeo tu in
scholam revocas, ego adhuc Saturnalia extendo)
librum misisti. Num potui longius hyperbaton
facere atque hoc ipso probare eum esse me, qui non
modo magister tuus, sed ne discipulus quidem debeam
dici? Sumam tamen personam magistri exseramque
in librum tuum ius, quod dedisti, eo liberius, quo
nihil ex meis interim missurus sum tibi, in quo te
ulciscaris. Vale.

---

ᵃ *Hyperbaton*, (lit. "transgression") was the grammarians'

birth, who were humble enough to desire and solicit those very honours, which they thus saw conferred upon a freedman, and promised to slaves.

Happy for me that my lot was not cast in those times, which I blush for as though I actually lived in them! And I doubt not, they raise the same sentiments in you. I know the honest warmth of your temper, which, though I may in some passages have been transported into a higher style than the epistolatory, will easily persuade you that I have expressed too little rather than too much indignation. Farewell.

## VII

### To Tacitus

Not as one master to another, nor as one scholar to another (as you are pleased to say), but as a master to his scholar—for you are the master, I the other party, witness your summoning me back to school, whilst I am prolonging my New Year's holiday—have you sent me your oration. Tell me, now, could I have stretched out an *hyperbaton*[a] further than in this sentence, or given a stronger proof, that far from being called your master, I am not even worthy to be called your pupil? However, I will assume the rôle of master and exert the authority you have given me over your piece; the more freely as I have nothing of my own to send you at present, upon which you may take your revenge. Farewell.

term for "a considerable clause interpolated between two connected parts of a sentence."

THE LETTERS OF PLINY

## VIII

### C. Plinius Romano Suo S.

Vidistine aliquando Clitumnum fontem? Si nondum (et puto nondum; alioqui narrasses mihi), vide,
quem ego (paenitet tarditatis) proxime vidi.

Modicus collis adsurgit antiqua cupressu nemorosus
et opacus. Hunc subter fons exit et exprimitur
pluribus venis, sed imparibus, eluctatusque, quem
facit, gurgitem lato gremio patescit purus et vitreus,
ut numerare iactas stipes et relucentis calculos possis.
Inde non loci devexitate, sed ipsa sui copia et quasi
pondere, impellitur fons[1] adhuc et iam amplissimum
flumen atque etiam navium patiens, quas obvias
quoque et contrario nisu in diversa tendentes trans-
mittit et perfert, adeo validus, ut illa, qua properat
ipse, quamquam per solum planum, remis non adiuve-
tur, idem aegerrime remis contisque superetur adversus. Iucundum utrumque per iocum ludumque
fluitantibus, ut flexerint cursum, laborem otio, otium
labore variare.

Ripae fraxino multa, multa populo vestiuntur, quas
perspicuus amnis velut mersas viridi imagine adnu-
merat. Rigor aquae certaverit nivibus, nec color
cedit. Adiacet templum priscum et religiosum.
Stat Clitumnus ipse amictus ornatusque praetexta.

[1] impellitur fons *Müller*, impellitur. Fons *edd.*

[a] It was customary to throw coins as votive offerings into
those fountains, lakes, etc., which were accounted sacred.
Suetonius mentions this practice, in the annual vows which
he says the Roman people made for the health of Augustus.
(Melm.)

114

## VIII

### To Romanus

Have you at last seen the source of the river Clitumnus? As I never heard you mention it, I imagine not; let me therefore advise you to do so immediately. It is but lately indeed I had that pleasure, and I condemn myself for not having seen it sooner.

At the foot of a little hill, covered with venerable and shady cypress trees, the river head is sent up out from the ground in several and unequal rills, and bursting forth forms a broad pool so clear and glassy that you may count the shining pebbles, and the little pieces of money which are thrown into it.[a] From thence it is carried off not so much by the declivity of the ground, as by its own volume and, as it were, density. As soon as it has quitted its source, it becomes a mighty river, navigable for large vessels, even when they are making up stream and have to contend against the current. This runs so strong, though the ground is level, that boats going with it have no occasion for rowing oars; while it is difficult to advance against it, even with the help of oars and poles. This vicissitude and labour and ease is exceedingly amusing when one sails up and down merely for pleasure.

The banks are thickly clad with ash and poplar trees, whose verdant reflections are as distinctly seen in the translucent stream, as if they were actually sunk in it. The water is cold as snow, and as white too. Near it is a primitive and holy temple, wherein stands the river-god Clitumnus clothed in a purple-

Praesens numen atque etiam fatidicum indicant
sortes. Sparsa sunt circa sacella complura totidem-
que di. Sua cuique veneratio, suum nomen, quibusdam vero etiam fontes. Nam praeter illum quasi
parentem ceterorum sunt minores capite discreti;
sed flumini miscentur, quod ponte transmittitur.
Is terminus sacri profanique. In superiore parte
navigare tantum, infra etiam natare concessum.
Balineum Hispellates, quibus illum locum divus
Augustus dono dedit, publice praebent, praebent et
hospitium. Nec desunt villae, quae secutae fluminis
amoenitatem margini insistunt.

In summa nihil erit, ex quo non capias voluptatem.
Nam studebis quoque; et leges multa multorum
omnibus columnis, omnibus parietibus inscripta, quibus fons ille deusque celebratur. Plura laudabis, non
nulla ridebis; quamquam tu vero, quae tua humanitas,
nulla ridebis. Vale.

## IX

### C. PLINIUS URSO SUO S.

OLIM non librum in manus, non stilum sumpsi,
olim nescio, quid sit otium, quid quies, quid denique

bordered robe. The lots kept here for divining sufficiently testify to the presence and oracular power of the deity. Several little chapels are scattered round, each containing the statue of a different god. Each of these has his peculiar worship and title; and some of them, too, their own springs. For, beside the principal one, which is, as it were, the parent of all the rest, there are several other lesser streams, which, taking their rise from distinct sources, lose themselves in the river; over which a bridge is built, that separates the sacred part from that which lies open to common use. Vessels are allowed to come above this bridge, but no person is permitted to swim, except below it. The Hispellates, to whom Augustus gave this place, maintain a bath, and an inn for travellers, at the expense of the corporation. And villas, wherever the river is most beautiful, are situated upon its banks.

In short, every object that presents itself will afford you entertainment. For you will also find food for study in the numerous inscriptions, by many hands all over the pillars and walls, in praise of the spring and its tutelar deity. Many of them you will admire, others you will laugh at; but I must correct myself when I say so; you are too good-natured I know, to laugh at any. Farewell.

## IX

### To Ursus

It is a long time since I have taken either a book, or a pen in my hand. It is long since I have known the sweets of leisure and repose; since I have known

illud iners quidem, iucundum tamen nihil agere,
nihil esse; adeo multa me negotia amicorum nec
secedere nec studere patiuntur. Nulla enim studia
tanti, ut amicitiae officium deseratur, quod religio-
sissime custodiendum studia ipsa praecipiunt. Vale.

## X

### C. PLINIUS FABATO PROSOCERO SUO S.

Quo magis cupis ex nobis pronepotes videre, hoc
tristior audies neptem tuam abortum fecisse, dum se
praegnantem esse puellariter nescit ac per hoc quaedam custodienda praegnantibus omittit, facit omit-
tenda. Quem errorem magnis documentis expiavit
in summum periculum adducta. Igitur, ut necesse
est graviter accipias senectutem tuam quasi paratis
posteris destitutam, sic debes agere dis gratias, quod
ita tibi in praesentia pronepotes negaverunt, ut
servarent neptem, illos reddituri, quorum nobis spem
certiorem haec ipsa quamquam parum prospere
explorata fecunditas facit.

Isdem nunc ego te quibus ipsum me hortor, moneo,
confirmo. Neque enim ardentius tu pronepotes,

in fine, that indolent but agreeable situation of doing nothing, and being nothing: so entirely has the pressure of business on my friends' account put a stop alike to my going into the country and my studying. For no studies are of consequence enough to supersede that duty of friendship which they themselves teach us most religiously to observe. Farewell.

## X

### To Fabatus, His Wife's Grandfather

Your concern to hear of your grand-daughter's miscarriage will be proportionate, I know, to your earnest desire that we should make you a great-grandfather. The inexperience of her youth rendered her ignorant that she was breeding: so that she not only omitted the proper precautions, but managed herself in a way extremely unsuitable to a person in her condition. But she has received a severe lesson, paying for her mistake by the utmost hazard of her life. So, though you cannot but feel it an affliction to be bereaved at your advanced age of the immediate prospect of posterity; yet it deserves your gratitude to the Gods, that while denying you great-grandchildren for the present, they preserved the life of your grand-daughter, as designing yet to bestow them; a blessing we may expect with more certainty, as she has given this proof, though an unhappy one indeed, of her being capable of bearing children.

I am offering you the reflections in which I seek exhortation, counsel, and strengthening for myself. You cannot more ardently wish to have great-

quam ego liberos cupio, quibus videor a meo tuoque
latere pronum ad honores iter et audita latius nomina
et non subitas imagines relicturus, nascantur modo et
hunc nostrum dolorem gaudio mutent.   Vale.

## XI

### C. Plinius Hispullae Suae S.

Cum affectum tuum erga fratris filiam cogito etiam
materna indulgentia molliorem, intellego prius tibi,
quod est posterius, nuntiandum, ut praesumpta
laetitia sollicitudini locum non relinquat.   Quamquam vereor, ne post gratulationem quoque in metum
redeas atque ita gaudeas periculo liberatam, ut simul,
quod periclitata sit, perhorrescas.   Iam hilaris, iam
sibi, iam mihi reddita incipit refici transmissumque
discrimen   convalescendo metiri.   Fuit   alioqui in
summo discrimine, impune dixisse liceat, fuit nulla
sua culpa, aetatis aliqua.   Inde abortus et ignorati
uteri triste experimentum.

Proinde, etsi non contigit tibi desiderium fratris
amissi aut nepote eius aut nepte solari, memento

---

ᵃ *imagines*, wax portrait masks of ancestors who had held
curule office (carried in their own and their descendants'
funeral processions), were kept in the atrium of the family
house, "arranged, and connected by coloured lines, in such a
way as to exhibit the family pedigree" (Seyffert).   Hence
"to have *imagines*" meant "to be of noble ancestry," in

grandchildren, than I do to have children; for
methinks as your offspring and mine they will in-
herit an easy path to honours, a fairly well-known
name, and an ancestral tree of no mushroom growth.[a]
May we but see them born, it will turn our present
sorrow into joy.   Farewell.


## XI

### To Hispulla

When I consider that you love your brother's
daughter with a more than maternal fondness, I see
I ought to give you my latest news first; that sentiments of joy may forestall and preclude anxiety.
Though I fear indeed, even after your transports of
gratulation you will feel some renewal of concern,
and in the midst of your joy for the danger she has
escaped, will tremble at the thought of that which
she has undergone.   She is now, however, in good
spirits, and again restored to herself and to me;
already she is making as rapid progress towards
recovery, as she did towards her late danger.   To
tell you the truth, she was in the utmost danger (be
it said without ill omen); for which no blame can be
laid on her, but a good deal on her youthfulness.
To this must be imputed her miscarriage, and the
sad result she has experienced of not knowing her
condition.
     But though you have not been vouchsafed the
consolation of a nephew or niece, to supply the loss
of your brother; remember, that comfort is rather

contrast to being *novus homo*, the first of your family to
attain curule rank.

tamen dilatum magis istud quam negatum, cum
salva sit, ex qua sperari potest. Simul excusa
patri tuo casum, cui paratior apud feminas venia
est. Vale.

## XII

### C. Plinius Miniciano Suo S.

Hunc solum diem excuso. Recitaturus est Titinius Capito, quem ego audire nescio magis debeam an
cupiam. Vir est optimus et inter praecipua saeculi
ornamenta numerandus; colit studia, studiosos amat,
fovet, provehit, multorumque, qui aliqua componunt,
portus, sinus, gremium,[1] omnium exemplum, ipsarum
denique litterarum iam senescentium reductor ac
reformator. Domum suam recitantibus praebet,
auditoria, non apud se tantum benignitate mira
frequentat; mihi certe, si modo in urbe est, defuit
nunquam.

Porro tanto turpius gratiam non referre, quanto
honestior causa referendae. An, si litibus tererer,
obstrictum esse me crederem obeunti vadimonia mea,
nunc, quia mihi omne negotium, omnis in studiis
cura, minus obligor tanta sedulitate celebranti, in

---

[1] gremium *Schaefer*, praemium *vulg.*

---

[a] Fabatus.

deferred than denied, since her life is preserved from whom it is to be expected. I beg also you will excuse this accident to your father,[a] whose indulgence is always more readily forthcoming when solicited by one of your sex. Farewell.


## XII

### To Minicianus

I beg you would excuse me this one day. Titinius Capito is going to recite, and I know not whether it is most my inclination, or my duty to attend him. He is a man of a most amiable disposition, and justly to be numbered among the brightest ornaments of our age; he cultivates the polite arts himself, and generously admires and encourages them in others. To many authors of merit, he is a haven, a refuge, a resting-place; to all, a model. In a word, he is the restorer and reformer of literature itself, now alas! falling into decrepitude. His house is at the disposal of everyone who wishes to give a recital; and it is not there only that he attends these assemblies with the most obliging good nature. I am sure at least he never missed one of mine if he happened to be at Rome.

Besides, it were the more unseemly not to return a favour, when I have such honourable cause. Should not I, if my business lay in lawsuits, think myself obliged to a man who kept the recognizances I had entered into for his appearance? And am I less indebted because my whole care and business is of the literary kind, for his assiduity on a point which,

123

quo obligari ego, **ne** dicam solo, certe maxime
possum ?

Quod si illi nullam vicem, nulla quasi mutua officia
deberem, sollicitarer tamen vel ingenio hominis
pulcherrimo et maximo et in summa severitate
dulcissimo vel honestate materiae. Scribit exitus
illustrium virorum, in iis quorundam mihi carissi-
morum. Videor ergo fungi pio munere, quorumque
exsequias celebrare non licuit, horum quasi fune-
bribus laudationibus seris quidem, sed tanto magis
veris interesse. Vale.

## XIII

### C. PLINIUS GENIALI SUO S.

PROBO, quod libellos meos cum patre legisti.
Pertinet ad profectum tuum a disertissimo viro
discere, quid laudandum, quid reprehendendum,
simul ita institui, ut verum dicere adsuescas. Vides,
quem sequi, cuius debeas implere vestigia. O te
beatum, cui contigit vivum atque idem optimum et
coniunctissimum exemplar, qui denique eum potissimum imitandum habes, cui natura esse te simillimum
voluit ! Vale.

if not the only, is however the principal instance wherein I can be obliged ?

But though I owed him no return, nor what I might call reciprocity of good offices ; yet not only the beauty of his extensive genius, as polite as it is severely correct, but the dignity of his subject, would forcibly invite my attendance.  He has written an account of the deaths of several illustrious persons, some of whom were my dear friends.  It is a pious office, methinks, as I could not be present at their obsequies, to attend this (as I may call it) their funeral oration ; which though a late, is however for that reason a more genuine tribute to their memories. Farewell.

## XIII

### To Genialis

I much approve of your having read my orations with your father.  It is important for your progress, to learn from a man of his eloquence what to admire and what to condemn, and by the same course of training to acquire the habit of speaking your real sentiments.  You see whose steps you ought to follow ; and happy are you in having a living model before you, which is at once the nearest and the noblest you can pursue !  Happy, in a word, that he whom nature designed you should most resemble, is, of all others, the person whom you should most imitate !  Farewell.

## XIV

### C. Plinius Aristoni Suo S.

Cum sis peritissimus et privati iuris et publici, cuius pars senatorium est, cupio ex te potissimum audire, erraverim in senatu proxime necne, non ut in prae-teritum (serum enim) verum ut in futurum, si quid simile inciderit, erudiar.

Dices: 'Cur quaeris, quod nosse debebas?' Priorum temporum servitus ut aliarum optimarum artium sic etiam iuris senatorii oblivionem quandam et ignorantiam induxit. Quotus enim quisque tam patiens, ut velit discere, quod in usu non sit habiturus? Adde, quod difficile est tenere, quae acceperis, nisi exerceas. Itaque reducta libertas rudes nos et imperitos deprehendit; cuius dulcedine accensi cogimur quaedam facere ante quam nosse.

Erat autem antiquitus institutum, ut a maioribus natu non auribus modo, verum etiam oculis disceremus, quae facienda mox ipsi ac per vices quasdam tradenda minoribus haberemus. Inde adulescentuli statim castrensibus stipendiis imbuebantur, ut imperare parendo, duces agere, dum sequuntur, adsuescerent, inde honores petituri adsistebant curiae

---

<sup>a</sup> That of Domitian.
<sup>b</sup> On the accession of Nerva, 96 A.D.

## XIV

### To Aristo

As you are equally versed in civil and constitutional law, which latter includes the procedure of the Senate, I am particularly desirous to have your opinion, whether or no I made a mistake in the House the other day. This I request for my better instruction, not as to what is passed, (for that is now too late,) but as regards questions of the same nature that may hereafter arise.

I can fancy your replying, "Why do you ask, what you ought to have known?" But our servitude under a former reign [a] cast a cloud of oblivion and ignorance over all branches of useful knowledge, and not excluding even the usages of the Senate; for who is so tame-spirited as to desire to learn an art of which he will be debarred the exercise? Besides, it is not easy to retain the knowledge one has acquired, without putting it in practice. Thus Liberty at her return [b] found us ignorant and inexperienced; and kindled by her charms, we are sometimes impelled to action, ere we know how to act.

But in the olden time it was an established rule that Romans should learn from their elders, not only by precept, but by example, the principles on which they themselves should one day act, and which they should in their turn transmit to the younger generation. Hence they were inured from boyhood to service in camp, that by being accustomed to obey, they might learn to command and by following others, be trained to play the leader. And hence, on becoming candidates for office, they used to stand

THE LETTERS OF PLINY

foribus et consilii publici spectatores ante quam
consortes erant. Suus cuique parens pro magistro,
aut cui parens non erat, maximus quisque et vetus-
tissimus pro parente. Quae potestas referentibus,
quod censentibus ius, quae vis magistratibus, quae
ceteris libertas, ubi cedendum, ubi resistendum, quod
silendi tempus, quis dicendi modus, quae distinctio
pugnantium sententiarum, quae exsecutio prioribus
aliquid addentium, omnem denique senatorium
morem, quod fidelissimum praecipiendi genus, exemplis docebantur.

At nos iuvenes fuimus quidem in castris, sed cum
suspecta virtus, inertia in pretio, cum ducibus
auctoritas nulla, nulla militibus verecundia, nusquam
imperium, nusquam obsequium, omnia soluta, turbata
atque etiam in contrarium versa, postremo obliviscen-
da magis quam tenenda. Iidem prospeximus curiam,
sed curiam trepidam et elinguem; cum dicere, quod
velles, periculosum, quod nolles, miserum esset.
Quid tunc disci potuit, quid didicisse iuvit, cum
senatus aut ad otium summum aut ad summum nefas
vocaretur, et modo ludibrio, modo dolori retentus,
numquam seria, tristia saepe censeret? Eadem mala
iam senatores, iam participes malorum multos per

---

*a* If any motion proposed in the Senate was thought too
general, and to include several distinct articles, some of which
might be approved, and others rejected, it was usual to
require that it might be divided. (Melm.)

*b* The fourth satire of Juvenal will serve as a comment
upon this passage, where he acquaints us that a turbot of a
most enormous size being brought to Domitian, he immediately convened the Senate, in order to consult in what manner it should be dressed. (Melm.)

128

at the senate-house doors, and were spectators, before they were members of the Council of State. The father of each youth served as his instructor, or, if he had none, some person of years and dignity supplied the place of a father. Thus they were taught by that surest method of instruction, example, how far the right of proposing any law to the Senate extended; what privileges a senator had in delivering his opinion; the powers of senators who are magistrates, and the independence of the rest; where it is proper to yield, and where to stand firm; how long to speak, and when to be silent; how to distinguish conflicting motions,[a] and how to discuss an amendment. In a word, they learnt by this means the whole conduct of a senator.

It is true, indeed, I myself served in the army as a young man; but it was at a time when courage was suspected, and cowardice at a premium; when the generals were without authority, and the soldiers without awe; when there was neither command nor obedience; when our whole military system was relaxed, disordered, and actually turned upside down—in short, when it was better to forget than to remember its lessons. I likewise went as a spectator to the Senate, but a Senate that was mute and fearful; since it was dangerous to speak one's real sentiments, and infamous to profess any others. What satisfaction in learning, or indeed what could be learnt, when the Senate was convened either for utter idleness or for business the most criminal; when they were kept sitting either for cruel or ridiculous purposes[b]; and when their resolutions were never serious, though often tragical. On becoming a senator, and a partaker of these miseries,

annos vidimus tulimusque: quibus ingenia nostra in
posterum quoque hebetata, fracta, contusa sunt.
Breve tempus (nam tanto brevius omne quanto
felicius tempus), quo libet scire, quid simus, libet
exercere, quod scimus.[1]

Quo iustius peto, primum ut errori, si quis est
error, tribuas veniam, deinde medearis scientia tua,
cui semper fuit curae sic iura publica ut privata, sic
antiqua ut recentia, sic rara ut adsidua tractare.
Atque ego arbitror illis etiam, quibus plurimarum
rerum agitatio frequens nihil esse ignotum patiebatur,
genus quaestionis, quod adfero ad te, aut non satis
tritum aut etiam inexpertum fuisse. Hoc et ego
excusatior, si forte sum lapsus, et tu dignior laude,
si potes id quoque docere, quod in obscuro est, an
didiceris.

Referebatur de libertis Afrani Dextri consulis
incertum sua an suorum manu, scelere an obsequio
peremti. Hos alius ('Quis?' inquis. Ego; sed
nihil refert) post quaestionem supplicio liberandos,
alius in insulam relegandos, alius morte puniendos
arbitrabatur. Quarum sententiarum tanta diversitas

---

[1] scimus *Reifferscheid. Mus. Rhen.* 1860, p. 636, sumus *vulg.*

I both witnessed and endured them for many years;
which so broke and damped my spirits, that they have
not even yet been able fully to recover themselves.
It is but a short time (for every period is shorter,
the happier it is) since we could take any pleasure
in knowing the rights and duties of our station, or in
putting that knowledge into practice.

Upon these grounds I may the more reasonably
ask you, in the first place, to condone my error (if I
have been guilty of one), and in the next, to remedy
it by your expert knowledge: for you have ever
been a devoted student of our laws both public and
private, ancient and modern, general and exceptional.
And I think the point upon which I am going to
consult you, is one that even those who by constant
and varied practice must have mastered every detail
of public business, have seldom or never had to
deal with. I shall be more excusable, therefore, if I
happen to have been mistaken: as you will deserve
so much the higher applause, if you can teach me a
lesson which it is not clear that you have learned
yourself.

The case before the House concerned the freedmen of the consul Afranius Dexter, who being
found murdered, it was uncertain whether he fell by
his own hands or by those of his people; and if the
latter, whether they acted in obedience to his
commands, or were prompted by their own villainy.
After they had been put to the question, a certain
senator (never mind his name, but if you wish to
know, it was myself) was for acquitting them;
another moved that they should be banished to an
island; and a third that they should be put to death.
These several verdicts were so extremely opposite,

erat, ut non possent esse nisi singulae. Quid enim
commune habet occidere et relegare? Non hercule
magis quam relegare et absolvere; quamquam
propior aliquanto est sententiae relegantis, quae
absolvit, quam quae occidit (utraque enim ex illis
vitam relinquit, haec adimit) cum interim, et qui
morte puniebant, et qui relegabant, una sedebant
et temporaria simulatione concordiae discordiam
differebant. Ego postulabam, ut tribus sententiis
constaret suus numerus, nec se brevibus induciis
duae iungerent. Exigebam ergo, ut, qui capitali
supplicio afficiendos putabant, discederent a relegante, nec interim contra absolventis mox dissensuri
congregarentur, quia parvulum referret, an idem
displiceret, quibus non idem placuisset. Illud etiam
mihi permirum videbatur, eum quidem, qui libertos
relegandos, servos supplicio adficiendos censuisset,
coactum esse dividere sententiam; hunc autem, qui
libertos morte multaret, cum relegante numerari.
Nam, si oportuisset dividi sententiam unius, quia
res duas comprehendebat, non reperiebam, quem ad
modum posset iungi sententia duorum tam diversa
censentium.

---

*a* Those in favour of a motion in the Senate signified the
same by ranging themselves on that side of the House where
the proposer was seated.

that it was impossible to put them to the vote
otherwise than separately. For what is there in
common between a sentence of banishment, and a
sentence of death? Nothing more, heaven knows,
than there is between a sentence of banishment and
an acquittal. (Albeit acquitting a person comes
much nearer to banishing him, than does sentencing
him to death; for both the former verdicts spare,
whereas the latter takes away, his life.) In the
meanwhile, those respectively in favour of death, and
of banishment, sate together on the same side of the
House: and by a temporary appearance of union,
suspended their real disagreement. I demanded,
that the three verdicts should be counted as three,
and that two of them should not coalesce by a
momentary truce; consequently, I insisted that
members who were for capital punishment should
move away <sup>a</sup> from the proposer of banishment; and
that those who would shortly be at variance should
not meanwhile group themselves in opposition to the
party for acquittal, merely to disunite again; for it was
not material that they all opposed the same motion,
since they did not support the same. It also seemed
to me very extraordinary that whereas he who
proposed banishment for freedmen and death for
the slaves was obliged to put two distinct motions
to the House; the proposer of a death-sentence upon
the freedmen should be reckoned along with him
who proposed to banish them. For if one and the
same senator's motion had to be divided, because
it comprehended two distinct things, I could not
see how the motions of two different persons, whose
views were diametrically opposed, could be taken
together.

Atque adeo permitte mihi sic apud te tamquam
ibi, sic peracta re tamquam adhuc integra rationem
iudicii mei reddere, quaeque tunc carptim multis
obstrepentibus dixi, per otium iungere. Fingamus
tres omnino iudices in hanc causam datos esse,
horum uni placuisse perire libertos, alteri relegari,
tertio absolvi; utrumne sententiae duae collatis
viribus novissimam periment, an separatim una-
quaeque tantundem quantum altera valebit, nec
magis poterit cum secunda prima conecti, quam
secunda cum tertia? Igitur in senatu quoque
numerari tamquam contrariae debent, quae tamquam
diversae dicuntur. Quodsi unus atque idem et
perdendos censeret et relegandos, num ex sententia
unius et perire possent et relegari? num denique
omnino una sententia putaretur, quae tam diversa
coniungeret? Quem ad modum igitur, cum alter
puniendos, alter censeat relegandos, videri potest una
sententia, quia dicitur a duobus, quae non videretur
una, si ab uno diceretur?

Quid? lex non aperte docet dirimi debere
sententias occidentis et relegantis, cum ita dis-
cessionem fieri iubet: ' Qui haec sentitis, in hanc
partem, qui alia omnia, in illam partem ite, qua sentitis ' ? Examina singula verba et expende: ' Qui
haec sentitis,' hoc est qui relegandos putatis, ' in
hanc partem,' id est in eam, in qua sedet, qui

Permit me then, notwithstanding the point is
determined, to go over it again as if it were still
undecided, and to lay before you those reasons at my
ease, which I offered to the House in the midst of
much interruption and clamour. Let us suppose
there had been only three judges appointed to hear
this cause, one of whom was of opinion that the
freedmen should die; the second that they should
be banished; and the third that they ought to be
acquitted: should the two former verdicts unite
their strength to the destruction of the latter? Or
should not each of them separately be balanced, and
the first and second be no more combined than the
second and third? They ought therefore to be
counted in the Senate likewise as contrary, since
they were delivered as conflicting opinions. Suppose
the same person had moved, that the freedmen be
banished and put to death as well; could they on
one individual's motion have suffered both punishments? Or could it possibly have been esteemed
as one motion, when it united two such contrary
proposals? How then can one man's vote for death
and another's for banishment, which could not be
deemed a single motion if proposed by a single
person, pass for such because it has two proposers?

Does not the law manifestly teach that we are to
separate a capital verdict from one of banishment,
by the formula employed when the House is ordered
to divide? "You who hold such an opinion come
to this side; you who hold any other go over to the
side of him whose opinion you follow." Let us
examine and weigh every clause: "You who are of
this opinion": that is, you who would banish the freedmen, "come on this side"; namely, where the

censuit relegandos. Ex quo manifestum est non posse in eadem parte remanere eos, qui interficiendos arbitrantur. 'Qui alia omnia.' Animadvertis, ut non contenta lex dicere 'alia' addiderit 'omnia.' Num ergo dubium est alia omnia sentire eos, qui occidunt, quam qui relegant? 'In illam partem ite, qua sentitis.' Nonne videtur ipsa lex eos, qui dissentiunt, in contrariam partem vocare, cogere, impellere? non consul etiam, ubi quisque remanere, quo transgredi debeat, non tantum solemnibus verbis, sed manu gestuque demonstrat?

At enim futurum est ut, si dividantur sententiae interficientis et relegantis, praevaleat illa, quae absolvit. Quid istud ad censentes? quos certe non decet omnibus artibus, omni ratione pugnare, ne fiat, quod est mitius. Oportet tamen eos, qui puniunt capite, et qui relegant, absolventibus primum, mox inter se comparari. Scilicet, ut in spectaculis quibusdam sors aliquem seponit ac servat, qui cum victore contendat, sic in senatu sunt aliqua prima, sunt secunda certamina, et ex duabus sententiis eam, quae superior exierit, tertia exspectat.

Quid, quod prima sententia comprobata ceterae perimantur? Qua ergo ratione potest esse nunc[1] unus atque idem locus sententiarum, quarum nullus est postea? Planius repetam. Nisi dicente sententiam eo, qui relegat, illi, qui puniunt capite, initio

---

[1] nunc *Schaefer,* non *codd.*

proposer **of** that motion is sitting.   From whence it
is clear that those who would execute the freedmen
cannot remain on that side.   "You who hold any
other" : observe, the Law is not contented with
barely saying *another*, but it adds *any*.   Now can
there be a doubt, whether they who declare for a
capital conviction are of *any* other opinion, than
those who propose exile ?   "Go over to the side of
him whose opinion you follow" : does not the Law
herself seem to summon, force and urge those who
differ to opposite sides ?  Does not the Consul
actually point out, not only by the customary formula,
but by waving his hand, where each man is to
remain, or to which side he must cross over ?

"But," it is objected, "if the House votes separately on the motions for death and for banishment,
the motion for acquittal will get a majority."   But
what is that to the parties who vote ?  Certainly it
ill becomes them to fight tooth and nail to defeat the
milder verdict.  "Still," they say, "those who would
condemn the accused either capitally or to banishment, should be first matched against those who would
acquit them, and afterwards against each other."
Thus, as in certain public games one competitor is
reserved and set apart by lot to engage with the
conqueror of the rest; so, it seems, in the Senate
there is a first and second combat, and of two motions,
the prevailing one has still a third to contend with.

How about the rule that when the first motion
proposed is carried, all the rest fall to the ground ?
On what principle then can motions be simultaneously put now, which cannot later be put at all ?
To repeat this more plainly ; unless those in favour
of the death-penalty immediately go over to the side

statim in alia discedant, frustra postea dissentient ab
eo, cui paulo ante consenserint.

Sed quid ego similis docenti? cum discere velim,
an sententias dividi an iri in singulas oportuerit?
Obtinui quidem, quod postulabam; nihilo minus
tamen quaero, an postulare debuerim. Quem ad
modum obtinui? Is, qui ultimum supplicium su-
mendum esse censebat, nescio an iure, certe aequitate
postulationis meae victus omissa sententia sua accessit
releganti veritus scilicet, ne, si dividerentur sententiae, quod alioqui fore videbatur, ea, quae
absolvendos esse censebat, numero praevaleret.
Etenim longe plures in hac una quam in duabus
singulis erant. Tum illi quoque, qui auctoritate eius
trahebantur, transeunte illo destituti reliquerunt
sententiam ab ipso auctore desertam secutique sunt
quasi transfugam, quem ducem sequebantur. Sic ex
tribus sententiis duae factae, tenuitque ex duabus
altera tertia expulsa, quae cum ambas superare non
posset, elegit, ab utra vinceretur. Vale.

## XV

### C. Plinius Iuniori Suo S.

Oneravi te tot pariter missis voluminibus, sed
oneravi, primum quia exegeras, deinde quia scripseras

of the "Noes" when a member proposes banishment, it will be vain for them to oppose him on a
future division, whom they have supported just before.

But why do I talk like one giving instruction,
when I wish to learn whether or no these motions
should have been taken separately? My demand
was at least successful; nevertheless, I ask, was it
justifiable? Would you know how I succeeded in it?
The proposer of the death penalty, overcome
probably by the legality, certainly by the equity of
my demand, dropped his own motion and went over
to the proposer of exile. He was afraid, to be sure,
that if the motions were taken separately (which he
saw would anyhow be the case), those for acquittal
would have a majority. And truly, the numbers
were far greater on that side than on either of the
other two, separately counted. The consequence
was, that those who had been influenced by his
authority, when they saw themselves forsaken by his
going over to the other party, gave up a motion
which they found abandoned by the first author, and
deserted, as it were, with their leader. Thus the
three motions were resolved into two; and of those
two one prevailed; while the rejected third, as it
could not vanquish both the others, had only to
choose to which of the two it would yield. Farewell.

## XV

### To Junior

I HAVE over-burthened you by sending you so
many volumes at once; but I have done so firstly at
your own request; and secondly because you wrote

tam graciles istic vindemias esse, ut plane scirem tibi
vacaturum, quod vulgo dicitur, librum legere. Eadem
ex meis agellis nuntiantur. Igitur mihi quoque
licebit scribere, quae legas, sit modo, unde chartae
emi possint ; quae si scabrae bibulaeve sint, aut non
scribendum, aut necessario, quidquid scripserimus
boni malive, delebimus. Vale.


## XVI

### C. Plinius Paterno Suo S.

Confecerunt me infirmitates meorum, mortes
etiam, et quidem iuvenum. Solacia duo nequaquam paria tanto dolori, solacia tamen, unum facilitas manumittendi (videor enim non omnino
immaturos perdidisse, quos iam liberos perdidi),
alterum, quod permitto servis quoque quasi testamenta facere eaque, ut legitima, custodio. Mandant
rogantque, quod visum ; pareo ut iussus. Dividunt,
donant, relinquunt dumtaxat intra domum ; nam
servis res publica quaedam et quasi civitas domus
est. Sed, quamquam his solaciis adquiescam, de-

---

* Slaves could not hold or bequeath property.

me word that the yield of your vineyards had been so poor, that I might be assured you would have *time*, as people say, to read a book. I have received the same bad accounts of my own little farms; and am myself therefore at full leisure to write books for you, provided I can but raise money enough to furnish me with good paper. For should I be reduced to the coarse and spongy sort, either I must not write at all, or whatever I compose, whether good or bad, must necessarily undergo one cruel blot. Farewell.


## XVI

### To Paternus

THE sickness which has lately run through my family, and carried off several of my domestics, some of them too in the prime of their years, has deeply afflicted me. I have two consolations, however, which though they are not equal to so considerable a grief, still they are consolations. One is, that I have always very readily manumitted my slaves (for their death does not seem altogether immature, if they lived long enough to receive their freedom); the other, that I have allowed them to make a kind of will, which I observe as religiously as if it were good in law.[a] I receive and obey their last requests, as so many authoritative commands, suffering them to dispose of their effects to whom they please; with this single restriction, that they leave them to some in my household, for to persons in their station the household takes the place of city and commonwealth. But though I solace myself with such reflections,

bilitor et frangor eadem illa humanitate, quae me, ut
hoc ipsum permitterem, induxit.

Non ideo tamen velim durior fieri. Nec ignoro
alios huius modi casus nihil amplius vocare quam
damnum eoque sibi magnos homines et sapientes
videri. Qui an magni sapientesque sint, nescio,
homines non sunt. Hominis est enim adfici dolore,
sentire, resistere tamen et solacia admittere, non
solaciis non egere. Verum de his plura fortasse,
quam debui, sed pauciora, quam volui. Est enim
quaedam etiam dolendi voluptas, praesertim si in
amici sinu defleas, apud quem lacrimis tuis vel laus
sit parata vel venia. Vale.


## XVII

### C. Plinius Macrino Suo S.

Num istic quoque immite et turbidum caelum?
Hic adsiduae tempestates et crebra diluvia. Tiberis
alveum excessit et demissioribus ripis alte super-
funditur. Quamquam fossa, quam providentissimus
imperator fecit, exhaustus premit valles, innatat
campis, quaque planum solum, pro solo cernitur.
Inde, quae solet flumina accipere et permixta de-
vehere, velut obvius sistere cogit atque ita alienis
aquis operit agros, quos ipse non tangit. Anio,

I am overpowered by those very sentiments of
humanity which led me to grant them that indulgence.

However, I do not therefore wish to become more
callous. Others, I know, describe misfortunes of this
kind by no higher term than "a pecuniary loss,"
and fancy they thereby shew themselves men of
sense and spirit. Their wisdom and magnanimity I
shall not dispute, but *men*, I am sure, they are not;
for it is the very essence of human nature to *feel*
those impressions of sorrow, which it yet endeavours
to resist, and to admit, not to be above, consolation.
But perhaps I have detained you too long upon this
subject—though not so long as I would. For there
is a certain luxury in grief; especially when we pour
out our sorrows in the bosom of a friend, who will
approve, or, at least, pardon our tears. Farewell


## XVII

### To Macrinus

Is the weather in your parts as rude and boisterous
as it is with us? All here is tempest and inundation.
The Tiber has overflowed its channel, and deeply
flooded its lower banks. Though drained by a
dyke, which the Emperor providently had cut, it
submerges the valleys, swims along the fields, and
entirely overspreads the flats. The streams which
it ordinarily receives and carries down commingled
to the sea, it now forcibly checks in their course,
by, so to speak, advancing to meet them; and thus
deluges with borrowed waters lands it cannot reach
itself. That most delightful of rivers, the Anio,

delicatissimus amnium ideoque adiacentibus villis velut invitatus retentusque, magna ex parte nemora, quibus inumbratur, fregit et rapuit; subruit montes et decidentium mole pluribus locis clausus, dum amissum iter quaerit, impulit tecta ac se super ruinas eiecit atque extulit.

Viderunt, quos excelsioribus terris illa tempestas non deprehendit, alibi divitum apparatus, et gravem supellectilem, alibi instrumenta ruris, ibi boves, aratra, rectores, hic soluta et libera armenta atque inter haec arborum truncos aut villarum trabes atque culmina varie lateque fluitantia. Ac ne illa quidem malo vacaverunt, ad quae non ascendit amnis. Nam pro amne imber adsiduus et deiecti nubibus turbines, proruta opera, quibus pretiosa rura cinguntur, quassata atque etiam decussa monumenta. Multi eius modi casibus debilitati, obruti, obtriti ; et aucta luctibus damna.

Ne quid simile istic pro mensura periculi, vereor teque rogo, si nihil tale, quam maturissime sollicitudini meae consulas, sed, et si tale, id quoque nunties. Nam parvulum differt, patiaris adversa an exspectes : nisi quod tamen est dolendi modus, non est timendi. Doleas enim, quantum scias accidisse, timeas, quantum possit accidere. Vale.

which seems invited and detained by the villas
upon its banks, has destroyed and carried away
much of the woods that shade its brink. It has
undermined mountains, and its channel being
blocked by the resulting landslides, it has wrecked
houses in the endeavour to regain its course, and
surges high above the ruins.

Dwellers in the uplands, who were out of reach of
this fearful inundation, have seen, here the household
gear and heavy furniture of lordly mansions, there
instruments of husbandry, elsewhere ploughs and
oxen with their drivers, elsewhere again herds of
cattle let loose and astray, together with trunks of
trees, or beams and gables of the neighbouring villas
—all floating about far and wide. Nor indeed have
even these uplands, to which the river did not
rise, escaped calamity. For long torrential rains,
and waterspouts hurled down from the clouds, have
destroyed all the enclosures on the valuable farms,
and shaken, and even overturned, public buildings.
Numbers have been maimed, crushed, or buried by
such accidents, and loss of property has been
aggravated by bereavements.

I am extremely uneasy lest this extensive disaster
should have spread to you; I beg therefore, if it has
not, you will immediately relieve my anxiety.
And indeed, I desire you would inform me though
it should; for there is little difference between
expecting misfortune and undergoing it; except
that grief has limits, whereas apprehension has
none. For we grieve only for what we know *has*
happened; but we fear all that possibly *may* happen.
Farewell.

## XVIII

### C. Plinius Rufino Suo S.

Falsum est nimirum, quod creditur vulgo, testamenta hominum speculum esse morum, cum Domitius Tullus longe melior apparuerit morte quam vita Nam, cum se captandum praebuisset, reliquit filiam heredem, quae illi cum fratre communis, quia genitam fratre adoptaverat. Prosecutus est nepotes plurimis iucundissimisque legatis, prosecutus etiam proneptem. In summa omnia pietate plenissima ac tanto magis, quoniam inexspectata sunt.

Ergo varii tota civitate sermones; alii fictum, ingratum, immemorem loquuntur seque ipsos, dum insectantur illum, turpissimis confessionibus produnt, ut qui de patre, avo, proavo quasi de orbo querantur, alii contra hoc ipsum laudibus ferunt, quod sit frustratus improbas spes hominum, quos sic decipere pro moribus temporum prudentia est. Addunt etiam non fuisse ei liberum alio testamento mori; neque enim reliquisse opes filiae, sed reddidisse, quibus auctus per filiam fuerat. Nam Curtilius Mancia perosus generum suum Domitium Lucanum (frater is Tulli) sub ea condicione filiam eius, neptem suam,

## XVIII

### To Rufinus

THERE is certainly no truth in the popular belief, that a man's will is the mirror of his character. We have an instance to the contrary in Domitius Tullus, who appears a much better man in his death than during his life. After having encouraged the attentions of legacy-hunters, he has left his estate to his brother's daughter, whom he had adopted as his own. He has complimented his grandsons, and also his great grand-daughter, by a number of very agreeable bequests. In a word, all the provisions of the will showed the utmost family feeling, and all the more as they were unexpected.

All Rome has been discussing this affair; some people charge Tullus with feigning, ingratitude, and unmindfulness; and while they thus complain of him as if, instead of leaving three generations of descendants, he had died without natural heirs, their invectives betray their own dishonest designs. Others, on the contrary, applaud him precisely for having disappointed the hopes of this infamous tribe of men, whom, considering the manners of the age, it is but prudence to deceive in this way. And they add, that he was not at liberty to leave any other will; for he did not bequeath, but restore, to his adopted daughter, wealth that accrued to him through her. For Curtilius Mancia, having taken a dislike to his son-in-law Domitius Lucanus (brother to Tullus) devised his estate to this young lady, his grand-daughter, upon condition that Lucanus, her father,

effecerat heredem, si esset manu patris emissa.
Emiserat pater, adoptaverat patruus, atque ita cir-
cumscripto testamento consors frater in patris po-
testatem emancipatam filiam adoptionis fraude re-
vocaverat et quidem cum opibus amplissimis.

Fuit alioqui fratribus illis quasi fato datum, ut
divites fierent invitissimis iis,[1] a quibus facti sunt.
Quin etiam Domitius Afer, qui illos in nomen
adsumpsit, reliquit testamentum ante octo et decem
annos nuncupatum adeoque postea improbatum sibi,
ut patris eorum bona proscribenda curaverit. Mira
illius asperitas, mira felicitas horum, illius asperitas,
qui numero civium exscidit, quem socium etiam in liberis habuit, felicitas horum, quibus successit in locum
patris, qui patrem abstulerat.

Sed haec quoque hereditas Afri ut reliqua cum
fratre quaesita transmittenda erat filiae fratris, a quo
Tullus ex asse heres institutus praelatusque filiae
fuerat, ut conciliaretur. Quo laudabilius testamentum
est, quod pietas, fides, pudor, scripsit, in quo denique omnibus adfinitatibus pro cuiusque officio gratia
relata est, relata et uxori. Accepit amoenissimas
villas, accepit magnam pecuniam uxor optima et
patientissima ac tanto melius de viro merita, quanto

[1] iis *add. Müller.*

[a] See iv. 2 n.

would renounce his paternal rights over her.[a]  He
did so, but her uncle adopted her.  In this way the
purpose of Mancia's will was defeated, and as the
brothers held their property in common, Lucanus,
despite the act of emancipation, got his daughter
under his dominion again, along with her handsome
fortune, by this trick of adoption.

It seems, indeed, to have been the fate of these
two brothers, to be enriched by those who had the
greatest aversion to them.  For Domitius Afer, by
whom they were adopted, left a will in their favour,
which he had made eighteen years before his death;
though he afterwards so entirely reversed his intention
as to be active in procuring the confiscation of their
father's estate.  There is something very strange
about his harsh conduct, and the good fortune of
the other two; strange on the one hand that
Domitius should cut off from the citizen order a
man with whom he went partner even in children;
and on the other, that these brothers should find a
second father in him who had ruined their first.

But it was highly just in Tullus, after having been
appointed sole heir by his brother, in preference to the
latter's own daughter, to make her amends by giving
her this estate which came to him from Afer, as well
as all the rest which he possessed in common with his
brother.  His will therefore is the more praise-worthy,
since it follows the dictates of family affection,
integrity and honour; since, finally, he has therein
acknowledged his obligations to all his relatives by
marriage, according to their respective good offices.
He has made a similar acknowledgement to his wife,
having bequeathed to that excellent and much-
enduring spouse his delightful villas, besides a

magis est reprehensa, quod nupsit. Nam mulier natalibus clara, moribus proba, aetate declivis, diu vidua, mater olim parum decore secuta matrimonium videbatur divitis senis ita perditi morbo, ut esse taedio posset uxori, quam iuvenis sanusque duxisset.

Quippe omnibus membris extortus et fractus tantas opes solis oculis obibat ac ne in lectulo quidem nisi ab aliis movebatur. Quin etiam (foedum miserandumque dictu) dentes lavandos fricandosque praebebat. Auditum frequenter ex illo, cum quereretur de contumeliis debilitatis suae, digitos se servorum suorum quotidie lingere. Vivebat tamen et vivere volebat sustentante maxime uxore, quae culpam inchoati matrimonii in gloriam perseverantia verterat.

Habes omnes fabulas urbis; nam sunt omnes fabulae Tullus. Exspectatur auctio. Fuit enim tam copiosus, ut amplissimos hortos eodem, quo emerat, die instruxerit plurimis et antiquissimis statuis. Tantum illi pulcherrimorum operum in horreis, quae neglegebantur. Invicem tu, si quid istic epistula

large sum of money. And indeed, she deserved so much the more at his hands, as she was highly censured for her marriage with him. It was thought indecorous for a woman of her high birth and character, long widowed of a husband by whom she had issue, to marry in her declining years a rich old man, who was so hopelessly diseased, that even a wife whom he had wedded in his youth and health might well have grown weary of him.

He had so entirely lost the use of all his limbs, that he could not move himself in bed without assistance; and all the enjoyment he had of his riches, was only to contemplate them. He was even reduced to the wretched necessity (which indeed one cannot mention without loathing as well as lamenting) of having his teeth washed and cleansed by others; and he used frequently to say, when he was complaining of the indecencies which his infirmities obliged him to suffer, that he was every day forced to lick his servants' fingers. Still, however, he lived, and was willing to accept of life which was mainly preserved to him by his wife, who, whatever censure she might incur by contracting the alliance, turned it to praise by her steadfast loyalty afterwards.

Now I have given you all the gossip of the town, where nothing is talked of but Tullus. We are all eagerly awaiting the sale of his effects. For he was so large a collector that he adorned a vast pleasure ground with a quantity of antique statuary the very day he purchased it, so numerous were the exquisite works of art which lay neglected in his store-rooms. If you have any local news worth communicating in return, I hope you will not refuse the trouble of

dignum, ne gravare scribere.[1] Nam cum aures
hominum novitate laetantur, tum ad rationem vitae
exemplis erudimur. Vale.

## XIX

### C. Plinius Maximo Suo S.

Et gaudium mihi et solacium in litteris, nihilque
tam laetum, quod his laetius, tam triste, quod
non per has sit minus triste. Itaque et infirmitate
uxoris, et meorum periculo, quorundam vero etiam
morte turbatus ad unicum doloris levamentum
studia confugi, quae praestant, ut adversa magis
intellegam, sed patientius feram. Est autem mihi
moris, quod sum daturus in manus hominum, ante
amicorum iudicio examinare, in primis tuo. Proinde,
si quando, nunc intende libro, quem cum hac
epistula accipies, quia vereor, ne ipse ut tristis
parum intenderim. Imperare enim dolori, ut
scriberem, potui, ut vacuo animo laetoque, non potui.
Porro ut ex studiis gaudium sic studia hilaritate
proveniunt. Vale.

## XX

### C. Plinius Gallo Suo S.

Ad quae noscenda iter ingredi, transmittere mare
solemus, ea sub oculis posita neglegimus, seu quia

[1] scribere *add. a.*

writing to me : not only as we all love to hear some new thing, but because our moral education is promoted by examples. Farewell.

## XIX

### To Maximus

LITERATURE proves both an entertainment and consolation to me ; and as there is no pleasure I prefer to it, so there is no pain it does not alleviate. Accordingly, distracted as I am by my wife's ill-health, the dangerous sickness of some of my servants, and the death of others, I fly to my studies, those sovereign composers of my grief. It is true, they give me a keener perception of misfortunes, but they teach me too how to bear them more patiently. It is an established rule with me, before I publish anything, to take the judgement of my friends upon it, especially yours. I beg therefore you would examine the speech I here send you with particular care, as I am afraid my dejection may have prevented me from doing so myself. For though I could command my grief so far as to write, I could not master it enough to write with ease and cheerfulness. Moreover, if study promotes a pleasing serenity, so does a cheerful mood promote study. Farewell.

## XX

### To Gallus

THOSE works of art or nature which are usually the motives of our travels by land or sea, are often overlooked and neglected if they lie within our

ita natura comparatum, ut proximorum incuriosi
longinqua sectemur, seu quod omnium rerum cupido
languescit, cum facilis occasio, seu quod differimus
tamquam saepe visuri, quod datur videre, quoties
velis cernere. Quacunque de causa permulta in
urbe nostra iuxtaque urbem non oculis modo, sed
ne auribus quidem novimus, quae si tulisset Achaia,
Aegyptus, Asia aliave quaelibet miraculorum ferax
commendatrixque terra, audita, perlecta, lustrata
haberemus.

Ipse certe nuper, quod nec audieram ante nec
videram, audivi pariter et vidi. Exegerat prosocer
meus, ut Amerina praedia sua inspicerem. Haec
perambulanti mihi ostenditur subiacens lacus nomine
Vadimonis; simul quaedam incredibilia narrantur.
Perveni ad ipsum. Lacus est in similitudinem
iacentis rotae circumscriptus et undique aequalis;
nullus sinus, obliquitas nulla, omnia dimensa, paria
et quasi artificis manu cavata et excisa. Color
caeruleo albidior, viridior et pressior, sulpuris odor
saporque medicatus, vis, qua fracta solidantur. Spatium modicum, quod tamen sentiat ventos et fluctibus
intumescat. Nulla in hoc navis (sacer enim), sed
innatant insulae herbidae omnes arundine et iunco

---

*a* " The water, as it evaporated, depositing a crust of
sulphurous or calcareous character " (Merrill).

154

reach; whether it be that we are naturally less inquisitive concerning those things which are near us, while we are pushed forward in pursuit of remote objects; or because the easiness of gratifying a desire is always sure to damp it; or, perhaps, that we defer from time to time viewing what we know we have an opportunity of seeing when we please. Whatever the reason be, it is certain there are several rarities in and near Rome which we have not only never seen, but even never so much as heard of: and yet if they had been the produce of Greece, or Egypt, or Asia, or any other country which offers us a rich display of wonders, we would long since have heard about them, read about them, and surveyed them ourselves.

For myself at least, I confess, I have lately become acquainted with one of these curiosities, to which I was an entire stranger before. My wife's grandfather desired I would view his estate near Ameria. As I was walking over his grounds I was shewn a lake that lies below them, called Vadimon, and given at the same time an incredible account of it. So I went close up to this lake. It is formed exactly circular; there is not the least obliquity or winding, but all is regular and even as if it had been hollowed and cut out by the hand of art. The colour of its water is a whitish-blue, verging upon green, and somewhat cloudy; it has the odour of sulphur and a strong medicinal taste, and possesses the property of cementing fractures.[a] Though it is but of moderate extent, yet the winds have a great effect upon it, throwing it into violent commotions. No vessels are suffered to sail here, as its waters are held sacred; but several grassy islands swim about it, covered

155

tectae, quaeque alia fecundior palus ipsaque illa extremitas lacus effert. Sua cuique figura ut modus; cunctis margo derasus, quia frequenter vel litori vel sibi illisae terunt terunturque. Par omnibus altitudo, par levitas; quippe in speciem carinae humili radice descendunt. Haec ab omni latere perspicitur eademque suspensa pariter et mersa. Interdum iunctae copulataeque et continenti similes sunt, interdum discordantibus ventis digeruntur; non numquam destitutae tranquillitate singulae fluitant.

Saepe minores maioribus velut cumbulae onerariis adhaerescunt, saepe inter se maiores minoresque quasi cursum certamenque desumunt; rursus omnes in eundem locum adpulsae, qua steterunt, promovent terram et modo hac, modo illac lacum reddunt auferuntque ac tum demum, cum medium tenuere, non contrahunt. Constat pecora herbas secuta sic in insulas illas ut in extremam ripam procedere solere nec prius intellegere mobile solum, quam litori abrepta quasi illata et imposita circumfusum undique lacum paveant, mox, quo tulerit ventus, egressa non magis se descendisse sentire, quam senserint ascendisse. Idem lacus in flumen egeritur, quod, ubi se paulisper oculis dedit, specu mergitur alteque con-

with reeds and rushes, and whatever other plants the more prolific neighbouring marsh and the borders of the lake produce. No two are alike in size or shape; but the edges of all of them are worn away by their frequent collision against the shore and one another. They have all the same depth, and the same buoyancy; for their shallow bases are formed like the hull of a boat. This formation is distinctly visible from every point of view; the hull lies half above and half below the water. Sometimes the islands cluster together and seem to form one entire little continent; sometimes they are dispersed by veering winds; at times, when it is calm, they desert their station and float up and down separately.

You may frequently see one of the larger islands sailing along with a lesser joined to it, like a ship with its long boat; or perhaps, seeming to strive which shall outswim the other; then again all are driven to one spot of the shore, which they thus advance, and now here, now there, diminish or restore the area of the lake; only ceasing to contract it anywhere, when they occupy the centre. Cattle have often been known, while grazing, to advance upon those islands as upon the border of the lake, without perceiving that they are on moving ground, till, being carried away from shore they are alarmed by finding themselves surrounded with water, as if they had been put on board ship; and when they presently land wherever the wind drives them ashore, they are no more sensible of disembarking than they had been of embarking. This lake empties itself into a river, which after running a little way above ground, sinks

ditum meat ac si quid, antequam subduceretur,
accepit, servat et profert.

Haec tibi scripsi, quia nec minus ignota quam
mihi nec minus grata credebam. Nam te quoque,
ut me, nihil aeque ac naturae opera delectant.
Vale.

## XXI

### C. Plinius Arriano Suo S.

Ut in vita sic in studiis pulcherrimum et hu
manissimum aestimo severitatem comitatemque
miscere, ne illa in tristitiam, haec in petulantiam
excedat. Qua ratione ductus graviora opera lusibus
iocisque distinguo. Ad hos proferendos et tempus
et locum opportunissimum elegi, utque iam nunc
adsuescerent et ab otiosis et in triclinio audiri, Iulio
mense, quo maxime lites interquiescunt, positis ante
lectos cathedris amicos collocavi.

Forte accidit, ut eo die mane in advocationem
subitam rogarer, quod mihi causam praeloquendi
dedit. Sum enim deprecatus, ne quis ut irreverentem
operis argueret, quod recitaturus, quamquam et
amicis et paucis, idem iterum amicis, foro et negotiis

---

[a] Apparently that the guests might jot down comments
during the reading.

into a cavern and pursues a subterraneous course and if anything is thrown in brings it up again where the stream emerges.

I have given you this account because I imagined it would not be less new, nor less agreeable to you than it was to me; as I know you take the same unique pleasure as myself, in contemplating the works of nature. Farewell.


## XXI

### To Arrianus

Nothing, in my opinion, gives a more amiable and becoming grace to our studies, as well as our manners, than to temper gravity with gaiety, lest the former should degenerate into austereness, and the latter run up into levity. Upon this maxim it is, that I diversify my more serious works with light and playful effusions. I had chosen a convenient place and season to introduce some of these; and designing to accustom them early to a disengaged audience, and to the dinner table, I invited my friends in July, when the courts of justice are usually shut up, and I placed writing-desks before their dining-couches.[a]

But as I happened that morning to be suddenly called on to plead a cause, I took occasion to preface my recital with an apology. I begged my audience not to infer that I slighted the affair in hand, because when on the point of reading my works, though merely to a small circle of friends, I had not kept clear of other friends and of legal business. I

non abstinuissem. Addidi hunc ordinem me et in scribendo sequi, ut necessitates voluptatibus, seria iucundis anteferrem ac primum amicis, tum mihi scriberem.

Liber fuit et opusculis varius et metris. Ita solemus, qui ingenio parum fidimus, satietatis periculum fugere. Recitavi biduo. Hoc adsensus audientium exegit. Et tamen, ut alii transeunt quaedam imputantque, quod transeant, sic ego nihil praetereo atque etiam non praeterire me, testor. Lego enim omnia, ut omnia emendem, quod contingere non potest electa recitantibus. At illud modestius et fortasse reverentius. Sed hoc simplicius et amantius. Amat enim, qui se sic amari putat, ut taedium non pertimescat; et alioqui quid praestant sodales, si conveniunt voluptatis suae causa? Delicatus ac similis ignoto est, qui amici librum bonum mavult audire quam facere.

Non dubito cupere te pro cetera mei caritate quam maturissime legere hunc adhuc musteum librum. Leges, sed retractatum, quae causa recitandi fuit; et tamen nonnulla iam ex eo nosti. Haec vel emendata postea vel, quod interdum longiore mora solet, deteriora facta quasi nova rursus et rescripta

added that I observed the same rule, as an author,
of giving precedence to the necessary over the
entertaining, the preference to the grave over the
gay, and of writing for my friends first, myself
afterwards.

The poems I read composed a variety of subjects
and measures. It is thus that we, who dare not
rely upon the single force of our genius, endeavour
to avoid giving our readers satiety. In compliance
with the unanimous demand of my audience, I read
for two days successively. And this although, just
as others omit their less shining passages, and make
a merit of doing so, I omit nothing, and actually
affirm that fact. I read the whole, that I may
correct the whole; which it is impossible those who
only read select passages should do. True, the latter
plan is more modest, perhaps more respectful; but
the former is more artless and affectionate. For to
be so confident of your friends' affection that you feel
no dread of wearying them, is a sure indication of
your own. Besides, what good do your company do
you if they assemble merely with a view to their
own entertainment. He who had rather find his
friend's performance correct, than make it so, is to
be considered as a stranger, or one who is too indolent
to give himself any trouble.

Your affection for me leaves me no room to doubt,
that you are impatient to read my yet unripened
book. You shall do so, when I have corrected it;
which was indeed the design of my recital. You are
already acquainted with some parts of it; but even
those, after they have been polished (or perhaps
spoiled, as is sometimes the case by over-keeping)
will seem new to you. For when a composition

cognosces. Nam plerisque mutatis ea quoque mutata videntur, quae manent. Vale.

## XXII

### C. Plinius Gemino Suo S.

Nostine hos, qui omnium libidinum servi sic aliorum vitiis irascuntur, quasi invideant, et gravissime puniunt, quos maxime imitantur? cum eos etiam, qui non indigent clementia ullius, nihil magis quam lenitas deceat. Atque ego optimum et emendatissimum existimo, qui ceteris ita ignoscit, tamquam ipse quotidie peccet, ita peccatis abstinet, tamquam nemini ignoscat. Proinde hoc domi, hoc foris, hoc in omni vitae genere teneamus, ut nobis implacabiles simus, exorabiles istis etiam, qui dare veniam nisi sibi nesciunt, mandemusque memoriae, quod vir mitissimus et ob hoc quoque maximus, Thrasea, crebro dicere solebat: 'Qui vitia odit, homines odit.'

Quaeris fortasse, quo commotus haec scribam. Nuper quidam—sed melius coram; quamquam ne tunc quidem. Vereor enim, ne id, quod improbo, eos sectari, carpere, referre huic, quod cum maxime praecipimus, repugnet. Quisquis ille, qualiscunque, sileatur, quem insignire exempli nihil, non insignire, humanitatis plurimum refert. Vale.

has been extensively altered, it contracts an air of novelty even in those parts which remain untouched. Farewell.

## XXII

### To Geminus

Have you ever observed a sort of people, who, though they are themselves slaves to every lust, shew a kind of jealous resentment against the vices of others; and are most severe upon those whom they most resemble? yet, surely tolerance, even in persons who have the least occasion for clemency themselves, is of all virtues the most becoming. To my mind, the best and most faultless character is his, who is as ready to pardon the rest of mankind, as though he daily transgressed himself; and at the same time as cautious to avoid a fault, as if he never forgave one. Be it our rule, then, at home, abroad, and in every sphere of conduct to be relentless to ourselves, placable to others, even such as forgive no failings but their own; remembering always what the humane, and therefore, as well as upon other accounts, the great Thrasea used frequently to say: "He who hates vice, hates mankind."

You will ask, perhaps what has moved me to these reflections? The other day, a certain person—but of that when we meet—though upon second thoughts, not even then, lest whilst I inveigh against and expose conduct I disapprove, I should act counter to that maxim I particularly recommend. Who therefore, and what he is, shall remain in silence: for to brand the man would point no moral, while to refrain is to take the side of humanity. Farewell.

## XXIII

### C. Plinius Marcellino Suo S.

Omnia mihi studia, omnes curas, omnia avocamenta exemit, excussit, eripuit dolor, quem ex morte Iuni Aviti gravissimum cepi. Latum clavum in domo mea induerat, suffragio meo adiutus in petendis honoribus fuerat, ad hoc ita me diligebat, ita verebatur, ut me formatore morum, me quasi magistro uteretur. Rarum hoc in adulescentibus nostris. Nam quotusquisque vel aetati alterius vel auctoritati ut minor cedit? Statim sapiunt, statim sciunt omnia, neminem verentur, imitantur neminem atque ipsi sibi exempla sunt.

Sed non Avitus, cuius haec praecipua prudentia, quod alios prudentiores arbitrabatur, haec praecipua eruditio, quod discere volebat. Semper ille aut de studiis aliquid aut de officiis vitae consulebat, semper ita recedebat ut melior factus et erat factus vel eo, quod audierat, vel quod omnino quaesierat.

Quod ille obsequium Serviano, exactissimo viro, praestitit! quem legatum tribunus ita et intellexit et cepit, ut ex Germania in Pannoniam transeuntem non ut commilito, sed ut comes adsectatorque sequeretur. Qua industria, qua modestia quaestor

---

<sup>a</sup> ii. 9, note.

## XXIII

### To Marcellinus

THE deep concern I am under for the death of Junius Avitus, has rendered me incapable of business, study or amusement. He was invested with the *a* laticlave in my house; my interest supported him whenever he stood for office; more than that, his affection and esteem for me were so great that he formed his manners and regulated his conduct by my example and direction. An uncommon proceeding, this, with the youth of our day; for which of them pays submission as an inferior to age or authority? These young gentlemen begin life as sages, and know everything from the first; there is no one they revere or imitate, as they are their own models.

But not so Avitus; he especially shewed his wisdom, in believing there were some who had more; and discovered his knowledge, in his desire to learn. He constantly sought advice on points relating to his studies, or his duties in life, and always went away with the feeling of being morally improved; and improved he was, if not by the advice he received, by the mere act of seeking it.

How implicitly he obeyed that strict disciplinarian, Servianus! During the latter's command as Legate, Avitus, who was tribune under him, so fully learnt his merit, and so endeared himself to him, that when Servianus was transferred from Germany to Pannonia, he attended him, not as a fellow-officer, but as a friend and admirer. How diligent, how respectful, he must have been as Quaestor, to make himself no

consulibus suis (et plures habuit) non minus iucun-
dus et gratus quam utilis fuit! Quo discursu, qua
vigilantia hanc ipsam aedilitatem, cui praereptus
est, petiit! quod vel maxime dolorem meum
exulcerat.

Obversantur oculis cassi labores et infructuosae
preces et honor, quem meruit tantum. Redit animo
ille latus clavus in penatibus meis sumptus: redeunt
illa prima, illa postrema suffragia mea, illi sermones,
illae consultationes. Adficior adulescentia ipsius,
adficior necessitudinum casu. Erat illi grandis natu
parens, erat uxor, quam ante annum virginem
acceperat; erat filia, quam paulo ante sustulerat.
Tot spes, tot gaudia dies unus in adversa convertit.
Modo designatus aedilis, recens maritus, recens pater
intactum honorem, orbam matrem, viduam uxorem,
filiam pupillam ignaramque patris reliquit.

Accedit lacrimis meis, quod absens et impendentis
mali nescius pariter aegrum, pariter decessisse cognovi, ne gravissimo dolori timore consuescerem. In
tantis tormentis eram, cum scriberem haec, scriberem
sola; neque enim nunc aliud aut cogitare aut loqui
possum. Vale.

---

a Lit. "had taken up from the ground"; the ceremony by which
a father admitted a new-born child (which he had the right to rear or
not, as he pleased) into the family.

less pleasing and acceptable, than useful, to the several Consuls he served under! With what energy and vigilance did he canvass for this very aedileship, from which he is now prematurely snatched—a circumstance that intensely aggravates my grief!

His wasted labours, his fruitless solicitations, and the office which he only merited, never enjoyed, are ever in my mind's eye. That memorable investiture of the laticlave under my roof; the first and the last occasions of my supporting his candidature; the conversations we have had, and the consultations we have held, all return fresh upon my mind. I am affected by his own youth, and the misfortune of his family. He had an aged parent; a wife, who was his virgin bride only a year ago; a daughter, whom he had only lately given a father's first embrace :ᵃ so many pleasing hopes, so many tender joys, were all reversed and destroyed in one day! When he was just elected aedile; when he was lately commenced husband and father, he had to leave his office untasted, his mother childless, his wife a widow, his daughter a mere infant, never to know a father's love.

But what increases my tears upon this melancholy occasion is that, being absent and unconscious of the impending stroke, I never knew of his sickness, till I heard of his death, and had no time to prepare myself for this cruel blow, by previously apprehending it! Such is the distress of my mind as I communicate these tidings. You must not wonder then that they are the whole subject of my letter; for I am not able at present to think or talk of anything else. Farewell.

THE LETTERS OF PLINY

## XXIV

### C. Plinius Maximo Suo S.

Amor in te meus cogit, non ut praecipiam (neque
enim praeceptore eges), admoneam tamen, ut, quae
scis, teneas et observes aut scias melius.

Cogita te missum in provinciam Achaiam, illam
veram et meram Graeciam, in qua primum humanitas, litterae, etiam fruges inventae esse creduntur,
missum ad ordinandum statum liberarum civitatum,
id est ad homines maxime homines, ad liberos maxime liberos, qui ius a natura datum virtute, meritis,
amicitia, foedere denique et religione tenuerunt.

Reverere conditores deos et numina deorum,
reverere gloriam veterem et hanc ipsam senectutem,
quae in homine venerabilis, in urbibus sacra. Sit apud
te honor antiquitati, sit ingentibus factis, sit fabulis
quoque. Nihil ex cuiusquam dignitate, nihil ex
libertate, nihil ex iactatione decerpseris. Habe ante
oculos hanc esse terram, quae nobis miserit iura, quae
leges non victis, sed petentibus dederit, Athenas
esse, quas adeas, Lacedaemonem esse, quam regas;
quibus reliquam umbram et residuum libertatis nomen
eripere durum, ferum, barbarum est. Vides a medicis,

---

*a* Achaia is so called in contrast to the province of Mace-
donia, not only as including most of Greece proper, but
because it contained Athens and Sparta.
*b* *i.e.* enjoying nominal independence, and more or less
autonomy under Roman rule.
*c* *i.e.* the " Laws of the Twelve Tables " (451–50 B.C.) on
which the whole of Roman jurisprudence was founded.
Previous to framing this code, the Romans sent com
missioners to study the laws of the chief Greek cities.

168

## XXIV

### To Maximus

THE love I bear you obliges me to give you, not indeed a precept (for you are far from needing a preceptor), but a reminder that you should resolutely act up to the knowledge you already have, or else improve it. Consider that you are sent to the province of Achaia, that real, genuine Greece[a] where politeness, learning, and even agriculture itself, are supposed to have first arisen. You are commissioned to superintend the affairs of free states;[b] in other words, of men who are in the fullest sense men, and freemen who are in the highest sense free; who have maintained the right they received from Nature, by courage, by virtue, by friendship—in fine, by civil treaties and religious sanctions.

You will revere their Divine Founders, and the workings of divine powers among them; their ancient glory, and even their very age, which as it is venerable in men, in states it is sacred. Cherish sentiments of respect for their antiquity, their colossal achievements, and even for their legends. Let no man's dignity, liberty, or vanity, suffer the least diminution at your hands. Remember it was from this land we derived our legal code,[c] that she gave us laws not by right of conquest, but as a favour. Remember it is Athens you approach; it is Lacedaemon you govern; and to snatch from such a people the shadow that remains, the name that is left, of their freedom, would be a harsh, cruel, nay, barbarous, act. Physicians, you see, though in

quamquam in adversa valetudine nihil servi ac liberi
differant, mollius tamen liberos clementiusque
tractari.

Recordare, quid quaeque civitas fuerit, non ut
despicias, quod esse desierit; absit superbia, asperitas.
Nec timueris contemptum. An contemnitur, qui
imperium, qui fasces habet, nisi humilis et sordidus,
et qui se primus ipse contemnit? Male vim suam
potestas aliorum contumeliis experitur, male terrore
veneratio adquiritur, longeque valentior amor ad
obtinendum, quod velis, quam timor. Nam timor
abit, si recedas, manet amor: ac sicut ille in odium
hic in reverentiam vertitur.

Te vero etiam atque etiam (repetam enim) meminisse oportet officii tui titulum ac tibi ipsi interpretari, quale quantumque sit ordinare statum liberarum
civitatum. Nam quid ordinatione civilius, quid
libertate pretiosius? Porro quam turpe, si ordinatio
eversione, libertas servitute mutetur!

Accedit, quod tibi certamen est tecum. Onerat te
quaesturae tuae fama, quam ex Bithynia optimam
revexisti, onerat testimonium principis, onerat tribunatus, praetura atque haec ipsa legatio quasi praemium
data. Quo magis nitendum est, ne in longinqua
provincia quam suburbana, ne inter servientes quam

---

<sup>a</sup> *i.e.* of local rights and institutions.

sickness there is no difference between slaves and
freemen, yet give the latter milder and more gentle
treatment.

Recollect each city's former greatness, but not
so as to despise her for having lost it. Far be
pride and asperity from my friend; nor fear that a
proper condescension can breed contempt. Can he
who is vested with the powers and bears the ensigns
of the state—can he be contemned, unless he is a
low, sordid being, and sets the example by his self-
contempt? To put affronts upon others is an ill
way of testing the force of your authority; ill-
gotten the homage inspired by terror; and love will
help you to gain your ends far more effectually than
fear. For while fear departs the moment you withdraw your presence, love abides! and as fear turns
to hatred, so does love to respect.

It behoves you then (I cannot but repeat it), to
recall again and again the terms of your commission,
and to make yourself clearly comprehend the nature
and importance of your task as comptroller of free
states. For what is more constitutional than such
control, or more precious than liberty? How infamous, then, his conduct, who tranforms controlling
into overturning [a] and liberty into slavery!

Moreover, you are your own rival. The reputation of having been an admirable Quaestor, which
you brought home from Bithynia; the approbation
of the Emperor; your conduct as Tribune and
Praetor; in a word, this very mission, which may be
looked upon as the reward of your services—all
these are so many weighty responsibilities. So much
the more must you endeavour to avoid the imputation, that you showed more honesty, sympathy, and

# THE LETTERS OF PLINY

liberos, ne sorte[1] quam iudicio missus, ne rudis et
incognitus quam exploratus probatusque humanior,
melior, peritior fuisse videaris, cum sit alioqui, ut
saepe audisti, saepe legisti, multo deformius amittere
quam non adsequi laudem.

Haec velim credas, quod initio dixi scripsisse me
admonentem, non praecipientem; quamquam praecipientem quoque. Quippe non vereor, in amore
ne modum excesserim. Neque enim periculum
est, ne sit nimium, quod esse maximum debet.
Vale.

¹ sorte *Aldus for the* forte *of M.*

---

" *sc.* of the Emperor, by whose appointment Maximus was
sent to Greece.

skill in a remote, than in a suburban province ; among
a subject, than among a free people ; when you held
office by lot, than when you did so by deliberate
choice [a]; whilst you were still a novice and unknown,
than after you had been tried and tested.    For,
speaking generally, the maxim you have often heard
and read holds true—'tis far more disfiguring to lose,
than to lack, men's praises.

Pray believe, what I began by saying, that I have
written as your monitor, not your preceptor, though
I have played the preceptor also.    For, to be sure, I
am not afraid of carrying affection beyond its just
limits : since there cannot be any danger of excess
where we ought to advance as far as possible.
Farewell.

# BOOK IX

# LIBER NONUS

## I

### C. Plinius Maximo Suo S.

Saepe te monui, ut libros, quos vel pro te vel in
Plantam, immo et pro te et in illum (ita enim materia
cogebat) composuisti, quam maturissime emitteres,
quod nunc praecipue morte eius audita et hortor et
moneo.   Quamvis enim legeris multis legendosque
dederis, nolo tamen quemquam opinari defuncto
demum inchoatos, quos incolumi eo peregisti.   **Salva
sit tibi constantiae fama.** Erit autem, si notum aequis
iniquisque fuerit non post inimici mortem scribendi
tibi natam esse fiduciam, sed iam paratam editionem
morte praeventam.   Simul vitabis illud

'Οὐχ ὁσίη φθιμένοισιν.'

Nam, quod de vivente scriptum, de vivente recitatum

---

*a Odyss.* 23. 412.

# BOOK IX

## I

### To Maximus

I HAVE frequently recommended it to you, to be as expeditious as possible in publishing what you have written either in defence of yourself, or against Planta; or rather indeed (as your materials demanded) what you drew up with both those views: but I particularly press this advice upon you *now* that I hear he is dead. For though you read this piece to several of your friends, and put it into the hands of others, yet I should regret extremely, that the world should suspect you only began after his death, what it is most certain you had finished during his life. Let not the character my friend has acquired of firmness and resolution be called in question. And it will; unless both the candid and the malicious shall know, that the death of your adversary did not give you confidence to compose this piece, but merely forestalled the appearance of a work you were on the point of giving to the world. And thus you will also avoid the imputation,

"With impious joy to triumph o'er the dead." [a]

For what you wrote and recited on the subject of a living personage, will be considered as published so

177

est, in defunctum quoque tamquam viventem adhuc
editur, si editur statim. Igitur, si quid aliud in
manibus, interim differ; hoc perfice, quod nobis,
qui legimus, olim absolutum videtur. Sed iam
videatur et tibi, cuius cunctationem nec res ipsa
desideret et temporis ratio praecidit. Vale.


## II

### C. Plinius Sabino Suo S.

Facis iucunde, quod non solum plurimas epistulas
meas, verum etiam longissimas flagitas; in quibus
parcior fui, partim quia tuas occupationes verebar,
partim quia ipse multum distringebar plerumque
frigidis negotiis, quae simul et avocant animum
et comminuunt. Praeterea nec materia plura scribendi dabatur. Neque enim eadem nostra condicio
quae M. Tulli, ad cuius exemplum nos vocas. Illi
enim et copiosissimum ingenium et ingenio qua
varietas rerum qua magnitudo largissime suppetebat,
nos quam angustis terminis claudamur, etiam tacente
me perspicis, nisi forte volumus scholasticas tibi
atque, ut ita dicam, umbraticas litteras mittere.
Sed nihil minus aptum arbitramur, cum arma vestra,
cum castra, cum denique cornua, tubas, sudorem,
pulverem, soles cogitamus. Habes, ut puto, iustam
178

too, provided you publish it at once. If therefore you have any other work upon your hands, let me intreat you to lay it aside, and give your last finishing touches to this performance. It seemed to me, indeed, when I formerly read it, to want no improvements; and so let it now seem to you; as neither the thing itself requires, nor the occasion will admit, of any farther delay. Farewell.

## II

### To Sabinus

Your request that I would write to you not only very frequent, but very long letters, is extremely agreeable to me. If I have forborne to do so, it is partly in consideration of your being much occupied, and partly from some very cold and uninteresting engagements of my own, which distract and at the same time dissipate my ideas. Besides I had not sufficient matter for frequent letters; and am by no means in the same situation that Tully was, whom you point out to me as an example. He not only possessed a most enlarged genius, but the times wherein he lived furnished a variety of noble occasions for exercising it. As for myself, you know (without my telling you) to what narrow limits I am confined; unless I should take into my head to write you rhetorical, and what I might call, *armchair letters*. But nothing seems to me more out of place, when I imagine you in the midst of arms and encampments, in short, inflamed with martial music and toiling in dust and heat. This is my apology, and I think a

excusationem, quam tamen dubito an tibi probari
velim. Est enim summi amoris negare veniam
brevibus epistulis amicorum, quamvis scias illis
constare rationem. Vale.

## III

### C. Plinius Paulino Suo S.

Alius alium, ego beatissimum existimo, qui bonae
mansuraeque famae praesumptione perfruitur certus-
que posteritatis cum futura gloria vivit. Ac mihi
nisi praemium aeternitatis ante oculos, pingue illud
altumque otium placeat. Etenim omnes homines
arbitror oportere aut immortalitatem suam aut mor-
talitatem cogitare, et illos quidem contendere, eniti,
hos quiescere, remitti nec brevem vitam caducis
laboribus fatigare, ut video multos, misera simul et
ingrata imagine industriae ad vilitatem sui pervenire.
Haec ego tecum, quae quotidie mecum, ut desinam
mecum, si dissenties tu ; quamquam non dissenties,
ut qui semper clarum aliquid et immortale mediteris.
Vale.

---

ᵃ Cf. Cowley :
    "What shall I do to be for ever known,
     And make the age to come my own ? "

reasonable one; however, I almost wish you would
not accept it. For to reject a friend's excuses for
writing briefly, be they ever so just, bespeaks the
warmest affection. Farewell.

### III

#### To Paulinus

MANKIND differ in their notions of supreme
happiness; but in my opinion it consists in the fore-
taste of an honest and abiding fame, the assurance of
being admired by posterity, the realization, while yet
living, of future glory.[a]  I confess if I had not the
reward of an immortal reputation in view, I should
choose to live in the lap of Leisure, as people say.
There seem to be but two points worthy our attention; either the endless duration of fame, or the
short extent of life. Those who are governed by the
former consideration, must pursue it with the full
exertion of the most laborious efforts; while such as
are influenced by the latter should quietly resign
themselves to repose, nor wear out a short life in
perishable pursuits: as some, we may observe, do, and
then sink at last into self-contempt, in the midst of
a wretched and fruitless course of false industry.
These are my daily reflections, which I communicate
to you, in order to renounce them if you do not join
with me in the same sentiments: as undoubtedly
you will, who are for ever meditating some glorious
and immortal enterprise. Farewell.

# THE LETTERS OF PLINY

## IV

### C. Plinius Macrino Suo S.

Vererer, ne immodicam orationem putares, quam cum hac epistula accipies, nisi esset generis eius, ut saepe incipere, saepe desinere videatur. Nam singulis criminibus singulae velut causae continentur. Poteris ergo, undecunque inceperis, ubicunque desieris, quae deinceps sequentur, et quasi incipientia legere et quasi cohaerentia meque in universitate longissimum, brevissimum in partibus iudicare. Vale.

## V

### C. Plinius Tironi Suo S.

Egregie facis (inquiro enim, et persevere) quod iustitiam tuam provincialibus multa humanitate commendas; cuius praecipua pars est honestissimum quemque complecti atque ita a minoribus amari, ut simul a principibus diligare. Plerique autem, dum verentur, ne gratiae potentium nimium impertire videantur, sinisteritatis atque etiam malignitatis famam consequuntur. A quo vitio tu longe recessisti (scio), sed temperare mihi non possum, quo minus

## IV

### To Macrinus

I should fear you would think the oration which you receive with this letter, immoderately long, but that it is of such a nature as to require several breaks; and as it consists of different charges, has the appearance of so many distinct speeches. Wherever therefore you begin or end, you may consider what follows, either as connected with what went before, or making of itself a new subject; so that you may look upon it as very long upon the whole, and yet as extremely short with respect to its particular parts. Farewell.

## V

### To Tiro

You are to be highly applauded for the courtesy by which as I am informed (and I make very strict enquiry), you commend your administration of justice to the people of your province; one principal branch of which virtue is to distinguish merit in every degree, and so to gain the love of the lower rank, as to preserve at the same time the regard of their superiors. But it is an error many have fallen into, that while they endeavour to avoid the appearance of favouring the great, they run into the contrary extreme, and gain the character of acting with ill manners, or ill nature. A mistake this, which you are far from committing, I well know: however, I cannot forbear throwing in a caution with

laudem similis monenti, quod eum modum tenes,
ut discrimina ordinum dignitatumque custodias;
quae si confusa, turbata, permixta sunt, nihil est
ipsa aequalitate inaequalius.   Vale.

## VI

### C. Plinius Calvisio Suo S.

Omne hoc tempus inter pugillares ac libellos
iucundissima quiete transmisi.  'Quem ad modum,'
inquis, 'in urbe potuisti?'  Circenses erant; quo
genere spectaculi ne levissime quidem teneor.  Nihil
novum, nihil varium, nihil quod non semel spectasse
sufficiat.  Quo magis miror tot milia virorum tam
pueriliter identidem cupere currentes equos, in-
sistentes curribus homines videre.  Si tamen aut
velocitate equorum aut hominum arte traherentur,
esset ratio nonnulla; nunc favent panno, pannum
amant, et si in ipso cursu medioque certamine hic
color illuc, ille huc transferatur, studium favorque
transibit, et repente agitatores illos, equos illos, quos
procul noscitant, quorum clamitant nomina, relin-
quent.

Tanta gratia, tanta auctoritas in una vilissima

---

ª The games in the Circus Maximus, chiefly consisting of
chariot-races, for which the Roman people had the same
passion as the English now have for football matches.

my applause, and recommending it to you, to conduct yourself in such a manner as to keep up the distinctions of rank and dignity. For to level and confound the different orders of mankind, is far from producing an equality among them; it is, in truth, the most unequal thing imaginable. Farewell.

## VI

### To Calvisius

I HAVE spent these several days past among my papers with the most pleasing tranquillity imaginable. You will ask how that can possibly be in the midst of Rome? Why, the Circensian Games *a* were taking place; a kind of entertainment for which I have not the least taste. They have no novelty, no variety, nothing, in short, one would wish to see twice. I am the more astonished that so many thousands *b* of grown men should be possessed again and again with a childish passion to look at galloping horses, and men standing upright in their chariots. If, indeed, they were attracted by the swiftness of the horses or the skill of the men, one could account for this enthusiasm. But in fact it is a bit of cloth they favour, a bit of cloth that captivates them. And if during the running the racers were to exchange colours, their partisans would change sides, and instantly forsake the very drivers and horses whom they were just before recognizing from afar, and clamorously saluting by name.

Such favour, such weighty influence, hath one

*b* The elder Pliny (*N.H.* xxxvi. 102) says that the Circus Maximus, as enlarged by Nero, held 250,000 spectators.

tunica, mitto apud vulgus, quod vilius tunica, sed
apud quosdam graves homines; quos ego cum
recordor in re inani, frigida, adsidua tam insatiabiliter
desidere, capio aliquam voluptatem, quod hac volup-
tate non capior. Ac per hos dies libentissime otium
meum in litteris colloco, quos alii otiosissimis
occupationibus perdunt. Vale.

## VII

### C. Plinius Romano Suo S.

Aedificare te scribis. Bene est; inveni patro-
cinium; aedifico enim iam ratione, quia tecum. Nam
hoc quoque non dissimile, quod ad mare tu, ego ad
Larium lacum.

Huius in litore plures villae meae, sed duae ut
maxime delectant ita exercent. Altera imposita
saxis more Baiano lacum prospicit, altera aeque
more Baiano lacum tangit. Itaque illam tragoediam, hanc appellare comoediam soleo; illam,
quod quasi cothurnis, hanc quod quasi socculis, sus-
tinetur. Sua utrique amoenitas, et utraque possi-
denti ipsa diversitate iucundior. Haec lacu propius,
illa latius utitur; haec unum sinum molli curvamine

---

a The charioteers and their teams were hired out by rival
companies or "factions," named from the colours of their
livery. The "Greens" and "Blues," introduced in early
Imperial times, eclipsed the two older Red and White

cheap tunic [a]—never mind it with the vulgar herd
who are more worthless than the tunics they wear—
but with certain grave personages. When I observe
such men thus insatiably fond of so silly, so low,
so uninteresting, so common an entertainment, I
congratulate myself that I am insensible to these
pleasures : and am glad to devote the leisure of this
season to literature, which others throw away upon
the most idle employment. Farewell.

## VII

### To Romanus

Your letter informs me that you are engaged in
building; 'tis mighty well; I have now found
patronage; for I am doing the same, and since I
have you, who shall deny I have reason on my side?
We are pretty much agreed likewise, I find, in our
situations; as you are building upon the sea-coast,
and I beside the Larian lake.

I have several villas upon this shore, but there are
two particularly, in which as I take most delight, so
they give me the most employment. They are
both situated in the manner of those at Baiae; one
of them stands upon a rock, and overlooks the lake;
the other touches it. The first, supported as it were
by the lofty buskin, I call my *Tragedy*; the other,
as resting upon the humble sock, my *Comedy*. Each
has its peculiar beauties, and recommends itself the
more to their owner by mere force of contrast. The
former enjoys a wider, the latter a nearer prospect of

factions, and had frantic partisans among all classes.
Caligula and Nero were devotees of the "Greens." See
Gibbon, c. xl. 2.

amplectitur, illa editissimo dorso duos dirimit; illic recta gestatio longo limite super litus extenditur, hic spatiosissimo xysto leviter inflectitur; illa fluctus non sentit, haec frangit; ex illa possis despicere piscantes, ex hac ipse piscari hamumque de cubiculo ac paene etiam de lectulo ut e navicula iacere. Hae mihi causae utrique, quae desunt, adstruendi ob ea quae supersunt. Sed quid ego rationem tibi? apud quem pro ratione erit idem facere. Vale.

## VIII

### C. Plinius Augurino Suo S.

Si laudatus a te laudare te coepero, vereor, ne non tam proferre iudicium meum quam referre gratiam videar. Sed, licet videar, omnia scripta tua pulcherrima existimo, maxime tamen illa, quae de nobis. Accidit hoc una eademque de causa. Nam et tu, quae de amicis, optime scribis, et ego, quae de me, ut optima lego. Vale.

the lake. This follows the gentle curve of a single
bay; the salient ridge upon which the other stands,
forms two. Here you have a straight alley
extending itself along the shore, there, a spacious
terrace that falls by a gentle descent towards it.
The former does not perceive the force of the waves;
the latter breaks them: from *that* you see the
fishermen at work below; from *this* you may fish
yourself, and throw your line out of your chamber,
and almost as you lie in bed, as out of a boat. It is
the beauties therefore these agreeable villas possess,
that tempt me to add to them those which are
wanting.—But I need not assign a reason to you;
who, undoubtedly, will think it a sufficient one that
you are about the same business. Farewell.

## VIII

### To Augurinus

WERE I to begin praising you from whom I have
received so much applause, I am afraid I should
seem not so much to profess my genuine opinion as
to confess my gratitude. Nevertheless I will not
scruple to say, that I think all your productions are
beautiful, but especially those of which I am the
subject. And the same reason will account both for
their deserving that character, and for my thinking
so: for as on the one hand you ever succeed best
when writing about your friends; so, on the other,
I always admire most what is written about myself.
Farewell.

## IX

### C. Plinius Coloni Suo S.

Unice probo, quod Pompeii Quintiani morte tam dolenter adficeris, ut amissi caritatem desiderio extendas, non ut plerique, qui tantum viventes amant, seu potius amare se simulant ac ne simulant quidem, nisi quos florentes vident. Nam miserorum non secus ac defunctorum obliviscuntur. Sed tibi perennis fides tantaque in amore constantia, ut finiri nisi tua morte non possit. Et hercule is fuit Quintianus, quem diligi deceat ipsius exemplo. Felices amabat, miseros tuebatur, desiderabat amissos. Iam illa quanta probitas in ore, quanta in sermone cunctatio, quam pari libra gravitas comitasque! quod studium litterarum, quod iudicium! qua pietate cum dissimillimo patre vivebat! quam non obstabat illi, quo minus vir optimus videretur, quod erat optimus filius!

Sed quid dolorem tuum exulcero? Quamquam sic amasti iuvenem, ut hoc potius quam de illo sileri velis, a me praesertim, cuius praedicatione putas vitam eius ornari, memoriam prorogari, ipsamque illam, qua est raptus, aetatem posse restitui. Vale.

## IX

### To Colo

I GREATLY approve your being so poignantly affected by the death of Pompeius Quintianus, as to keep alive by your regrets your love for a lost friend. Far different from the majority, who love, or rather, who counterfeit love to, none but the living; nor even counterfeit it, save to those whom they see in the height of prosperity! For the unfortunate they forget as quickly as they do the dead. But *your* fidelity is perennial, and the constancy of your affection can only end with your life. Quintianus, most certainly, well deserved to meet with that generous warmth from his friends, of which he was himself so bright an example. He loved them in prosperity; he protected them in adversity; he lamented them in death. How honest was his countenance! how deliberate his speech! how equally did he hold the balance between dignity and courtesy! how fond was he of learning! how judicious his sentiments! how dutiful his commerce with a father of a very different character! how completely did he surmount the difficulty of proving himself a good son, without forfeiting the title of a good man!

But I must not sharpen your affliction—yet I know your affection for this excellent youth was such, that you had rather endure such a recital, than have his virtues passed over in silence; especially by me, whose applause, you imagine, will adorn his actions, extend his fame, and restore him, as it were, to that life from which he is unhappily snatched. Farewell.

# THE LETTERS OF PLINY

## X

### C. PLINIUS TACITO SUO S.

CUPIO praeceptis tuis parere ; sed aprorum tanta penuria est, ut Minervae et Dianae, quas ais pariter colendas, convenire non possit. Itaque Minervae tantum serviendum est, delicate tamen ut in secessu et aestate. In via plane non nulla leviora statimque delenda ea garrulitate, qua sermones in vehiculo seruntur, extendi. His quaedam addidi in villa, cum aliud non liberet. Itaque poëmata quiescunt, quae tu inter nemora et lucos commodissime perfici putas. Oratiunculam unam, alteram retractavi ; quamquam id genus operis inamabile, inamoenum magisque laboribus ruris quam voluptatibus simile. Vale.

## XI

### C. PLINIUS GEMINO SUO S.

EPISTULAM tuam iucundissimam accepi, eo maxime, quod aliquid ad te scribi volebas, quod libris inseri posset. Obveniet materia, vel haec ipsa quam mon-
192

# X

## To Tacitus

I should like extremely well to follow your advice; but there is such a scarcity of boars, that it is impossible to reconcile Minerva with Diana, who, you think, ought to be worshipped together. I must content myself then with paying my service to the former; and even that half-heartedly, considering it is holiday time and summer weather. I composed, indeed, a few trifles in my journey hither, which are only fit to be destroyed, as they are written with the same negligence and inattention that one usually chats upon the road. Since I came to my villa, I have made some few additions to them, not finding myself in a humour for work of more consequence. Thus my poetry, which you imagine is carried on with so much advantage amidst the silence and solemnity of woods and groves, is, in truth, at a stand. I have revised a small oration or two; though that kind of work is disagreeable and unentertaining enough, and has a much nearer affinity with rustic labours, than with rural pleasures. Farewell.

# XI

## To Geminus

Your letter was particularly agreeable to me, as it mentioned your desire that I would address some epistle to you which might appear in my published correspondence. I shall find matter either in the

stras, vel potior alia. Sunt enim in hac offendicula
non nulla : circumfer oculos, et occurrent.

Bibliopolas Lugduni esse non putabam, ac tanto
libentius ex litteris tuis cognovi venditari libellos
meos, quibus peregre manere gratiam, quam in urbe
collegerint, delector. Incipio enim satis absolutum
existimare, de quo tanta diversitate regionum discreta
hominum iudicia consentiunt. Vale.

## XII

### C. Plinius Iuniori Suo S.

Castigabat quidam filium suum, quod paulo sump-
tuosius equos et canes emeret. Huic ego iuvene
digresso ; 'Heus tu, numquamne fecisti, quod a
patre corripi posset? fecisti, dico, non interdum
facis, quod filius tuus, si repente pater ille, tu filius,
pari gravitate reprehendat? Non omnes homines
aliquo errore ducuntur? non hic in illo sibi, in hoc
alius, indulget?'

Haec tibi admonitus immodicae severitatis exemplo
pro amore mutuo scripsi, ne quando tu quoque filium
tuum acerbius duriusque tractares. Cogita et illum
puerum esse et te fuisse atque ita hoc, quod es pater,

subject you indicate or some preferable one. For *yours* contains some points of offence; look about you, and they will be obvious.

As I did not imagine there were any booksellers at Lyons, I am so much the more pleased to learn from your letter that my volumes are sold there. I rejoice to find they retain the favour abroad, which they gained at home; and I begin to flatter myself they are finished compositions, since persons living in entirely different localities are agreed in their sentiments concerning them. Farewell.

## XII

### To Junior

A certain friend of mine lately corrected his son with great severity before me, for being something too profuse in the article of dogs and horses. "And pray," said I to him (when the youth was withdrawn), "did you never do anything yourself which deserved your father's correction? Nay, are you not sometimes even now guilty of acts which your son, were your relations suddenly reversed, might with equal gravity reprove? Are not all mankind subject to errors of some kind? have we not each of us our particular foibles in which we fondly indulge ourselves?"

The great affection subsisting between us, has induced me to set this instance of unreasonable severity before you, as a caution not to treat *your* son with too much rigour and austerity. Consider he is but a boy, and that there was a time when you

utere, ut memineris et hominem esse te et hominis patrem.   Vale.

## XIII

### C. Plinius Quadrato Suo S.

Quanto studiosius intentiusque legisti libros, quos de Helvidi ultione composui, tanto impensius postulas, ut perscribam tibi, quaeque extra libros quaeque circa libros, totum denique ordinem rei, cui per aetatem non interfuisti.

Occiso Domitiano statui mecum ac deliberavi esse magnam pulchramque materiam insectandi nocentes, miseros vindicandi, se proferendi.   Porro inter multa scelera multorum nullum atrocius videbatur, quam quod in senatu senator senatori, praetorius consulari, reo iudex manus intulisset.   Fuerat alioqui mihi cum Helvidio amicitia, quanta potuerat esse cum eo, qui metu temporum nomen ingens, pares virtutes secessu tegebat, fuerat cum Arria et Fannia, quarum altera Helvidi noverca, altera mater novercae.   Sed non ita me iura privata ut publicum fas et indignitas facti et exempli ratio incitabat.

---

a *i.e.* his speech against Publicius Certus, revised, enlarged, and divided into "books."   See iv. 21, vii. 30.

b Sept. 18, 96 A.D.          c See iii. 16.

were so too. In exerting, therefore, the authority of
a father, remember always that you are a man, and
the parent of a man. Farewell.

## XIII

### To Quadratus

THE pleasure and attention with which you read
my books *a* *On the Avenging of Helvidius,* has made
you, it seems, more earnest in requesting I would
fully inform you of particulars not included in, yet
relevant to, my work, and, in short, of the whole
course of the affair, as you were too young to
witness it.

When Domitian was killed,*b* I judged, on mature
consideration, that a glorious opportunity now offered
of pursuing the guilty, vindicating the injured, and
advancing one's own career. Further, amidst the
many crimes whereof many had been guilty, none
appeared to me more atrocious, than that one who
was at once an ex-praetor and a judge, a senator,
should in the very senate itself have laid violent hands
upon a senator and ex-consul, who then stood arraigned
before him. Apart from this, I had maintained with
Helvidius the closest friendship that was possible
with one who, fearing the tyranny of the times,
endeavoured to hide his glory and his no less glorious
virtues, by a retired life. I had been intimate, too,
with Arria and her daughter Fannia,*c* who was step-
mother to Helvidius. But it was not so much private
attachments as the rights of the public, indignation
at the crime, and the importance of establishing
a precedent, that incited me to action.

Ac primis quidem diebus redditae libertatis pro se quisque inimicos suos, dumtaxat minores, incondito turbidoque clamore postulaverant simul et oppresserant. Ego et modestius et constantius arbitratus immanissimum reum non communi temporum invidia, sed proprio crimine urgere, cum iam satis primus ille impetus defervisset et languidior in dies ira ad iustitiam redisset, quamquam tum maxime tristis amissa nuper uxore mitto ad Anteiam (nupta haec Helvidio fuerat), rogo, ut veniat, quia me recens adhuc luctus limine contineret. Ut venit, 'Destinatum est' inquam 'mihi maritum tuum non inultum pati. Nuntia Arriae et Fanniae' (ab exsilio redierant); 'consule te, consule illas, an velitis adscribi facto, in quo ego comite non egeo; sed non ita gloriae meae faverim, ut vobis societate eius invideam.' Perfert Anteia mandata, nec illae morantur.

Opportune senatus intra diem tertium. Omnia ego semper ad Corellium retuli, quem providentissimum aetatis nostrae sapientissimumque cognovi; in hoc tamen contentus consilio meo fui, veritus ne vetaret; erat enim cunctantior cautiorque. Sed non sustinui inducere in animum, quo minus illi eodem die facturum me indicarem, quod an facerem

---

*a* *i.e.* of Nerva's reign.
*b* Tacitus also uses *constans* in this sense, *Hist.* iii. 1, (Church and Brodribb.) *c* See x. 2 n.
198

In the first days of restored liberty [a] every man
had singled out his personal enemy (though it must be
confessed, those only of a lower rank) and in the
midst of much clamour and confusion, no sooner accused, than crushed him.   But for myself, I thought
it the more moderate and also the more effectual [b]
course against a defendant so steeped in crime, to
rely not on the universal detestation of the last reign,
but on a specific indictment.   When, therefore, that
first outburst of rage had fairly subsided and daily
declining resentment gave way to justice, though I was
at that time saddened by the recent loss of my wife,[c]
I sent to Anteia, the widow of Helvidius, and desired
her to come to me, as my recent mourning obliged
me to keep at home.   When she arrived, "I am
resolved," I said, "not to suffer your husband to
remain unavenged.   Pray make this known to Arria
and Fannia" (they had returned from exile), "and
consider along with them whether you will jointly
lodge an accusation.   Not that I want an associate, but I am not so fond of my own renown as
to grudge your participating in it."   Anteia carried
my message to those ladies, who at once embraced
the proposal.

It happened very opportunely, that the Senate
met the next day but one.   I never acted without
consulting Corellius, in whom I recognised the most
far-seeing and the wisest man of our time.   However, in the present case, I contented myself with
following my own plan, which I feared he would
veto, as he was of a very slow and cautious temper.
But I could not prevail with myself to forbear
acquainting him, on the day of the event, that I
was about to take a step, on which I did not consult

non deliberabam, expertus usu de eo, quod desti-
naveris, non esse consulendos, quibus consultis
obsequi debeas. Venio in senatum, ius dicendi peto,
dico paulisper maximo adsensu. Ubi coepi crimen
attingere, reum destinare, adhuc tamen sine nomine,
undique mihi reclamari. Alius : 'Sciamus, quis sit,
de quo extra ordinem referas,' alius : 'Quis est ante
relationem reus?' alius : 'Salvi simus, qui super
sumus.' Audio imperturbatus, interritus ; tantum
susceptae rei honestas valet, tantumque ad fiduciam
vel metum differt, nolint homines, quod facias, an
non probent.

Longum est omnia, quae tunc hinc inde iacta
sunt, recensere. Novissime consul : 'Secunde,
sententiae loco dices, si quid volueris.' 'Permiseras'
inquam, 'quod usque adhuc omnibus permisisti.'
Resido. Aguntur alia. Interim me quidam ex consularibus amicis secreto accuratoque sermone quasi
nimis fortiter incauteque progressum corripit, revocat, monet, ut sistam : adiecit etiam notabilem
me futuris principibus. 'Esto' inquam, 'dum malis.'

---

*a* Ordinarily, motions were put to the Senate by the
presiding Consul, who then called upon the members, in
formal order, to express their opinions. But any Senator
might bring in a private motion by leave of the House.
*b* Lit. "out of the regular order," *i.e.* by the privilege
explained above. *c sc.* Domitian's reign of terror.
*d* "'Tis very remarkable, that when any senator was asked
his opinion in the house, he had the privilege of speaking as
long as he pleased upon any other affair." (Melm.)
*e* Nerva had not yet adopted an heir. His choice of
Trajan (97 A.D.) put an end to wide-spread anxiety.

anyone; experience having taught me the unwisdom of consulting on a predetermined affair those whose judgment you are bound to follow, if you do consult them. The Senate being assembled, I came into the house, and begged leave to introduce a motion; [a] I spoke for a few moments with universal assent. When I began to touch upon the charge, and indicate whom I intended to accuse (though as yet without mentioning him by name) I was attacked on all sides. " Let us know," says one, " who is the object of this extraordinary motion." [b] " Who is it," asked another, "that is thus actually put on trial before the question of indicting him has been submitted to the House?" " Let us be safe," added a third, "who have survived." [c] I heard all this unruffled and undismayed; such strength is derived from a good cause, and so much difference it makes with respect to confidence or fear, whether the world deprecates, or disapproves, your action.

It would be too tedious to relate all that was thrown out by different sides upon this occasion. At length the Consul said, " You will be at liberty, Secundus, to speak on whatever you wish to propose, when you are called upon to give your opinion on the business of the day." [d] " The permission you granted and now withdraw," said I, " you never yet refused to any," and so sat down; when immediately the House went upon other affairs. In the meanwhile, one of my consular friends took me aside, and with great earnestness telling me he thought I had carried on this affair with more boldness than prudence, used every method of reproof and persuasion, to prevail with me to desist. He even added that I should find myself a marked man under future Emperors. [e] " So be it,"

Vix ille discesserat, rursus alter: 'Quid audes? quo ruis? quibus te periculis obiicis? quid praesentibus confidis incertus futurorum? lacessis hominem iam praefectum aerarii et brevi consulem, praeterea qua gratia, quibus amicitiis fultum!' Nominat quendam, qui tunc ad orientem amplissimum et famosissimum exercitum non sine magnis dubiisque rumoribus obtinebat. Ad haec ego: '"Omnia praecepi atque animo mecum ante peregi"[1] nec recuso, si ita casus attulerit, luere poenas ob honestissimum factum, dum flagitiosissimum ulciscor.'

Iam censendi tempus. Dicit Domitius Apollinaris, consul designatus, dicit Fabricius Veiento, Fabius Postumius, Vettius Proculus, collega Publici Certi, de quo agebatur, uxoris autem meae, quam amiseram, vitricus, post hos Ammius Flaccus. Omnes Certum nondum a me nominatum ut nominatum defendunt, crimenque quasi in medio relictum defensione suscipiunt. Quae praeterea dixerint, non est necesse narrare; in libris habes. Sum enim cuncta ipsorum verbis persecutus

Dicunt contra Avidius Quietus, Cornutus Tertullus; Quietus, iniquissimum esse querelas dolentium excludi, ideoque Arriae et Fanniae ius

[1] Verg. *Aen.* vi. 105.

---

[a] *sc.* of Saturn; see x. 3 A, note *b*.

quoth I, "if they are bad Emperors." He had scarce left me, when a second came up : " For God's sake," said he, " what are you attempting ? Will you ruin yourself ? Do you consider to what hazards you are exposed ? Why will you presume on the present situation of public affairs, when it is so uncertain what turn they may hereafter take ? You are attacking a man who is actually at the head of the treasury,[a] and will shortly be Consul. Besides, consider what credit he has, and with what powerful friendships he is supported !" Upon which he named a certain person, who (not without several strong and suspicious rumours) was then commanding a powerful army in the east. I replied,

" 'All I've foreseen, and oft in thought revolv'd ;'

and am willing, if so it falls out, to suffer pains and penalties for an honourable action, provided I avenge an infamous one."

The time for the members to give their opinion was now arrived. Domitius Apollinaris, the consul elect, spoke first; after him Fabricius Veiento, Fabius Postumius, Vettius Proculus, (my late wife's step-father, and the colleague of Publicius Certus, on whom the debate turned,) and lastly Ammius Flaccus. They all defended Certus, as if I had named him (tho' I had not yet done so), and thus as it were took up the challenge of my accusation. I need not relate what they said further, as you can read it all word for word in my speech.

Avidius Quietus and Cornutus Tertullius spoke in the opposite sense. The former observed, that it was extremely unjust not to hear the complaints of those in distress, and therefore that Arria and

querendi non auferendum, nec interesse, cuius ordinis quis sit, sed quam causam habeat; Cornutus,
datum se a consulibus tutorem Helvidi filiae petentibus matre eius et vitrico; nunc quoque non sustinere
deserere officii sui partes, in quo tamen et suo dolori
modum imponere et optimarum feminarum perferre
modestissimum adfectum; quas contentas esse ad-
monere senatum Publici Certi cruentae adulationis
et petere, si poena flagitii manifestissimi remittatur,
nota certe quasi censoria inuratur. Tum Satrius
Rufus medio ambiguoque sermone 'Puto' inquit,
'iniuriam factam Publicio Certo, si non absolvitur;
nominatus est ab amicis Arriae et Fanniae, nominatus ab amicis suis. Nec debemus solliciti esse;
idem enim nos, qui bene sentimus de homine,
iudicaturi sumus; si innocens est, sicuti et spero
et malo, donec aliquid probetur, credo poteritis
absolvere.'

Haec illi, quo quisque ordine citabantur. Venitur
ad me; consurgo, utor initio, quod in libro est,

---

a A reply to the plea above, *salvi simus, qui supersumus*,
against any further prosecutions of *Senators*, so many of
whom had perished in that way under Domitian.

b Towards Domitian, at whose desire he brought a capital
charge against Helvidius.

c During the Republic, the list of senators was revised
once in five years by the Censors, who affixed a mark (*nota*)
to the names of those whom they thought proper to degrade.
Annual revision of the list, and expulsion of any senator at
discretion had now become part of the emperor's prerogative,

Fannia ought not to be denied the privilege of laying their grievances before the house; and that the point to be considered was not the rank of the person, but the merit of the cause.[a] Cornutus told the house, that as he was appointed guardian to the daughter of Helvidius by the consuls, upon the petition of her mother and her step-father, he could not bring himself to abandon the duty of his trust on this occasion. In fulfilling it, however, he would restrain his personal indignation, and report the extremely moderate sentiments of those excellent ladies. They desired no more, he said, than to bring to the Senate's notice the bloodshed which Certus procured in his obsequiousness,[b] with the request that, if the legal penalty of his notorious crime were remitted, at least Certus might be branded with some disgrace equivalent to degradation by the Censors.[c] Satrius Rufus then expressed himself in neutral and ambiguous terms. " I am of opinion," said he, " that injustice will be done to Certus, if he is not acquitted (I do not scruple to name him, since the friends of Arria and Fannia, as well as his own, have done so). Nor has the Senate any grounds for anxiety; for we, who think well of the man, are to be his judges. If he is innocent (as I hope and wish, and till something be proved against him, shall believe he is), it will be in your power to acquit him."

Thus they delivered their several opinions, in the order in which they were called upon. When it came to my turn, I rose up, and using the same exordium as appears in the published speech, I replied to them

and he might be induced to degrade Certus if the senate expressed condemnation of him.  (Merrill.)

respondeo singulis. Mirum qua intentione, quibus
clamoribus omnia exceperint, qui modo reclamabant;
tanta conversio vel negotii dignitatem, vel proven-
tum orationis, vel actoris constantiam subsecuta
est. Finio. Incipit respondere Veiento; nemo
patitur; obturbatur, obstrepitur adeo quidem, ut
diceret: 'Rogo, patres conscripti, ne me cogatis
implorare auxilium tribunorum.' Et statim Murena
tribunus: 'Permitto tibi, vir clarissime Veiento,
dicere.' Tunc quoque reclamatur. Inter moras
consul citatis nominibus et peracta discessione mittit
senatum, acp aene adhuc stantem temptantemque
dicere Veientonem reliquit. Multum ille de hac
(ita vocabat) contumelia, questus est Homerico
versu:

> Ὦ γέρον, ἦ μάλα δή σε νέοι τείρουσι μαχηταί.[1]

Non fere quisquam in senatu fuit, qui non me
complecteretur, exoscularetur, certatimque laude
cumularet, quod intermissum iamdiu morem in
publicum consulendi susceptis propriis simultatibus
reduxissem, quod denique senatum invidia liberassem,
qua flagrabat apud ordines alios, quod severus in
ceteros senatoribus solis dissimulatione quasi mutua
parceret.

[1] *Il.* viii. 102.

---

*a* Theoretically, the Tribunes could still control the procedure of the Senate by interposing their veto. Veiento
appealed to them to protect him in exercising his right of
giving his opinion (*ius censendi*).

*b* *i.e.* introducing a bill, which had become virtually a
prerogative of the Emperor. See next note.

severally. It is surprising with what attention, with what applause I was heard by those who just before were exclaiming against me; such a wonderful conversion was wrought either by the importance of the affair, the successful progress of the speech, or the resolution of the advocate. After I had finished, Veiento began to reply; not a soul would hear him; the general clamour raised against him was so over-powering that he was reduced to saying, "I hope, my lords, you will not oblige me to implore the assistance of the Tribunes." *a* Immediately the Tribune Murena cried out, "You have my leave, most illustrious Veiento, to proceed." But still the uproar was renewed. In the interval the Consul put the question severally to the rest, and having taken a division, dismissed the Senate, leaving Veiento in the midst, still attempting to speak. He made great complaints of this affront (as he called it) applying the following lines of Homer to himself:

" Great perils, father, wait th' unequal fight;
  Those younger champions will oppress thy might."

There was scarce a man in the House that did not embrace and kiss me, and vie in loading me with praises. They extolled me because, at the risk of exciting private animosities, I had revived the custom so long disused, of consulting the Senate in the interest of the public *b*; in fine, because I had wiped off that reproach which was thrown upon the Senate by the other orders of citizens, that while severe towards the rest of the community, it let its own members escape its justice by a sort of mutual connivance.

Haec acta sunt absente Certo; abfuit enim, seu tale aliquid suspicatus, sive, ut excusabatur, infirmus. Et relationem quidem de eo Caesar ad senatum non remisit; obtinui tamen, quod intenderam. Nam collega Certi consulatum, successorem Certus accepit; planeque factum est, quod dixeram in fine, 'Reddat praemium sub optimo principe, quod a pessimo accepit.'

Postea actionem meam, utcunque potui, recollegi, addidi multa. Accidit fortuitum, sed non tamquam fortuitum quod editis libris Certus intra paucissimos dies implicitus morbo decessit. Audivi referentes hanc imaginem menti eius, hanc oculis oberrasse, tamquam videret me sibi cum ferro imminere. Verane haec, adfirmare non ausim; interest tamen exempli, ut vera videantur.

Habes epistulam, si modum epistulae cogites, libris, quos legisti, non minorem; sed imputabis tibi, qui contentus libris non fuisti. Vale.

---

*a* From Vespasian's time, the *ius relationis*, *i.e.* the right to submit a motion to the Senate, belonged to the Emperor : *relationem remittere* was the technical term for his doing so at the request of the Senate itself (addressed to him through the Consuls). We gather that Pliny's motion for leave to prosecute Certus was carried by a large majority, but that the Senate could not proceed further without a formal

All this was transacted in the absence of Certus;
who kept out of the way either because he suspected
something of the kind was on foot, or (as was said in
his excuse) that he was really indisposed. Caesar
did not, it is true, refer his case to the Senate.[a]
But I obtained nevertheless, what I aimed at, for
his colleague was appointed to a consulship, while
he himself was superseded. And thus, the wish
with which I concluded my speech, was actually accomplished: "May he be obliged," said I, "to
renounce under a virtuous prince that reward he
received under an infamous one."[b]

Some time after I reconstituted my speech as well
as I could, and considerably enlarged it. It chanced
(though such an event seemed more than a co-
incidence) that a few days after I had published
those books, Certus was taken ill and died. I heard
reports that he not only imagined, but actually saw,
a figure haunting him—and the apparition was none
other than myself, threatening him with a sword.
Whether this story is true or not, I cannot venture
to affirm; but with a view to pointing a moral, 'tis
important that it should be accounted true.

And here you have a letter which, if you consider
the limits of a letter, is as long as the books you have
perused. But you must blame yourself for that,
since the books did not suffice you. Farewell.

*relatio* from Nerva, whose policy was to let bygones be
bygones, and who accordingly allowed the matter to drop.
[b] *i.e.* "May Nerva deprive him of the treasurership
Domitian gave him."

### XIV

#### C. Plinius Tacito Suo S.

Nec ipse tibi plaudis, et ego nihil magis ex fide quam de te scribo. Posteris an aliqua cura nostri, nescio, nos certe meremur, ut sit aliqua, non dico ingenio (id enim superbum), sed studio et labore et reverentia posterorum. Pergamus modo itinere instituto, quod ut paucos in lucem famamque provexit ita multos e tenebris et silentio protulit. Vale.

### XV

#### C. Plinius Falconi Suo S.

Refugeram in Tuscos, ut omnia ad arbitrium meum facerem. At hoc ne in Tuscis quidem; tam multis undique rusticorum libellis et tam querulis inquietor, quos aliquanto magis invitus quam meos lego: nam et meos invitus. Retracto enim actiunculas quasdam, quod post intercapedinem temporis et frigidum et acerbum est. Rationes quasi absente me negleguntur. Interdum tamen equum conscendo et patrem familiae hactenus ago, quod aliquam

## XIV

### To TACITUS

You do not blow your own trumpet, and I, for my part, never write more sincerely than when I write about you. Whether future generations will pay us some regard, I know not; but let us anyhow earn some regard, I will not say by our genius (that would be arrogant) but by our zeal, our labours, and our reverence for posterity. Let us but proceed in the course we have begun; which, as it has conducted some few to the sunshine of fame, so it has led out numbers from nameless obscurity. Farewell.

## XV

### To FALCO

I fled to my Tuscan estate in order to do just as I pleased; but that privilege is denied me even here, so greatly am I harassed by showers of petitions—which are so many complaints—from my various tenants. I look over their papers with more reluctance than my own; for, to confess the truth, it is with great unwillingness I review even them. I am revising, however, some little orations; an employment which, after a length of time has intervened, is but of a very cold and unentertaining kind. In the meanwhile my private affairs are neglected as much as if I were absent. Yet I sometimes so far act the part of a careful master of a family, as to mount my horse and ride about my

partem praediorum, sed pro gestatione percurro. Tu consuetudinem serva nobisque sic rusticis urbana acta perscribe. Vale.

## XVI

### C. Plinius Mamiliano Suo S.

Summam te voluptatem percepisse ex isto copiosissimo genere venandi non miror, cum historicorum more scribas numerum iniri non potuisse. Nobis venari nec vacat, nec libet; non vacat, quia vindemiae in manibus; non libet, quia exiguae. Devehimus tamen pro novo musto novos versiculos tibique iucundissime exigenti, ut primum videbuntur defervisse, mittemus. Vale.

## XVII

### C. Plinius Genitori Suo S.

Recepi litteras tuas, quibus quereris taedio tibi fuisse quamvis lautissimam cenam, quia scurrae, cinaedi, moriones mensis inerrabant. Vis tu remittere aliquid ex rugis? Equidem nihil tale habeo,

farms, but merely in lieu of taking exercise in my *allée*.
As for you, I hope you will keep up your old custom,
and give your rustic friend an account of what is
going forward in town.    Farewell.

## XVI

### To Mamilianus

It is no wonder a chace on the vast scale you
mention afforded you infinite pleasure, "the number of
the slain " (as you write in true historian phrase) " was
not to be counted."    As for myself, I have neither
leisure nor inclination for sports of that kind : not
leisure because I am in the midst of my vintage ;
not inclination because it has proved an extreme bad
one this season.    However, I shall be able, I hope, to
*draw off* some new verses, in default of new wine,
for your entertainment, which (since you request
them in so agreeable a manner) I will not fail to
send you as soon as they shall be thoroughly *settled*.
Farewell.

## XVII

### To Genitor

I have received your letter, in which you complain
of being highly disgusted lately at an entertainment,
though exceeding splendid, by a set of buffoons,
fools, and wanton prostitutes, who were playing
their antic tricks round the tables.    But let me
advise you to smooth your brow a little.    I confess,
indeed, I admit nothing of this kind at my own

habentes tamen fero. Cur ergo non habeo? Quia
nequaquam me ut inexspectatum festivumve delectat,
si quid molle a cinaedo, petulans a scurra, stultum a
morione profertur. Non rationem, sed stomachum
tibi narro. Atque adeo quam multos putas esse,
quos aeque ea, quibus ego et tu capimur et ducimur,
partim ut inepta, partim ut molestissima offendant!
Quam multi, cum lector aut lyristes aut comoedus
inductus est, calceos poscunt aut non minore cum
taedio recubant, quam tu ista (sic enim appellas)
prodigia perpessus es! Demus igitur alienis oblectationibus veniam, ut nostris impetremus. Vale.

## XVIII

### C. Plinius Sabino Suo S.

Qua intentione, quo studio, qua denique memoria
legeris libellos meos, epistula tua ostendit. Ipse
igitur exhibes negotium tibi, qui elicis et invitas, ut
quam plurima communicare tecum velim. Faciam,
per partes tamen et quasi digesta, ne istam ipsam

house; however, I bear with it in others. "And why then (you will be ready to ask) "should you not have them yourself?" The truth is, because the soft gestures from a wanton, the pleasantries from a buffoon, or the folly from a professed fool, give me no entertainment, as they give me no surprise. It is my taste, you see, not my principles, that I plead against them. And indeed, what numbers are there, think you, who distaste the entertainments which you and I are most delighted with, and consider them either trivial or wearisome! How many are there, who as soon as a reader, a musician, or a comedian is introduced, either take their leave of the company, or if they continue at the table, show as much dislike to this kind of diversions, as you did at those *monsters*, as you call them! Let us bear therefore, my friend, with others in their amusements, that they, in return, may shew indulgence to ours.    Farewell.

## XVIII

### To Sabinus

With what care and attention you have read my works, and how perfectly treasure them in your memory, your letter is a sufficient testimony.    Do you consider then, what a troublesome affair you are bringing upon your hands, when you kindly entice me, by every friendly art, to communicate to you as many of them as possible?    I cannot, certainly, refuse your request; but shall comply with it, however, at different intervals, and observe some kind of

memoriam, cui gratias ago, adsiduitate et copia
turbem oneratamque et quasi oppressam cogam
pluribus singula, posterioribus priora dimittere.
Vale.


## XIX

### C. PLINIUS RUSONI SUO S.

SIGNIFICAS legisse te in quadam epistula mea
iussisse Verginium Rufum inscribi sepulcro suo:

> ' Hic situs est Rufus, pulso qui Vindice quondam
>     Imperium adseruit non sibi, sed patriae.'

Reprehendis, quod iusserit, addis etiam melius
rectiusque Frontinum, quod vetuerit omnino monumentum sibi fieri, meque ad extremum, quid de
utroque sentiam, consulis. Utrumque dilexi, miratus sum magis, quem tu reprehendis, atque ita miratus, ut non putarem satis unquam laudari posse,
cuius nunc mihi subeunda defensio est. Omnes ego,
qui magnum aliquod memorandumque fecerunt, non
modo venia, verum etiam laude dignissimos iudico
si immortalitatem, quam meruere, sectantur victuri-
que nominis famam supremis etiam titulis prorogare
nituntur.

216

succession. For I would not by too copious and too frequent a supply, over-burthen and confound a memory to which I already owe so many acknowledgments; nor, in short, pour in such an unreasonable quantity, as to oblige it to discharge what it had before received, in order to retain what follows. Farewell.

## XIX

### To Ruso

You have read, it seems, in a letter of mine,[a] that Virginius Rufus directed the following lines to be inscribed upon his tomb:

" Here Rufus lies, who raised in victory's hour
  His country, not himself, to sovran power: "

for which you blame him, adding that Frontinus acted much more worthily in forbidding any monument whatsoever to be erected to his memory. And in the conclusion of your letter you desire my sentiments upon each. I loved them both; but I confess I admired *him* more whom you condemn; and to such a degree, that so far from imagining I ever should have occasion to rise up in his defence, I thought he could never be sufficiently applauded. In my opinion, every man who has acted a great and memorable part, deserves not only to be excused but extolled, if he pursues that glorious immortality of fame he has merited and endeavours to perpetuate an everlasting remembrance of himself, even by an epitaph.

a vi. 10. Cf. ii. 1.

Nec facile quemquam nisi Verginium invenio,
cuius tanta in praedicando verecundia quanta
gloria ex facto. Ipse sum testis, familiariter ab eo
dilectus probatusque, semel omnino me audiente
provectum, ut de rebus suis hoc unum referret, ita
secum aliquando Cluvium locutum: 'Scis, Vergini,
quae historiae fides debeatur; proinde si quid in
historiis meis legis aliter ac velis, rogo ignoscas.'
Ad hoc ille: 'Tune, Cluvi, ignoras, ideo me fecisse,
quod feci, ut esset liberum vobis scribere, quae
libuisset?'

Age dum, hunc ipsum Frontinum in hoc ipso,
in quo tibi parcior videtur et pressior, comparemus.
Vetuit exstrui monumentum; sed quibus verbis?
'Impensa monumenti supervacua est; memoria nostri
durabit, si vita meruimus.' An restrictius arbitraris
per orbem terrarum legendum dare duraturam
memoriam suam, quam uno in loco duobus versiculis
signare, quod feceris? Quamquam non habeo propositum illum reprehendendi, sed hunc tuendi;
cuius quae potest apud te iustior esse defensio quam
ex collatione eius, quem praetulisti? Meo quidem
iudicio neuter culpandus, quorum uterque ad gloriam
pari cupiditate, diverso itinere contendit, alter, dum
expetit debitos titulos; alter, dum mavult videri
contempsisse. Vale.

---

*a* Consul under Caligula; *legatus pro praetore* of Spain
under Galba. Tacitus, Plutarch, and Suetonius seem to have
drawn upon his (lost) history of his own times for their
accounts of Galba, Otho, and Vitellius.

Yet hardly could I name a man, who had performed such great achievements, so modestly reserved upon the subject of his own actions, as Virginius was. I can bear him witness (and I had the happiness to enjoy his intimacy and affection) that I never but once heard him mention his own conduct; and that was, in giving an account of a conversation which passed between him and Cluvius [a]: "You well know, Virginius," (said Cluvius to him,) "the fidelity required in an historian; you will pardon me therefore, I hope, if you should meet with any thing in my works, that is not agreeable to you." "O Cluvius," he replied, "can you be ignorant that what I did, was done in order that you historians might enjoy the liberty of writing what you please?"

But let us compare Frontinus with him in that very instance wherein you think the former is more modest and reserved. He forbid a monument to be erected to him, it is true; but in what words? "The expense of a monument," says he, "is superfluous; my memory will endure if my actions deserve it." Is there less vanity, do you think, thus to put on record for all the world to read that his memory would endure; than to mark upon a single tombstone, in two lines, the actions one has performed? It is not, however, my design to condemn your favourite; I only mean to defend Virginius; and what defence can be more prevailing with you, than one drawn from a comparison between him and the person you prefer? In my own opinion, indeed, neither of them is blameworthy, since they both pursued glory with equal passion, but by different roads; the former in desiring those monumental honours he had merited: the latter in rather choosing the appearance of despising them. Farewell.

## XX

C. Plinius Venatori Suo S.

Tua vero epistula tanto mihi iucundior fuit, quanto
longior erat, praesertim cum de libellis meis tota
loqueretur; quos tibi voluptati esse non miror, cum
omnia nostra perinde ac nos ames.

Ipse cum maxime vindemias graciles quidem,
uberiores tamen quam exspectaveram, colligo, si
colligere est, non numquam decerpere uvam, torcu-
lum invisere, gustare de lacu mustum, obrepere
urbanis, qui nunc rusticis praesunt meque notariis
et lectoribus reliquerunt. Vale.

## XXI

C. Plinius Sabiniano Suo S

Libertus tuus, cui succensere te dixeras, venit
ad me, advolutusque pedibus meis, tamquam tuis
haesit. Flevit multum, multumque rogavit, multum
etiam tacuit; in summa, fecit mihi fidem poeni-
tentiae. Vere credo emendatum, quia deliquisse se
sentit

## XX

### To Venator

THE longer your letter was, so much the more agreeable I thought it, especially as it turned entirely upon my works. I am not at all surprised you should find a pleasure in them, since I know you have the same affection for every thing that belongs to me, as you have for myself.

The getting in of my vintage (which though it has proved but a slender one this season, is, however, more plentiful than I expected) particularly employs me at present. If indeed I can with any propriety say so, who only gather a grape now and then, visit the vine-press, taste the must in the vat, and saunter to my town-servants; who being now engaged in assisting their rustic fellows, have wholly abandoned me to my readers and my secretaries. Farewell.

## XXI

### To Sabinianus

YOUR freedman, whom you lately mentioned as having displeased you, has been with me; he threw himself at my feet and clung there with as much submission as he could have done at yours. He earnestly requested me with many tears, and even with the eloquence of silent sorrow, to intercede for him; in short, he convinced me by his whole behaviour, that he sincerely repents of his fault. And I am persuaded he is thoroughly reformed, because he seems entirely sensible of his delinquency.

Irasceris, scio; et irasceris merito, id quoque scio; sed tunc praecipua mansuetudinis laus, cum irae causa iustissima est. Amasti hominem et, spero, amabis; interim sufficit, ut exorari te sinas. Licebit rursus irasci, si meruerit, quod exoratus excusatius facies. Remitte aliquid adulescentiae ipsius, remitte lacrimis, remitte indulgentiae tuae; ne torseris illum, ne torseris etiam te. Torqueris enim, cum tam lenis irasceris.

Vereor, ne videar non rogare, sed cogere, si precibus eius meas iunxero. Iungam tamen tanto plenius et effusius, quanto ipsum acrius severiusque corripui destricte minatus numquam me postea rogaturum. Hoc illi, quem terreri oportebat, tibi non idem. Nam fortasse iterum rogabo, impetrabo iterum; sit modo tale, ut rogare me, ut praestare te deceat. Vale.

## XXII

### C. Plinius Severo Suo S.

Magna me sollicitudine adfecit Passenni Pauli valetudo et quidem plurimis iustissimisque de causis.

I know you are angry with him, and I know too, it is not without reason; but clemency can never exert itself with more applause, than when there is the justest cause for resentment. You once had an affection for this man, and, I hope, will have again : in the meanwhile, let me only prevail with you to pardon him. If he should incur your displeasure hereafter, you will have so much the stronger plea in excuse for your anger, as you shew yourself more exorable to him now. Allow something to his youth, to his tears, and to your own natural mildness of temper : do not make him uneasy any longer, and I will add too, do not make yourself so; for a man of your benevolence of heart cannot be angry without feeling great uneasiness.

I am afraid, were I to join my entreaties with his, I should seem rather to compel, than request you to forgive him. Yet I will not scruple to do it; and so much the more fully and freely as I have very sharply and severely reproved him, positively threatening never to interpose again in his behalf. But though it was proper to say this to him, in order to make him more fearful of offending, I do not say it to you. I may, perhaps, again have occasion to intreat you upon his account, and again obtain your forgiveness; supposing, I mean, his error should be such as may become me to intercede for, and you to pardon. Farewell.

## XXII

### To Severus

I have been much alarmed by the ill state of health of Passennus Paulus, as indeed I had many and just reasons. He has a most excellent and

Vir est optimus, honestissimus, nostri amantissimus ;
praeterea in litteris veteres aemulatur, exprimit,
reddit, Propertium in primis, a quo genus ducit, vera
soboles eoque simillima illi, in quo ille praecipuus.
Si elegos eius in manus sumpseris, leges opus
tersum, molle, iucundum et plane in Properti domo
scriptum.

Nuper ad lyrica deflexit, in quibus ita Horatium,
ut in illis illum alterum effingit. Putes, si quid in
studiis cognatio valet, et huius propinquum. Magna
varietas, magna mobilitas. Amat ut qui verissime,
dolet ut qui impatientissime, laudat ut qui beni-
gnissime, ludit ut qui facetissime, omnia denique
tamquam singula absolvit

Pro hoc ego amico, pro hoc ego ingenio non
minus aeger animo, quam corpore ille, tandem
illum, tandem me recepi. Gratulare mihi, gratulare

generous heart, of which I have the happiness to share the warmest friendship. In his writings he very successfully emulates the antients, whose spirit and manner he has closely imitated and happily restored; especially that of Propertius, to whom he is no less related by genius, than by blood, as he particularly resembles that poet in his chief excellency. When you read his elegies, whatever is elegant, tender, and agreeable, will conspire to charm you; as you will clearly discover they derive their lineage from Propertius.

He has lately made some attempts in the lyric kind, in which he as successfully copies the manner of Horace as in his elegies he has that of the other poet just mentioned. You would imagine, were there such a thing as a kindred in genius, that the blood of Horace likewise flowed in his veins. He displays a most wonderful variety and versatility; when he describes the passion of love, you perceive his heart is entirely possessed by the most tender sentiments; when he paints the emotions of grief, you see his breast is penetrated with the deepest sorrow; when he enters upon topics of panegyric, it is with all the ardour of the warmest benevolence; when he diverts himself with subjects of pleasantry, it is in the spirit of the most agreeable gaiety; in short, whatever species of poetry he engages in, he executes it with such a masterly hand, that one would imagine it were the single branch to which he had applied himself.

The dangerous indisposition of such a friend and such a genius afflicted me in mind no less than him in body. But at length *he* is recovered, and *my* peace is restored. Congratulate me, my friend, and

etiam litteris ipsis, quae ex periculo eius tantum discrimen adierunt, quantum ex salute gloriae consequentur. Vale.

## XXIII

### C. Plinius Maximo Suo S.

Frequenter agenti mihi evenit, ut centumviri, cum diu se intra iudicum auctoritatem gravitatemque tenuissent, omnes repente quasi victi coactique consurgerent laudarentque ; frequenter e senatu famam, qualem maxime optaveram, rettuli ; numquam tamen maiorem cepi voluptatem, quam nuper ex sermone Corneli Taciti. Narrabat sedisse secum circensibus proximis equitem Romanum. Hunc post varios eruditosque sermones requisisse : ' Italicus es, an provincialis?' Se respondisse: ' Nosti me et quidem ex studiis.' Ad hoc illum, ' Tacitus es an Plinius?' Exprimere non possum, quam sit iucundum mihi, quod nomina nostra quasi litterarum propria, non hominum, litteris redduntur, quod uterque nostrum his etiam ex studiis notus, quibus aliter ignotus est.

Accidit aliud ante pauculos dies simile. Recumbebat mecum vir egregius, Fabius Rufinus, super eum

congratulate also literature itself, which ran as great
a hazard by his danger, as it will receive glory by his
recovery.   Farewell.


## XXIII

### To Maximus

It has frequently happened, as I have been
pleading before the centumviri, that those judges,
after having preserved as long as possible the gravity
and solemnity suitable to their character, have at
length as though overcome and compelled, suddenly
risen up with one consent to applaud me.   I have
often likewise gained as much glory in the senate, as
my utmost wishes could desire : but I never was
touched with a more sensible pleasure than by an
account which I lately received from Cornelius
Tacitus.   He informed me, that at the last Circensian
games, he sat next to a Roman knight, who, after
much discourse had passed between them upon
various points of learning, asked him if he was an
Italian or a provincial?   Tacitus replied, "Your
acquaintance with literature must have informed
you who I am."   "Ay!" said the knight, "Pray
then is it Tacitus or Pliny I am talking with?"   I
cannot express how highly I am pleased to find,
that our names, as if they were rather the proper
appellatives of letters than of men, are ascribed to
literature itself ; and that those very pursuits render
us known to those, who would be ignorant of us by
any other means.

An accident of the same nature happened to me a
few days ago.  Fabius Rufinus, a person of dis-

municeps ipsius, qui illo die primum venerat in urbem; cui Rufinus demonstrans me : 'Vides hunc?' Multa deinde de studiis nostris.   Et ille 'Plinius est' inquit.   Verum fatebor, capio magnum laboris mei fructum.   An, si Demosthenes iure laetatus est, quod illum anus Attica ita noscitavit, 'Οὗτός ἐστι Δημοσθένης,' ego celebritate nominis mei gaudere non debeo? Ego vero et gaudeo et gaudere me dico. Neque enim vereor, ne iactantior videar, cum de me aliorum iudicium non meum profero, praesertim apud te, qui nec ullius invides laudibus et faves nostris.   Vale

## XXIV

### C. Plinius Sabiniano Suo S.

Bene fecisti, quod libertum aliquando tibi carum reducentibus epistulis meis in domum, in animum recepisti.   Iuvabit hoc te ; me certe iuvat, primum quod te tam tractabilem [1] video, ut in ira regi possis, deinde quod tantum mihi tribuis, ut vel auctoritati

---

[1] tam tractabilem *M, Müller,* talem *a, Bipons.*

tinguished merit, was placed next to me at table;
and above him a fellow-townsman of his, who was
just then come to Rome for the first time. Rufinus
desired his friend to take notice of me, and fell to
expatiating upon the subject of my eloquence; to
whom the other immediately replied, "That must
undoubtedly be Pliny." To own the truth, I look
upon these instances as a very considerable recompense of my labours. Had Demosthenes reason
to be pleased with the old woman of Athens crying
out on recognizing him "There goes Demosthenes!"
and may I not be allowed to congratulate myself
upon the extensive reputation my name has acquired? Yes, my friend, I will rejoice in it, and
without scruple own that I do. As I only mention
the judgement of others concerning me, not the
opinion I conceive of myself, I am not afraid of
incurring the censure of vanity; especially from you,
who, as you envy no man's reputation, so you are
particularly zealous for mine. Farewell.

## XXIV

### To Sabinianus

I greatly approve of your having, under conduct
of my [a] letter, received again into your family and
favour, a freed-man, whom you once admitted into a
share of your affection. It will afford you, I doubt not,
great satisfaction. It certainly, at least, has me,
both as it is a proof that you are capable of being
governed in your anger, and as it is an instance of
your paying so much regard to me, as either to obey

[a] ix. 21.

meae pareas vel precibus indulgeas. Igitur et laudo
et gratias ago; simul in posterum moneo, ut te
erroribus tuorum, etsi non fuerit, qui deprecetur,
placabilem praestes. Vale.

## XXV

### C. Plinius Mamiliano Suo S.

Quereris de turba castrensium negotiorum et,
tamquam summo otio perfruare, lusus et ineptias
nostras legis, amas, flagitas meque ad similia condenda
non mediocriter incitas. Incipio enim ex hoc genere
studiorum non solum oblectationem, verum etiam
gloriam petere post iudicium tuum, viri gravissimi,
eruditissimi ac super ista verissimi. Nunc me rerum
actus modice, sed tamen distringit; quo finito
aliquid earundem Camenarum in istum benignis-
simum sinum mittam. Tu passerculis et columbulis
nostris inter aquilas vestras dabis pennas, si tamen et
sibi et tibi placebunt, si tantum sibi, continendos
cavea nidove curabis. Vale.

## XXVI

### C. Plinius Iuperco Suo S.

Dixi de quodam oratore seculi nostri recto quidem
et sano, sed parum grandi et ornato, ut opinor, apte:

230

my authority or to yield to my entreaty. You will accept therefore, at once, both of my applause and my thanks. At the same time, I must advise you for the future to be placable towards erring servants, though there should be none to interpose in their behalf. Farewell.

## XXV

### To Mamilianus

Though you complain of the crowd of military affairs which press upon you, yet, as if you were enjoying the most uninterrupted leisure, you read, admire and demand my poetical trifles and not a little encourage me still to persevere in them. I begin, indeed, to pursue this kind of study, not only with a view to my amusement, but my glory, since they have approved themselves to the judgement of a man of your gravity and learning, and what is more than all, of your veracity. At present I have some causes upon my hands, which (though not very deeply indeed, however) engage me; when I shall have dispatched these, I will again trust my Muse in your candid bosom. You will suffer my little doves and sparrows to take wing among your eagles, if you should have the same good opinion of them as they have of themselves; if not, you will kindly confine them to their cage or their nests. Farewell.

## XXVI

### To Lupercus

I said once (and I think not improperly) of a certain orator of the present age, whose compositions are extremely regular and correct, but by no means

'Nihil peccat, nisi quod nihil peccat.' Debet enim orator erigi, attolli, interdum etiam effervescere, efferri ac saepe accedere ad praeceps. Nam plerumque altis et excelsis adiacent abrupta; tutius per plana, sed humilius et depressius iter; frequentior currentibus quam reptantibus lapsus, sed his non labentibus nulla, illis non nulla laus, etiamsi labantur. Nam ut quasdam artes ita eloquentiam nihil magis quam ancipitia commendant. Vides, qui per funem in summa nituntur, quantos soleant excitare clamores, cum iam iamque casuri videntur. Sunt enim maxime mirabilia, quae maxime insperata, maxime periculosa, utque Graeci magis exprimunt, παράβολα. Ideo nequaquam par gubernatoris est virtus, cum placido et cum turbato mari vehitur; tunc admirante nullo illaudatus, inglorius subit portum; at, cum stridunt funes, curvatur arbor, gubernacula gemunt, tunc ille clarus et dis maris proximus.

Cur haec? Quia[1] visus es mihi in scriptis meis adnotasse quaedam ut tumida, quae ego sublimia, ut improba, quae ego audentia, ut nimia, quae ego plena arbitrabar. Plurimum autem refert, reprehendenda

[1] Cur haec? Quia *Dpa*, *K* ii., Haec, quia *M*, *K* i.

sublime and ornamented, "His only fault is, that he has none." For the true orator should be bold and elevated, and sometimes even flame out and be hurried away with all the warmth and violence of passion, in short, he should frequently soar to great, and even dangerous heights. For precipices are generally near whatever is towering and exalted, whereas the plain affords a safer, but for that reason a more humble and inglorious path; they that run are more likely to stumble than they that creep; but the latter gain no honour by not slipping, while the former even fall with glory. It is with eloquence as with some other arts; she is never more pleasing than when she hazards most. Have you not observed what acclamations our rope-dancers excite at the instant when they seem on the point of falling? Whatever is most unexpected and hazardous, or, as the Greeks strongly express it, desperate, has always the greatest share of our admiration. The pilot's skill is by no means equally proved in a calm, as in a storm; in the former case he tamely enters the port, unnoticed and un-applauded; but when the cordage creaks, the mast bends, and the rudder groans, then is it that he shines forth in full lustre, and is adored as little inferior to a sea-god.

The reason of my making this observation is, because, if I mistake not, you have condemned some passages in my writings as tumid which I thought sublime, excessive which I deemed bold, and over-loaded which seemed to me copious. But it is material to consider, whether your criticism turns upon such points as are real faults, or only striking

adnotes an insignia. Omnis enim advertit, quod eminet et exstat ; sed acri intentione diiudicandum est, immodicum sit an grande, altum an enorme. Atque, ut Homerum potissimum attingam, quem tandem alterutram in partem potest fugere ''Ἀμφὶ δὲ σάλπιγξεν μέγας οὐρανός·'[1] 'ἠέρι δ' ἔγχος ἐκέκλιτο'[2] et totum illud, 'οὔτε θαλάσσης κῦμα τόσον βοάᾳ'[3]? Sed opus est examine et libra, incredibilia sint haec et immania an magnifica et coelestia. Nec nunc ego me his similia aut dixisse aut posse dicere puto. Non ita insanio ; sed hoc intellegi volo, laxandos esse eloquentiae frenos, nec angustissimo gyro ingeniorum impetus refringendos.

At enim alia condicio oratorum, alia poetarum. Quasi vero M. Tullius minus audeat. Quamquam hunc omitto ; neque enim ambigi puto. Sed Demosthenes ipse, ille norma oratoris et regula, num se cohibet et comprimit, cum dicit illa notissima :

[1] *Il.* xxi. 388.   [2] *Il.* v. 356.   [3] *Il.* xiv. 394.

[a] Speaking of Mars. (Melm.)

and remarkable expressions. Whatever is salient is sure to be criticized; but it requires a very nice judgement to distinguish the bounds between extravagance and grandeur; between a just and enormous height. To give instances out of Homer, by preference—what reader, whether he incline to one side or the other, can fail to remark—

" Heav'n in loud thunder bids the trumpet sound,
  And wide beneath them groans the rending
      ground."

Again,
          " His spear on clouds reclined." *a*

So in that whole passage :

" Not half so loud the bellowing deeps resound."

It requires, I say, a very delicate hand to poise these metaphors, and determine whether they are fantastic and absurd, or truly majestic and sublime. Not that I think anything which I have written or can write, admits of comparison with these. I am not extravagant enough to say so; what I would be understood to contend for is, that we should throw up the reins to eloquence, nor restrain the daring flights of genius within too narrow a compass.

But it will be said, perhaps, there is a wide difference between orators and poets. As if, forsooth, Tully were not as bold in his figures as any of the poets ! But not to mention particular instances from him, since in his case, I imagine, there can be no dispute; does Demosthenes himself, that model and standard of true oratory, does Demosthenes check and repress the fire of his genius, in that well-known passage which begins thus: " Ye infamous

Ἄνθρωποι μιαροὶ καὶ κόλακες, καὶ ἀλάστορες,[1] et rursus: Οὐ λίθοις ἐτείχισα τὴν πόλιν οὐδὲ πλίνθοις ἐγώ,[2] et statim Οὐκ ἐκ μὲν θαλάττης τὴν Εὔβοιαν προβαλέσθαι τῆς Ἀττικῆς.[3] Et alibi: Ἐγὼ δὲ οἶμαι μέν, ὦ ἄνδρες Ἀθηναῖοι, νὴ τοὺς θεούς, ἐκεῖνον μεθύειν τῷ μεγέθει τῶν πεπραγμένων.[4]

Iam quid audentius illo pulcherrimo ac longissimo excessu? Νόσημα γάρ.[5] Quid haec? breviora superioribus, sed audacia paria, Τότε ἐγὼ μὲν τῷ Πύθωνι θρασυνομένῳ καὶ πολλῷ ῥέοντι καθ᾽ ἡμῶν.[6] Ex eadem nota: Ὅταν δὲ ἐκ πλεονεξίας καὶ πονηρίας τίς, ὥσπερ οὗτος, ἰσχύσῃ, ἡ πρώτη πρόφασις καὶ μικρὸν πταῖσμα ἅπαντα ἀνεχαίτισε καὶ διέλυσε.[7]

Simile his: Ἀπεσχοινισμένος ἅπασι τοῖς ἐν τῇ πόλει δικαίοις γνώσεσι τριῶν δικαστηρίων.[8] Et ibidem: Σὺ τὸν εἰς ταῦτα ἔλεον προύδωκας, Ἀριστόγειτον, μᾶλλον δὲ ἀνῄρηκας ὅλως. μὴ δὴ πρὸς οὓς αὐτὸς ἑάλωκας λιμένας, καὶ προβόλων ἐνέπλησας, πρὸς τούτους ὁρμίζου.[9] Et dixerat: Δέδοικα μὴ δόξητέ τισι τὸν ἀεὶ βουλόμενον εἶναι πονηρὸν τῶν ἐν τῇ πόλει παιδοτριβεῖν.[10] Et deinceps: Τούτῳ δ᾽ οὐδένα ὁρῶ τῶν τόπων τούτων βάσιμον ὄντα, ἀλλὰ πάντα ἀπόκρημνα, φάραγγας, βάραθρα.[11] Nec satis: Οὐδὲ γὰρ τοὺς

---

[1] *Dem.* xviii. 296.    [2] *ib.* 299.
[3] *ib.* 301.    [4] *ib.* iv. 49.    [5] *ib.* xix. 259.
[6] *ib.* xviii. 136.    [7] *ib.* ii. 9.    [8] *ib.* xxv. 28.
[9] *ib.* 84.    [10] *ib.* 7.    [11] *ib.* 76.

---

[a] *lit.* "throws off" as a horse does his rider when he rears and tosses up his neck.

flatterers, ye evil genii?"—And again, "It is neither
with stones nor bricks that I have fortified this city."
And afterwards: "Was it not well done to throw
the rampart of Euboea in front of Attica on the
seaward side?" And in another place: "O my
Countrymen, I think, by the immortal gods, that he
is intoxicated with the grandeur of his own actions."

But what can be more daring and beautiful than
that long digression, which begins in this manner:
"A terrible disease, O my countrymen, has seized
upon all Greece?"—The following passage, likewise,
though something shorter, is conceived in the same
boldness of metaphor:—"Then it was I rose up in
opposition to the daring Pytho, who *poured forth a
torrent* of menaces against you." The subsequent
stricture is of the same stamp: "When a man has
strengthened himself, as Philip has, by avarice and
wickedness, the first pretence that offers itself, the
least false step, overthrows him *a* and brings all to
ruin.

So in the same style with the foregoing is this:—
"*Railed off*, as it were, from all the privileges of
society, by the concurrent judgements of three
tribunals in the city." And in the same place: "O
Aristogiton! you have betrayed that mercy which
used to be shewn to offences of this nature, or rather
indeed, you have wholly exhausted it. In vain then
would you *fly* for refuge to a port, which you have
*shut up*, and *choked with piles*."—He had said before:
"I am afraid you will appear in the judgement
of some to be *setting up a public seminary* of faction."
And later on—"I see *no footing for him in any of
these places;* but all is *precipice, gulf*, and *profound
abyss.*" And again: "Nor do I imagine that our

προγόνους ὑπολαμβάνω τὰ δικαστήρια ταῦτα οἰκοδομῆσαι,
ἵνα τοὺς τοιούτους ἐν αὐτοῖς μοσχεύητε.[1] Adhuc : Εἰ δὲ
κάπηλός ἐστι πονηρίας καὶ παλιγκάπηλος καὶ με. αβολεύς.[2]
Et mille talia ; ut praeteream, quae ab Aeschine [3]
θαύματα, non ῥήματα, vocantur.

In contrarium incidi. Dices, hunc quoque ab isto
culpari. Sed vide, quanto maior sit, qui reprehen-
ditur, ipso reprehendente ; et maior ob haec quoque.
In aliis enim vis, in his granditas eius elucet. Num
autem Aeschines ipse iis, quae in Demosthene
carpebat, abstinuit ? Χρὴ γάρ, ὦ ἄνδρες Ἀθηναῖοι, τὸ
αὐτὸ φθέγγεσθαι τὸν ῥήτορα καὶ τὸν νόμον· ὅταν δ' ἑτέραν
μὲν φωνὴν ἀφιῇ ὁ νόμος, ἑτέραν δὲ ὁ ῥήτωρ.[4]—Alio loco :
Ἔπειτα ἀναφαίνεται περὶ πάντων ἐν τῷ ψηφίσματι πρὸς
τῷ κλέμματι γράψας τὰ πέντε τάλαντα, τοὺς πρέσβεις
ἀξιῶν τοὺς Ὠρείτας μὴ ἡμῖν ἀλλὰ Καλλίᾳ διδόναι. ὅτι
δὲ ἀληθῆ λέγω, ἀφελὼν τὸν κομπόν, καὶ τὰς τριήρεις, καὶ
τὴν ἀλαζονείαν, ἐκ τοῦ ψηφίσματος ἀνάγνωθι.[5] Iterum
alio : Καὶ μὴ ἐᾶτε αὐτὸν εἰς τοὺς τοῦ παρανόμου λόγους
περιίστασθαι.[6] Quod adeo probavit, ut repetat, Ἀλλὰ
ἐγκαθήμενοι καὶ ἐνεδρεύοντες ἐν τῇ ἐκκλησίᾳ εἰσελαύνετε
αὐτὸν εἰς τοὺς τοῦ παρανόμου λόγους, καὶ τὰς ἐκτροπὰς
αὐτοῦ τῶν λόγων ἐπιτηρεῖτε.[7] An illa custoditius

[1] *Dem.* xxv. 48.   [2] *ib.* 46.   [3] Aesch. *Ctes.* 167.
[4] *ib.* 16.   [5] *ib.* 101.   [6] *ib.* 206.
[7] *Timarch.* 176.

ancestors erected those courts of judicature, that men of his character should be *propagated* there;"— And afterwards: "If he deals in, and retails, and peddles wickedness."—And a thousand other passages which I might cite to the same purpose: not to mention those expressions which Aeschines says are not *words*, but *wonders*.

You will tell me I have lighted on an adverse instance, since Demosthenes is condemned by Aeschines for running into these figurative expressions. But observe, I intreat you, how far superior the former orator is to his criticizer, and superior, too, in virtue of these very passages: for in others, the strength of his genius discovers itself: in those above quoted, the sublimity of it shines out. But does Aeschines himself avoid what he reproves in Demosthenes? "The orator," says he, "Athenians, and the law, ought to *speak* the same language; but when the *voice* of the law declares one thing, and that of the orator another."—And in another place: " he afterwards manifestly discovered the design he had, of concealing his fraud under cover of the decree, having expressly declared therein, that the embassadors sent to the Oretae gave the five talents, not to you, but to Callias. And that you may be convinced what I say is the truth (after having *stripped* the decree of its *pomp*, its *galleys*, and *braggadocio*) read the clause itself." And in another part: "Suffer him not to *break cover* and *wander* out of the limits of the question:" a metaphor he is so fond of, that he repeats it again: "But sitting firm and lying in ambush in the assembly *drive* him into the merits of the question, and observe well how he *doubles*." Is his style more reserved and

# THE LETTERS OF PLINY

pressiusque? Σὺ δὲ ἑλκοποιεῖς,[1] ἢ συλλαβόντες ὡς λῃστὴν
τῶν πραγμάτων διὰ τῆς πολιτείας πλέοντα τιμωρήσασθε,[2]
et alia.

Exspecto, ut quaedam ex hac epistula, ut illud,
'gubernacula gemunt,' et 'dis maris proximus,'
iisdem notis, quibus ea, de quibus scribo, confodias.
Intellego enim, me, dum veniam prioribus peto, in
illa ipsa, quae adnotaveras, incidisse. Sed confodias
licet, dummodo iam nunc destines diem, quo et
de illis et de his coram exigere possimus. Aut
enim tu me timidum, aut ego te temerarium
faciam. Vale.

## XXVII

### C. Plinius Paterno Suo S.

Quanta potestas, quanta dignitas, quanta maiestas,
quantum denique numen sit historiae, cum frequenter alias tum proxime sensi. Recitaverat
quidam verissimum librum partemque eius in alium
diem reservaverat. Ecce amici cuiusdam orantes
obsecrantesque, ne reliqua recitaret. Tantus au-
diendi, quae fecerint, pudor, quibus nullus faciendi,
quae audire erubescunt. Et ille quidem praestitit,

[1] Aesch. *Ctes.* 208.        [2] *ib.* 253.

240

simple when he says : " But you are *manufacturing wounds*," or, " will you not seize and punish this political *pirate*, who *cruises* about the state ? "—with many other passages of the like nature.

And now I expect you will make the same strictures upon certain expressions in this letter, as you did upon those I have been endeavouring to defend. The rudder that *groans,* and the pilot compared to a *sea-god,* will not, I imagine, escape your erasures : for I perceive while I am suing for indulgence to my former offences, I have fallen into the very turn of figure that you condemn. But blot these expressions if you please, provided you will immediately appoint a day when we may meet to discuss both my letter and my speech in person : you will then either teach *me* to be less daring, or I shall learn *you* to be more bold. Farewell.


## XXVII

### To Paternus

I have had many occasions to observe the power, the dignity, the majesty, and I will add too, even the *divine* efficacy there is in history ; but I never met with so strong an instance of it as lately. An author had recited part of an historical performance, which he had drawn up with the utmost regard to truth, reserving the remainder for another day. When behold ! the friends of a certain person came to him and earnestly conjured him not to recite the rest ; so much are men ashamed to hear those actions repeated which they yet do not blush to commit ! The historian complied (as he well might, without any

quod rogabatur; sinebat fides.   Liber tamen ut
factum ipsum manet, manebit legeturque semper
tanto magis, quia non statim.   Incitantur enim
homines ad agnoscenda, quae differuntur.   Vale.


## XXVIII

### C. Plinius Romano Suo S.

Post longum tempus epistulas tuas, sed tres
pariter recepi, omnes elegantissimas, amantissimas,
et quales a te venire, praesertim desideratas, oportebat.   Quarum una iniungis mihi iucundissimum mi-
nisterium, ut ad Plotinam, sanctissimam feminam,
litterae tuae perferantur.   Perferentur.   Eadem
commendas Popilium Artemisium.   Statim praestiti,
quod petebat.   Indicas etiam modicas te vindemias
collegisse.   Communis haec mihi tecum, quamquam
in diversissima parte terrarum, querela est.

Altera epistula nuntias multa te nunc dictare,
nunc scribere, quibus nos tibi repraesentes.   Gratias
ago; agerem magis, si me illa ipsa, quae scribis aut
dictas, legere voluisses.   Et erat aequum ut te mea
ita me tua scripta cognoscere, etiamsi ad alium
quam ad me pertinerent.   Polliceris in fine, cum
certius de vitae nostrae ordinatione aliquid audieris,

---

<sup>a</sup> The Empress, Trajan's wife.

breach of honour) with their request. But however, the history, like the action, remains, and will ever remain. And will be read too with so much the greater curiosity as the publication of it is delayed: for nothing raises the inquisitive disposition of mankind so much as to defer the gratification of it. Farewell.

## XXVIII

### To Romanus

Your letters have at length reached me, but I received three at once; all breathing the very spirit of elegance and friendship, and such as I had reason to expect from you, especially after having wished for them so long. In one, you enjoin me the very agreeable commission of forwarding your letter to that excellent lady, the virtuous Plotina [a]: I will take care to do so. At the same time you recommend to me Popilius Artemisius; and I have at once performed his request. You tell me also your vintage has proved extremely moderate. That complaint, notwithstanding we are separated by such distant countries, is common to us both.

Your second letter informs me, that you are employed in dictating and writing your impressions of myself. I am much obliged to you; and should be more so, if you would give me the pleasure of reading your performance. It were but just indeed, that as I communicate to you all my compositions, you should suffer me to partake of yours, even though they should turn upon another subject than myself. You promise me in the close of your letter, that as soon as you shall be informed with certainty, in what

futurum te fugitivum rei familiaris statimque ad nos
evolaturum, qui iam tibi compedes nectimus, quas
perfringere nullo modo possis.

Tertia epistula continebat esse tibi redditam
orationem pro Clario, eamque visam uberiorem,
quam dicente me, audiente te fuerit. Est uberior;
multa enim postea inserui. Adicis alias te litteras
curiosius scriptas misisse; an acceperim, quaeris.
Non accepi et accipere gestio. Proinde prima
quaque occasione mitte adpositis quidem usuris, quas
ego (num parcius possum?) centesimas computabo.
Vale

## XXIX

### C. Plinius Rustico Suo S.

Ut satius est unum aliquid insigniter facere quam
plurima mediocriter, ita plurima mediocriter, si non
possis unum aliquid insigniter. Quod intuens ego
variis me studiorum generibus nulli satis confisus
experior. Proinde, cum hoc vel illud leges, ita
singulis veniam ut non singulis dabis. An ceteris

manner I intend to dispose of myself, you will make an elopement from your family, and immediately fly to me: I am already preparing certain chains for you, which, when I have you here, you will by no means be able to break through.

I learn from your third, that my oration in behalf of Clarius has been delivered to you, which appears, it seems, more full than when you heard it pronounced. It is so, I confess: for I afterwards very considerably enlarged it. You mention having sent me another letter, which you say was written with some pains, and desire to know if I have received it: I have not, but impatiently wish for its arrival. To make me amends, write to me upon the first opportunity, and pay me with full interest, which I shall compute at *one per cent. monthly*; tell me, can I acquit you upon more reasonable terms? Farewell.

## XXIX

### To Rusticus

As it is far better to excel in any single art, than to arrive only at a mediocrity in several; so on the other hand, a moderate skill in several is to be preferred, where one cannot attain to excellency in any. Upon this maxim it is, that I have attempted compositions of various sorts, as I could not expect to carry any particular one to its highest point of excellency. I hope, therefore, when you read any performance of mine, you will consider it with that indulgence which is due to an author, who has not confined himself to a single manner of writing, but has struck out into different kinds. In every other

artibus excusatio in numero, litteris durior lex, in
quibus difficilior effectus est? Quid autem ego de
venia quasi ingratus? Nam, si ea facilitate proxima
acceperis qua priora, laus potius speranda quam
venia obsecranda est. Mihi tamen venia sufficit.
Vale.

## XXX

### C. Plinius Gemino Suo S.

Laudas mihi et frequenter praesens et nunc
per epistulas Nonium tuum, quod sit liberalis in
quosdam. Et ipse laudo, si tamen non in hos
solos. Volo enim eum, qui sit vere liberalis, tri-
buere patriae, propinquis, adfinibus, amicis, sed
amicis dico pauperibus, non ut isti, qui iis potissimum donant, qui donare maxime possunt. Hos
ego viscatis hamatisque muneribus non sua promere
puto, sed aliena corripere. Sunt ingenio simili,
qui, quod huic donant, auferunt illi famamque
liberalitatis avaritia petunt. Primum est autem
suo esse contentum, deinde, quos praecipue scias
indigere, sustentantem foventemque orbe quodam
societatis ambire. Quae cuncta si facit iste, usque-

art quantity pleads some excuse for the quality; and shall literature, the most difficult of all, be tried by a severer law? But whilst I am bespeaking your candour, am I not bringing my gratitude in question? For, if you receive these last pieces with the same indulgence that you have all my former, I have more reason to hope for your applause, than to sue for your pardon. However, your pardon will be sufficient. Farewell.

## XXX

### To Geminus

You have frequently in conversation, and lately in a letter, commended your friend Nonius to me for his liberality to some particular persons; I shall join with you in his applause, if his bounty is not confined to those only. I would have the man of true generosity assist his country, his kindred, his relations, and his friends; his friends I mean in distress; not like those who chiefly bestow their presents where there is the greatest ability to make returns. I do not look upon such, as parting with any thing of their own; on the contrary, I consider their bounties as only so many disguised baits, thrown out with a design of catching the property of others. Much of the same character are those, who rob Peter to pay Paul, and seek a reputation for munificence by the practice of avarice. The first principle of genuine liberality is to be contented with what you have; and after that, to cherish and embrace all the most indigent of your acquaintance, in one comprehensive circle of benevolence. If your friend observes this rule in its full extent, he is entirely to

quaque laudandus est ; si unum aliquid, minus quidem,
laudandus tamen. Tam rarum est etiam imperfectae
liberalitatis exemplar. Ea invasit homines habendi
cupido, ut possideri magis quam possidere videantur.
Vale.

## XXXI

### C. PLINIUS SARDO SUO S.

POSTQUAM a te recessi, non minus tecum, quam
cum apud te fui. Legi enim librum tuum identidem repetens ea maxime (non enim mentiar),
quae de me scripsisti, in quibus quidem percopiosus
fuisti. Quam multa, quam varia, quam non eadem
de eodem nec tamen diversa dixisti ! Laudem
pariter et gratias agam ? Neutrum satis possum
et, si possem, timerem, ne arrogans esset ob ea
laudare, ob quae gratias agerem. Unum illud
addam, omnia mihi tanto laudabiliora visa, quanto
iucundiora, et tanto iucundiora, quanto laudabiliora
erant. Vale.

## XXXII

### C. PLINIUS TITIANO SUO S.

QUID agis ? quid acturus es ? Ipse vitam iucundissimam, id est, otiosissimam, vivo. Quo fit, ut

be commended; if he only partially pursues it, still he deserves (in a less degree indeed, however, he deserves) applause: so uncommon is it to meet with an instance of generosity even of the most imperfect kind! The lust of lucre has so totally seized upon mankind, that their wealth seems rather to possess them, than they to possess their wealth. Farewell.

## XXXI

### To Sardus

I still continued with you, notwithstanding we had parted: for I entertained myself with reading over your book. And I frequently went over with particular fondness (I honestly own it) those passages of which I am the subject: a subject upon which, indeed, you have been extremely copious. What a number and variety of remarks, all different, yet all consistent, have you made on one and the same person! Will you suffer me to mingle my applauses with my acknowledgements? I can do neither sufficiently; and if I could, there would be something, I fear, of vanity, in making that the subject of my praise, which is, in truth the object of my thanks. I will only add then, that the pleasure I received from your performance raised its merit in my eyes; and its merit heightened that pleasure. Farewell.

## XXXII

### To Titianus

What are you doing? And what do you propose to do? As for myself, I pass my life in the most agreeable, that is, in the most disengaged manner

scribere longiores epistulas nolim, velim legere;
illud tamquam delicatus, hoc tamquam otiosus.
Nihil est enim aut pigrius delicatis aut curiosius
otiosis. Vale.

## XXXIII

### C. PLINIUS CANINIO SUO S.

INCIDI in materiam veram, sed simillimam fictae
dignamque isto laetissimo, altissimo planeque poëtico
ingenio, incidi autem, dum super cenam varia mira-
cula hinc inde referuntur. Magna auctoris fides;
tametsi quid poëtae cum fide? Is tamen auctor, cui
bene vel historiam scripturus credidisses.

Est in Africa Hipponensis colonia mari proxima;
adiacet navigabile stagnum; ex hoc in modum
fluminis aestuarium emergit, quod vice alterna, prout
aestus aut repressit aut impulit, nunc infertur mari,
nunc redditur stagno. Omnis hic aetas piscandi,
navigandi, atque etiam natandi studio tenetur,
maxime pueri, quos otium ludusque sollicitat. His
gloria et virtus altissime provehi; victor ille, qui
longissime ut litus ita simul nantes reliquit. Hoc
certamine puer quidam audentior ceteris in ulteriora

imaginable. I do not find myself, therefore, in the
humour to write a long letter, though I am to read
one. I am too much a man of pleasure for the
former, and just idle enough for the latter ; for none
are more indolent, you know, than the voluptuous,
or have more curiosity than those who have nothing
to do. Farewell.

## XXXIII

### To Caninius

I HAVE met with a story, which, though true, has
all the air of fable, and would afford a very proper
subject for your lively, elevated, and truly poetical
genius. It was related to me the other day at table,
where the conversation happened to turn upon
various kinds of miraculous events. The person who
gave the account, was a man of unsuspected veracity:—but what has a poet to do with truth?
However, you might venture to rely upon his
testimony, even though you had the character of
a faithful historian to support.

There is in Africa a town called Hippo, situated
not far from the sea-coast : it stands upon a navigable lake, from whence an estuary is discharged
after the manner of a river, which ebbs and flows
with the sea. Persons of all ages divert themselves
here with fishing, sailing or swimming ; especially
boys, whom love of play and idleness bring hither.
The contest among them is, who shall have the glory
of swimming farthest ; and he that leaves the shore
and his companions at the greatest distance, gains
the victory. It happened in one of these trials of
skill, that a certain boy, more bold than the rest,

251

tendebat. Delphinus occurrit et nunc praecedere
puerum, nunc sequi, nunc circumire, postremo subire,
deponere, iterum subire trepidantemque perferre
primum in altum, mox flectit ad litus redditque
terrae et aequalibus. Serpit per coloniam fama;
concurrere omnes, ipsum puerum tamquam miraculum
adspicere, interrogare, audire, narrare.

Postero die obsident litus, prospectant mare, et si
quid mari simile. Natant pueri; inter hos ille, sed
cautius. Delphinus rursus ad tempus, rursus ad
puerum [venit]. Fugit ille cum ceteris. Delphinus,
quasi invitet et revocet, exilit, mergitur, variosque
orbes implicitat expeditque. Hoc altero die, hoc
tertio, hoc pluribus, donec homines innutritos mari
subiret timendi pudor: accedunt et adludunt et
appellant, tangunt etiam pertrectantque praebentem.
Crescit audacia experimento. Maxime puer, qui
primus expertus est, adnatat natanti, insilit tergo,
fertur ref]erturque, agnosci se, amari putat, amat ipse;

---

* This animal is celebrated by several of the ancients for
its philanthropy, and Pliny the elder, in particular, relates
this very story, among other instances, in confirmation of
that notion. See Plin. *Hist. Nat.* l. 9, c. 8. (Melm.)

launched out towards the opposite shore.   He was
met by a dolphin,[a] who sometimes swam before him,
and sometimes behind him, then played round him,
and at last took him upon his back, then let him
down, and afterwards took him up again : and thus
carried the poor frightened boy out into the deepest
part ; when immediately he turns back again to the
shore, and lands him among his companions.   The
fame of this remarkable accident spread through the
town, and crowds of people flocked round the boy
(whom they viewed as a kind of prodigy) to ask him
questions, hear his story and repeat it.

The next day the shore was lined with multitudes
of spectators all attentively observing the ocean, and
(what indeed is almost itself an ocean) the lake.   In
the meanwhile the boys swam as usual, and among the
rest, the youth I am speaking of went into the lake,
but with more caution than before.   The dolphin
punctually appeared again and came to the boy, who
together with his companions swam away with the utmost precipitation.   The dolphin, as it were, to invite
and recall them, bounded and dived up and down,
winding about in a thousand different circles.   This
he practised for several days together, till the people
(accustomed from their infancy to the sea) began to
be ashamed of their timidity.   They ventured therefore to advance nearer, playing with him and calling
him to them, while he, in return, suffered himself to
be touched and stroked.   Use rendered them more
courageous : the boy, in particular, who first made
the experiment, swam by the side of him, and leap-
ing upon his back, was carried to and fro in that
manner : he fancies the dolphin knows and is fond of
him, and he returns its fondness.   There seemed

neuter timet, neuter timetur; huius fiducia, mansue-
tudo illius augetur. Nec non alii pueri dextra
laevaque simul eunt hortantes monentesque. Ibat
una (id quoque mirum) delphinus alius tantum
spectator et comes. Nihil enim simile aut faciebat
aut patiebatur, sed alterum illum ducebat reducebat-
que, ut puerum ceteri pueri.

Incredibile, tam verum tamen quam priora, del-
phinum gestatorem collusoremque puerorum in terram quoque extrahi solitum harenisque siccatum, ubi
incaluisset, in mare revolvi. Constat Octavium
Avitum, legatum proconsulis in litus educto religione
prava superfudisse unguentum, cuius illum novitatem
odoremque in altum refugisse nec nisi post multos
dies visum languidum et maestum, mox redditis viribus priorem lasciviam et solita ministeria repetisse.
Confluebant ad spectaculum omnes magistratus,
quorum adventu et mora modica res publica novis
sumptibus atterebatur. Postremo locus ipse quietem
suam secretumque perdebat. Placuit occulte inter-
fici ad quod coibatur.

Haec tu qua miseratione, qua copia deflebis,

---

now, indeed, to be no fear on either side, the confidence of the one and the tameness of the other mutually increasing; the rest of the boys in the meanwhile swimming on either hand, encouraging and cautioning their companion. It is very remarkable, that this dolphin was followed by a second, which seemed only as a spectator and attendant on the former; for he did not at all submit to the same familiarities as the first, but only conducted him backwards and forwards, as the boys did their comrade.

But what is incredible, yet no less true than the rest, this dolphin who thus played with the boys and carried them upon his back, would come upon the shore, dry himself in the sand, and as soon as he grew warm, roll back into the sea. 'Tis known that Octavius Avitus, deputy governor of the province, from an absurd piece of superstition, poured some precious ointment over him as he lay on the shore,[a] the novelty and smell of which made him retire into the ocean, and it was not till after several days that he was seen again, when he appeared dull and languid; however he recovered his strength and continued his usual wanton tricks. All the magistrates round the country flocked hither to view this sight, the entertainment of whom upon their arrival, and during their stay, was an additional expense, which the slender finances of this little community could ill afford; besides, the quiet and retirement of the place was utterly destroyed. It was thought proper therefore to remove the occasion of this concourse, by privately killing the poor dolphin.

And now, with what a flow of tenderness will you describe this sad catastrophe! and how will your

# THE LETTERS OF PLINY

ornabis, attolles! Quamquam non est opus adfingas aliquid aut adstruas; sufficit, ne ea, quae sunt vera, minuantur. Vale.

## XXXIV

### C. Plinius Tranquillo Suo S.

Explica aestum meum. Audio me male legere, dumtaxat versus; orationes enim commodius, sed tanto minus versus. Cogito ergo recitaturus familiaribus amicis experiri libertum meum. Hoc quoque familiare, quod elegi non bene, sed melius lecturum, si tamen non fuerit perturbatus. Est enim tam novus lector quam ego poëta. Ipse nescio, quid illo legente interim faciam, sedeam defixus et mutus et similis otioso an ut quidam, quae pronuntiabit, murmure, oculis, manu prosequar. Sed puto me non minus male saltare quam legere. Iterum dicam, explica aestum meum vereque rescribe, num sit melius pessime legere quam ista vel non facere vel facere. Vale

genius adorn and heighten this moving story! Though, indeed, it does not require any fictitious embellishments; it will be sufficient to place the real circumstances in their full light. Farewell.


## XXXIV

### To Tranquillus

I am under a wondrous difficulty, which you must settle. I have not, I am told, a good manner of reading verses: my talent lying chiefly in reciting orations, I succeed so much the worse, it seems, in poetry. I design therefore, as I am to recite some poems to my familiar friends, to make trial of my freedman for that purpose. It is treating them, I own, with familiarity, to employ a person who does not read well himself; however, he will perform, I know, better than I can, provided his fears do not disconcert him, for he is as unpractised a reader as I am a poet. Now the perplexing question is, how I shall behave while he is reading; whether I shall sit silent in a fixed and indolent posture, or follow him as he pronounces, with my eyes, hands and voice; a manner which some, you know, practise. But I fancy I have as little gift for pantomime as for reading. I repeat it again, therefore, you must extricate me out of this wondrous difficulty, and write me word whether you honestly think it would be better to read ever so ill, than to practise or omit any of the weighty circumstances abovementioned. Farewell.

# THE LETTERS OF PLINY

## XXXV

### C. Plinius Atrio[1] Suo S.

Librum, quem misisti, recepi et gratias ago. Sum
tamen hoc tempore occupatissimus. Ideo nondum
eum legi, cum alioqui validissime cupiam ; sed eam
reverentiam cum litteris ipsis tum scriptis tuis debeo,
ut sumere illa nisi vacuo animo irreligiosum putem.
Diligentiam tuam in retractandis operibus valde
probo. Est tamen aliquis modus, primum quod
nimia cura deterit magis quam emendat, deinde
quod nos a recentioribus revocat simulque nec
absolvit priora et inchoare posteriora non patitur.
Vale.

## XXXVI

### C. Plinius Fusco Suo S.

Quaeris, quem ad modum in Tuscis diem aestate
disponam.

Evigilo, cum libuit, plerumque circa horam
primam, saepe ante, tardius raro. Clausae fenestrae
manent. Mire enim silentio et tenebris ab iis, quae
avocant, abductus et liber et mihi relictus, non oculos
animo sed animum oculis sequor, qui eadem quae

[1] Atrio *D*, Appio *pr*, Oppio *a*, Attio *K*.

258

## XXXV

### To Atrius

I have received your book, and return you thanks
for it; but am at present so much engaged, that I
have not time to read it; which, however, I impatiently wish to do. I have that high reverence for
letters in general, and for your compositions in
particular, that I think it a sort of profanation to
approach them but with a mind entirely disengaged.
I extremely approve of your care in revising your
works; remember, however, this exactness has its
limits: too much polishing rather weakens than
strengthens a performance. Besides, this excessive
delicacy, while it calls one off from other pursuits,
not only prevents any new attempts, but does not
even finish what it has begun. Farewell.

## XXXVI

### To Fuscus

You desire to know in what manner I dispose of
my day in summer-time at my Tuscan villa.

I rise just when I find myself in the humour,
though generally with the sun; often indeed sooner,
but seldom later. When I am up, I continue to keep
the shutters of my chamber-windows closed. For
under the influence of darkness and silence, I find
myself wonderfully free and abstracted from those
outward objects which dissipate attention, and left to
my own thoughts; nor do I suffer my mind to
wander with my eyes, but keep my eyes in subjection

mens vident, quotiens non vident alia. Cogito, si quid in manibus, cogito ad verbum scribenti emendantique similis nunc pauciora, nunc plura, ut vel difficile, vel facile componi tenerive potuerunt. Notarium voco et die admisso, quae formaveram dicto. Abit rursusque revocatur rursusque remittitur.

Ubi hora quarta vel quinta (neque enim certum dimensumque tempus), ut dies suasit, in xystum me vel cryptoporticum confero, reliqua meditor et dicto. Vehiculum ascendo. Ibi quoque idem quod ambulans aut iacens; durat intentio mutatione ipsa refecta. Paulum redormio, dein ambulo, mox orationem Graecam Latinamve clare et intente non tam vocis causa quam stomachi lego; pariter tamen et illa firmatur. Iterum ambulo, ungor, exerceor, lavor. Cenanti mihi, si cum uxore vel paucis, liber legitur; post cenam comoedus aut lyristes; mox cum meis ambulo, quorum in numero sunt eruditi

to my mind, which in the absence of external
objects, see those which are present to the mental
vision. If I have any composition upon my hands,
this is the time I choose to consider it, not only with
respect to the general plan, but even the style and
expression, which I settle and correct as if I were
actually writing. In this manner I compose more or
less as the subject is more or less difficult, and I find
myself able to retain it. Then I call my secretary,
and, opening the shutters, I dictate to him what I
have composed, after which I dismiss him for a little
while, and then call him in again and again dismiss
him.

About ten or eleven of the clock (for I do not
observe one fixed hour), according as the weather
recommends, I betake myself either to the terrace,
or the covered portico, and there I meditate and
dictate what remains upon the subject in which I am
engaged. From thence I get into my chariot, where
I employ myself as before, when I was walking or in
my study; and find this changing of the scene
preserves and enlivens my attention. At my return
home I repose myself a while; then I take a walk;
and after that, read aloud and with emphasis some
Greek or Latin oration, not so much for the sake of
strengthening my elocution as my digestion; though
indeed the voice at the same time finds its account
in this practice. Then I walk again, am anointed,
take my exercises, and go into the bath. At supper,
if I have only my wife, or a few friends with me,
some author is read to us; and after supper we are
entertained either with music, or an interlude.
When that is finished, I take my walk with my
domestics, in the number of which I am not without

Ita variis sermonibus vespera extenditur, et quamquam longissimus dies cito conditur.

Non numquam ex hoc ordine aliqua mutantur
Nam, si diu iacui vel ambulavi, post somnum demum
lectionemque non vehiculo, sed, quod brevius, quia
velocius, equo gestor. Interveniunt amici ex proximis
oppidis partemque diei ad se trahunt interdumque
lassato mihi opportuna interpellatione subveniunt.
Venor aliquando, sed non sine pugillaribus, ut,
quamvis nihil ceperim, non nihil referam.    Datur et
colonis, ut videtur ipsis, non satis temporis, quorum
mihi agrestes querelae litteras nostras et haec urbana
opera commendant.    Vale.


## XXXVII

### C. PLINIUS PAULINO SUO S.

NEC tuae naturae est translaticia haec et quasi
publica officia a familiaribus amicis contra ipsorum
commodum exigere, et ego te constantius amo, quam
ut verear, ne aliter, ac velim, accipias, nisi te
Kalendis statim consulem videro ; praesertim cum
me necessitas locandorum praediorum in [1] plures

---

[1] in add. *Müller.*

some persons of literature. Thus we pass our evenings in various conversation; and the day, even when it is at the longest, is quickly spent.

Upon some occasions, I change the order in certain of the articles above mentioned. For instance, if I have lain longer or walked more than usual, after my second sleep and reading aloud, instead of using my chariot I get on horseback; by which means I take as much exercise and lose less time. The visits of my friends from the neighbouring towns claim some part of the day; and sometimes by a seasonable interruption, they relieve me, when I am fatigued. I now and then amuse myself with sporting, but always take my tablets into the field, that though I should catch nothing, I may at least bring home something. Part of my time, too (though not so much as they desire), is allotted to my tenants: and I find their rustic complaints give a zest to my studies and engagements of the politer kind. Farewell.

## XXXVII

### To Paulinus

As you are not of a disposition to expect from your friends the common ceremonies of the world, when they cannot observe them without inconvenience to themselves; so I too warmly love you to be apprehensive you will take otherwise than I wish you should, my not waiting upon you on the first day on your entrance upon the consular office; especially as I am detained here by the necessity of letting my

annos ordinatura detineat, in qua mihi nova consilia sumenda sunt. Nam priore lustro, quamquam post magnas remissiones, reliqua creverunt. Inde plerisque nulla iam cura minuendi aeris alieni, quod desperant posse persolvi; rapiunt etiam consumuntque, quod natum est, ut qui iam putent se non sibi parcere.

Occurrendum ergo augescentibus vitiis et medendum est. Medendi una ratio, si non nummo, sed partibus locem ac deinde ex meis aliquos operis exactores custodes fructibus ponam. Et alioqui nullum iustius genus reditus, quam quod terra, coelum, annus refert. At hoc magnam fidem, acres oculos, numerosas manus poscit. Experiendum tamen et quasi in veteri morbo quaelibet mutationis auxilia temptanda sunt.

Vides, quam non delicata me causa obire primum consulatus tui diem non sinat; quem tamen hic quoque ut praesens votis, gaudio, gratulatione celebrabo. Vale.

farms upon long leases. I am obliged to enter upon an entire new method with my tenants: for during the last five years, though I made them very considerable abatements, they have run greatly in arrear. For this reason several of them not only take no sort of care to lessen a debt, which they despaired of paying in full; but even seize and consume all the produce of the lands, in the belief that it would now be no advantage to themselves to spare it.

I must therefore obviate this increasing evil, and endeavour to find out some remedy against it. The only one I can think of is, not to let at a money-rent, but on condition of receiving a fixed share of the produce; and then to place some of my servants to overlook the tillage, and to keep a watch on the crops. And indeed, there is no sort of revenue more equitable, than what arises from the bounty of the soil, the seasons and the climate. 'Tis true, this method will require great integrity and diligent attendance in the person I appoint my bailiff, and put me to the expense of employing many hands. However, I must hazard the experiment; and, as in an inveterate distemper, try every change of remedy.

You see, it is not any pleasurable indulgence, that prevents my attending you on the first day of your consulship. I shall celebrate it nevertheless, as much as if I were present, and pay my vows for you here, with all the warmest sentiments of joy and congratulation. Farewell.

## XXXVIII

### C. Plinius Saturnino Suo S.

Ego vero Rufum nostrum laudo, non quia tu, ut
ita facerem, petisti, sed quia ille est dignissimus.
Legi enim librum omnibus numeris absolutum, cui
multum apud me gratiae amor ipsius adiecit. Iudi-
cavi tamen. Neque enim soli iudicant, qui maligne
legunt. Vale.

## XXXIX

### C. Plinius Mustio Suo S.

Haruspicum monitu reficienda est mihi aedes
Cereris in praediis in melius et in maius, vetus sane
et angusta, cum sit alioqui stato die frequentissima.
Nam Idibus Septembribus magnus e regione tota
coit populus, multae res aguntur, multa vota susci-
piuntur, multa redduntur; sed nullum in proximo
suffugium aut imbris aut solis. Videor ergo munifice
simul religioseque facturus, si aedem quam pulcherrimam exstruxero, addidero porticus aedi, illam ad
usum deae, has ad hominum.

Velim ergo emas quattuor marmoreas columnas,
cuius tibi videbitur generis, emas marmora, quibus

---

_a_ Soothsayers who practised the (originally Etruscan)
method of divination by inspection of the sacrificial victim's
entrails.

## XXXVIII

### To Saturninus

Yes, I sincerely applaud our friend Rufus; not because you desire me; but because I think he highly merits approbation. I have read his very finished performance, to which my affection for the author added a considerable recommendation. Yet it did not blind my judgement; for the malicious, is not, I trust, the only judicious reader. Farewell

## XXXIX

### To Mustius

In compliance with the advice of the *haruspices*,[a] I intend to repair and enlarge the temple of Ceres, which stands upon my estate. It is indeed not only very ancient, but small, considering how thronged it is upon a certain anniversary On the 13th of September, great numbers of people from all the country round assemble there, many affairs are transacted, and many vows paid and offered; but there is no shelter hard by against rain or sun. I imagine then, I shall do at once an act of piety and munificence, if at the same time that I rebuild the temple on the noblest scale, I add to it a spacious portico; the first for the service of the Goddess, the other for the use of the people.

I beg therefore you would purchase for me four marble pillars, of whatever kind you shall think proper; as also a quantity of marble for laying the

solum, quibus parietes excolantur. Erit etiam vel faciendum vel emendum ipsius deae signum, quia antiquum illud e ligno quibusdam sui partibus vetustate truncatum est.

Quantum ad porticus, nihil interim occurrit, quod videatur istinc esse repetendum ; nisi tamen ut formam secundum rationem loci scribas. Neque enim possunt circumdari templo ; nam solum templi hinc flumine et abruptissimis ripis, hinc via cingitur. Est ultra viam latissimum pratum, in quo satis apte contra templum ipsum porticus explicabuntur ; nisi quid tu melius inveneris, qui soles locorum difficultates arte superare. Vale.

## XL

### C. PLINIUS FUSCO SUO S.

SCRIBIS pergratas tibi fuisse litteras meas, quibus cognovisti, quem ad modum in Tuscis otium aestatis exigerem ; requiris quid ex hoc in Laurentino hieme permutem. Nihil, nisi quod meridianus somnus eximitur, multumque de nocte vel ante vel post diem sumitur, et si agendi necessitas instat, quae frequens hieme, non iam comoedo vel lyristae post cenam

---

[a] ix. 36.

floor and incrusting the walls. You must likewise either buy a statue of the Goddess, or procure one to be made; for age has maimed, in some parts, the ancient one of wood which stands there at present.

With respect to the portico, I do not at the moment recollect there is any thing you can send me that will be serviceable; unless you will sketch me out a plan suitable to the situation of the place. It is not practicable to build it round the temple, because it is encompassed on one side by the river, whose banks are exceedingly steep; and on the other, by the high road. Beyond this road lies a very large meadow, in which the portico may be conveniently enough placed, opposite to the temple; unless you, who are accustomed to conquer the inconveniences of nature by art, can propose some better situation. Farewell.

## XL

### To Fuscus

You are much pleased, I find, with the account I gave you in my former letter,[a] of the manner in which I spend my summer holidays in my Tuscan villa; and desire to know what alteration I make in my method, when I am at my Laurentine villa in the winter. None at all, except depriving myself of my sleep at noon, and considerably abridging my nocturnal repose, either after sunset or before sunrise: and if I have any forensic business impending (which in winter very frequently happens) instead of having interludes or music after supper

iocus, sed illa, quae dictavi, identidem retractantur,
ac simul memoriae frequenti emendatione proficitur.
Habes aestate, hieme consuetudinem; nunc[1] addas
huc licet ver et autumnum, quae inter hiemem aesta-
temque media, ut nihil de die perdunt, ita de nocte
parvulum acquirunt.   Vale.

[1] nunc *add. Casaub.*

I meditate upon what I have dictated, and by often revising it in my own mind, fix it in my memory. Thus I have given you my scheme of life in summer and winter ; to which you may add the intermediate seasons of spring and autumn.   As at those times I lose nothing of the day, so I steal but little from the night.   Farewell.

# BOOK X

# LIBER DECIMUS

## I

### C. Plinius Traiano Imperatori

Tua quidem pietas, imperator sanctissime, opta-
verat, ut quam tardissime succederes patri : sed di
immortales festinaverunt virtutes tuas ad gubernacula rei publicae, quam susceperas, admovere. Precor ergo, ut tibi et per te generi humano prospera
omnia, id est digna saeculo tuo, contingant. Fortem
te et hilarem, imperator optime, et privatim et
publice opto.

## II

### C. Plinius Traiano Imperatori

Exprimere, domine, verbis non possum, quantum
mihi gaudium attuleris, quod me dignum putasti
iure trium liberorum. Quamvis enim Iuli Serviani,
optimi viri tuique amantissimi, precibus indulseris,

---

[a] Nerva, who had adopted Trajan three months previously,
died on Jan. 28, 98 A.D. Trajan received the news of his

# BOOK X

## I

### To the Emperor Trajan

Your filial affection, most pious Emperor, made you wish it might be late ere you succeeded your Father. But the immortal gods have hastened the advancement of those virtues to the helm of the commonwealth, which had already so successfully shared in the conduct of it.[a] May you then, and the world through your means, enjoy every prosperity, in other words, everything worthy of your reign ; to which let me add my wishes, most excellent Emperor, upon a private as well as public account, that your health and spirits may be preserved firm and unbroken.

## II

### To the Emperor Trajan

You have occasioned me, Sir, an inexpressible pleasure, by thinking me worthy of enjoying the privilege which the laws confer on those who have three children.[b] For though it was an indulgence to the request of your very affectionate and worthy friend Servianus, that you granted this favour ; yet

accession at Cologne, and did not return to Rome for nearly two years.    [b] See ii. 13, note, vii, 16, note.

tamen etiam ex rescripto intellego libentius hoc
ei te praestitisse, quia pro me rogabat.   Videor
ergo summam voti mei consecutus, cum inter initia
felicissimi principatus tui probaveris me ad pe-
culiarem indulgentiam tuam pertinere ; eoque magis
liberos concupisco, quos habere etiam illo tristissimo
saeculo volui, sicut potes duobus matrimoniis meis
credere.   Sed di melius, qui omnia integra bonitati
tuae reservarunt ; malui[1] hoc potius tempore me
patrem fieri, quo futurus essem et securus et
felix.


### III A

#### C. PLINIUS TRAIANO IMPERATORI

UT primum me, domine, indulgentia vestra
promovit ad praefecturam aerarii Saturni, omnibus
advocationibus, quibus alioqui   numquam   eram
promiscue   functus, renuntiavi, ut   toto   animo
delegato mihi officio vacarem.   Qua ex causa, cum
patronum me provinciales optassent contra Marium

---

[1] malui *Av. a, Bipons*, maluere *Ernesti, Müller*.

---

[a] Of Domitian.   On Pliny's marriages see Introduction.
[b] The only public treasury until the time of Augustus, who
created two others, with separate sources of revenue.   The
*aerarium Saturni* (so called from its office being in the temple

I have the satisfaction to find by the words of your rescript that you complied the more willingly, as his application was in my behalf. I cannot but look upon myself as in possession of my utmost wish, after having thus received, at the entrance of your auspicious government, so distinguishing a mark of your peculiar favour; at the same time that it considerably heightens my desire of leaving a family behind me. I was not without this inclination even in that former most cruel reign:[a] as my two marriages will easily incline you to believe. But the Gods decreed it better, by reserving every valuable privilege to be bestowed by your kindness. I prefer to become a father only *now*, when I can be secure and happy in my fatherhood.

## III A

### To the Emperor Trajan

When, Sir, by the joint indulgence of your august Father and yourself, I was promoted to the head of the treasury of Saturn,[b] I immediately renounced all engagements of the bar (which indeed I never undertook promiscuously), that no avocations might call off my attention from the post to which I was appointed. For this reason when the people of Africa petitioned that I might undertake their cause against Marius Priscus,[c] I excused myself from that

---

of Saturn), after various changes of administration under the emperors, was placed by Nerva under the charge of two "prefects of the treasury," who were appointed by the emperor and held office for three years.

[c] See ii. 11; iii. 4, 9; vi. 29.

Priscum, et petii veniam huius muneris et impetravi.
Sed, cum postea consul designatus censuisset, agendum nobiscum, quorum erat excusatio recepta, ut
essemus in senatus potestate pateremurque nomina
nostra in urnam conici, convenientissimum esse
tranquillitati saeculi tui putavi praesertim tam
moderatae voluntati amplissimi ordinis non repugnare. Cui obsequio meo opto ut existimes constare
rationem, cum omnia facta dictaque mea probare
sanctissimis moribus tuis cupiam.

## III B

### TRAIANUS PLINIO

ET civis et senatoris boni partibus functus es obsequium amplissimi ordinis, quod iustissime exigebat,
praestando. Quas partes impleturum te secundum
susceptam fidem confido.

## IV

### C. PLINIUS TRAIANO IMPERATORI

INDULGENTIA tua, imperator optime, quam plenissimam experior, hortatur me, ut audeam tibi etiam
pro amicis obligari; inter quos sibi vel praecipuum

---

a When provincials sought to prosecute a governor, an
advocate for them was ordinarily chosen by lot, out of several
nominated by the Senate. This form was observed when, as

office ; and accordingly my excuse was admitted.
But when afterwards the consul elect proposed that
the Senate should apply again to those of us who
had put in an excuse and endeavour to prevail with
us to place ourselves at its disposal, and suffer our
names to be thrown into the urn,[a] I thought it most
suitable to that tranquillity and good order which so
happily distinguishes your times, not to oppose
(especially in so reasonable an article) the will of
that august assembly. And, as I am desirous that
all my words and actions may be approved by your
exemplary virtue, I hope you will think my compliance was proper.

## III b

### The Emperor Trajan to Pliny

You acted as becomes a good citizen and a worthy
senator, by paying obedience to the just injunctions
of that august body ; and I have full confidence
you will faithfully discharge the part you have
undertaken.

## IV

### To the Emperor Trajan

The ample experience, Sir, I have had of your
unbounded generosity to me, in my own person,
encourages me to hope I may be yet farther obliged
to it, in favour of my friends. Voconius Romanus

in this case, the provincials asked for some particular
advocate.

locum vindicat Voconius Romanus, ab ineunte
aetate condiscipulus et contubernalis meus. Quibus
ex causis et a divo patre tuo petieram, ut illum
in amplissimum ordinem promoveret. Sed hoc
votum meum bonitati tuae reservatum est, quia
mater Romani liberalitatem sestertii quadragiens,[1]
quod conferre se filio codicillis ad patrem tuum
scriptis professa fuerat, nondum satis legitime
peregerat ; quod postea fecit admonita a nobis.
Nam et fundos emancipavit et cetera, quae in
emancipatione implenda solent exigi, consummavit.

Cum sit ergo finitum, quod spes nostras morabatur,
non sine magna fiducia subsigno apud te fidem pro
moribus Romani mei, quos et liberalia studia
exornant, et eximia pietas, qua et hanc ipsam
matris liberalitatem et statim patris hereditatem
et adoptionem a vitrico meruit. Auget haec et
natalium et paternarum facultatum splendor ; quibus singulis multum commendationis accessurum
etiam ex meis precibus indulgentiae tuae credo.
Rogo ergo, domine, ut me exoptatissimae mihi
gratulationis compotem facias et honestis, ut spero,
adfectibus meis praestes, ut non in me tantum,
verum et in amico gloriari iudiciis tuis possim.

quadragiens *B*, quadringenties *a*.

(my school-fellow and early companion) claims the first rank in that number; in consequence of which I petitioned your sacred Father to promote him to the dignity of the Senatorial order. But the completion of my request is reserved to your goodness; for his mother had not then executed a deed of gift of the four millions of sesterces which she engaged to give him, in her petition to the Emperor your late father: [a] this, however, on a reminder from me she has since done, having realized a sufficient estate in land, with all the necessary formalities.

The difficulties therefore being removed which deferred our wishes, it is with full confidence I venture to assure you of the merit of my friend Romanus, heightened and adorned as it is, not only by the liberal and polite arts, but by his extraordinary tenderness to his parents. It is to that virtue he owes the present liberality of his mother; as well as his immediate succession to his late father's estate, and his having been adopted by his stepfather. To these personal qualifications, the wealth and rank of his family give an increase of lustre; as I persuade myself it will be some additional recommendation to your favour, that I solicit in his behalf. Let me then intreat you, Sir, to put it in my power to congratulate Romanus, on an occasion so highly agreeable to me; and at the same time to gratify an eager, and I hope a laudable ambition of being able to boast, that your favourable regards are extended not only to myself, but also to my friend.

*a* Property to the value of 1,200,000 sesterces was a necessary qualification for senatorial rank.

# THE LETTERS OF PLINY

## V

### C. Plinius Traiano Imperatori

Proximo anno, domine, gravissima valitudine usque ad periculum vitae vexatus iatralipten adsumpsi; cuius sollicitudini et studio tuae tantum indulgentiae beneficio referre gratiam possum. Quare rogo, des ei civitatem Romanam. Est enim peregrinae condicionis manumissus a peregrina. Vocatur ipse Harpocras; patronam habuit Thermuthin Theonis, quae iam pridem defuncta est. Item rogo, des ius Quiritium libertis Antoniae Maximillae, ornatissimae feminae, Hediae et Harmeridi, quod a te petente patrona peto.

## VI

### C. Plinius Traiano Imperatori

Ago gratias, domine, quod et ius Quiritium libertis necessariae mihi feminae et civitatem Romanam Harpocrati, iatraliptae meo, sine mora indulsisti. Sed, cum annos eius et censum, sicut praeceperas, ederem, admonitus sum a peritioribus debuisse me

---

<sup>a</sup> An *iatraliptes*, or "doctor-trainer," practised a treatment consisting of dieting, exercises, and massage.

<sup>b</sup> Freedmen of citizens, if manumitted with the full legal formalities (*iusta manumissio*) became *ipso facto* citizens; those of aliens kept, of course, the status of their patrons.

<sup>c</sup> A woman, though herself a citizen, could not give *iusta manumissio*, but must use one of the informal methods, by which the freedman gained only the "Latin franchise"

282

# V

## TO THE EMPEROR TRAJAN

HAVING been attacked last year by a severe and
dangerous illness, I employed a physician [a] whose
care and diligence, Sir, I cannot sufficiently reward,
but by your gracious assistance. I intreat you therefore to make him a citizen of Rome; for he is the
freedman of an alien. [b] His name is Harpocras; his
patroness (who has been dead a considerable time)
was Thermuthis, the daughter of Theon. I farther
intreat you to bestow the full privileges of a Roman
citizen [c] upon Hedia and Harmeris, the freedwomen
of Antonia Maximilla, a lady of high rank. It is at
her desire [d] I make this request.

# VI

## TO THE EMPEROR TRAJAN

I return you thanks, Sir, for your ready compliance
with my desire, in granting the complete privileges
of a Roman to the freedwomen of a lady to whom I
am allied, and making Harpocras my physician a
citizen of Rome. But when, agreeably to your
directions, I gave in an account of his age and estate,
I was informed by those who are better skilled in
these affairs than I pretend to be, that as he is an

(vii. 16, note, x. 104, note). Persons who already had this
*ius Latinorum* became full citizens by the addition of the *ius
Quiritium*; hence Pliny asks the latter for Antonia's freedwomen, but *civitas* for the alien Harpocras.
   [d] Certain legal disqualifications attended the non-fulfilment
of this condition.

ante ei Alexandrinam civitatem impetrare, deinde
Romanam, quoniam esset Aegyptius.  Ego autem,
quia inter Aegyptios ceterosque peregrinos nihil
interesse credebam, contentus fueram hoc solum
scribere tibi, esse eum [1] a peregrina manumissum
patronamque eius iam pridem decessisse.  De qua
ignorantia mea non queror, per quam stetit, **ut** tibi
pro eodem homine saepius obligarer.

Rogo itaque, ut beneficio tuo legitime frui possim,
tribuas ei et Alexandrinam civitatem et Romanam.
Annos eius et censum, ne quid rursus indulgentiam
tuam moraretur, libertis tuis, quibus iusseras, misi.

## VII

### TRAIANUS PLINIO

CIVITATEM Alexandrinam secundum institutionem
principum non temere dare proposui.  Sed, cum
Harpocrati, iatraliptae tuo, iam civitatem Romanam
impetraveris, huic quoque petitioni tuae negare non
sustineo.  Tu, ex quo nomo sit, notum mihi facere
debebis, ut epistulam tibi ad Pompeium Plantam,
praefectum Aegypti, amicum meum, mittam.

---

[1] esse eum *B*, etsi eum *Av.*, scilicet eum *a*.

---

a The citizens of Alexandria and other Greek cities in
Egypt formed a distinct class from the Egyptians belonging

Egyptian, I ought first to have obtained for him the freedom of Alexandria,[a] before he was made free of Rome. I confess, indeed, as I was ignorant of any difference in this case between Egyptians and other aliens, I contented myself with only acquainting you, that he had been manumitted by a foreign lady, long since deceased. However, it is an ignorance I cannot regret, since it affords me an opportunity of receiving from you a double obligation in favour of the same person.

That I may legally therefore enjoy the benefit of your goodness, I beg you would be pleased to grant him the freedom of the city of Alexandria, as well as that of Rome. And that your gracious intentions may not meet with any farther obstacles, I have taken care, as you directed, to send an account to your freedmen of his age and fortune.

## VII

### The Emperor Trajan to Pliny

It is my resolution, in pursuance of the maxim observed by the princes my predecessors, to be extremely cautious in granting the freedom of the city of Alexandria: however, since you have obtained of me the freedom of Rome for your physician Harpocras, I cannot refuse you this other request. You must let me know to what district he belongs, that I may give you a letter to my good friend Pompeius Planta, governor of Egypt.

to the forty-seven nomes (provinces). Neither the Ptolemies, nor their successors the Roman emperors, ever granted the Alexandrian citizenship to these Egyptians, except in very special circumstances. (Hardy.)

## VIII

### C. Plinius Traiano Imperatori

Cum divus pater tuus, domine, et oratione
pulcherrima et honestissimo exemplo omnes cives
ad munificentiam esset cohortatus, petii ab eo, ut
statuas principum, quas in longinquis agris per plures
successiones traditas mihi, quales acceperam, custodie-
bam, permitteret in municipium transferre adiecta
sua statua. Quod cum[1] ille mihi cum plenissimo
testimonio indulserat, ego statim decurionibus scripseram, ut adsignarent solum, in quo templum pecunia
mea exstruerem; illi in honorem operis ipsius elec-
tionem loci mihi obtulerant. Sed primum mea, deinde
patris tui valetudine, postea curis delegati a vobis
officii retentus nunc videor commodissime posse in
rem praesentem excurrere. Nam et menstruum
meum Kalendis Septembris finitur, et sequens mensis
complures dies feriatos habet.

Rogo ergo ante omnia permittas mihi opus, quod
incohaturus sum, exornare et tua statua, deinde, ut
hoc facere quam maturissime possim, indulgeas

---

[1] quod cum *Gruterus*, quodque *a*, B.

## VIII

### To the Emperor Trajan

AFTER your late sacred Father, Sir, had, in a noble speech as well as by his own generous example, exhorted and encouraged the public to acts of munificence, I implored his permission to remove to my township the several statues which I had of the former emperors; and at the same time begged the liberty of adding his own to the number. For these statues had come down to me as family heirlooms, and I had kept them just as they were on my distant estate. He was pleased to grant my request and at the same time to give me a very ample testimony of his approbation.

I immediately therefore wrote to the town council, that they would allot a piece of ground, upon which I might build a temple at my own expense; but as a mark of honour to my design, they offered me the choice of any site I thought proper. However, my own indisposition in the first place, and afterward that of your father, and later the duties of that post with which you were both pleased to intrust me, prevented my going on with that design. But I have now, I think, a convenient opportunity of making an excursion to this place, as my month's attendance ends on the first of September, and there are several holidays in the month following.

My first request then is, that you would permit me to adorn the temple I am going to erect, with your statue, besides the rest; and next (in order to execute my design with all the expedition possible) that you would indulge me with leave of absence.

commeatum.  Non est autem simplicitatis meae
dissimulare apud bonitatem tuam obiter te plurimum
collaturum utilitatibus rei familiaris meae.  Agrorum
enim, quos in eadem regione possideo, locatio cum
alioqui cccc excedat, adeo non potest differri, ut
proximam putationem novus colonus facere debeat.
Praeterea continuae sterilitates cogunt me de remissi-
onibus cogitare ; quarum rationem nisi praesens inire
non possum.

Debebo ergo, domine, indulgentiae tuae et pietatis
meae celeritatem et status ordinationem, si mihi ob
utraque haec dederis commeatum xxx dierum.  Neque
enim angustius tempus praefinire possum, cum et
municipium et agri, de quibus loquor, sint ultra
centesimum et quinquagesimum lapidem.

## IX

### TRAIANUS PLINIO

ET privatas[1] multas et omnes publicas causas
petendi commeatus reddidisti ; mihi autem vel sola
voluntas tua suffecisset.  Neque enim dubito te, ut
primum potueris, ad tam districtum officium reversurum.  Statuam poni mihi a te eo, quo desideras,

[1] privatas *add. Catan.*

It would ill become the sincerity I profess, were I to conceal from so kind a master that your complying with this desire will at the same time be extremely serviceable to me in my own private affairs. It is absolutely necessary I should not defer any longer the letting of my lands in that province ; for besides that they amount to above four hundred thousand sesterces annually, the time for dressing the vineyards is approaching, and *that* care must fall upon my new tenants. Moreover, the badness of the vintage for several years past obliges me to think of making some abatements in my rents ; which I cannot possibly settle unless I am present.

I shall be indebted then to your indulgence, Sir, both as accelerating this public act of piety, and giving me the opportunity of settling my private affairs, if you will be pleased to grant me leave to be absent for thirty days. I cannot limit a shorter time, as the town and the estate of which I am speaking lie above an hundred and fifty miles from Rome.

## IX

### TRAJAN TO PLINY

You have given me many private reasons, and all, moreover, with a bearing on the public welfare, why you desire leave to be absent; but I need no other than that it is your inclination : and I doubt not of your returning as soon as possible to the duty of an office, which so much requires your attendance. As I would not seem to check any instance of your

loco, quamquam eiusmodi honorum parcissimus, tamen
patior, ne impedisse cursum erga me pietatis tuae
videar.

## X

### C. PLINIUS TRAIANO IMPERATORI

EXPRIMERE, domine, verbis non possum, quanto
me gaudio adfecerint epistulae tuae, ex quibus
cognovi, te Harpocrati, iatraliptae meo etiam Alexandrinam civitatem tribuisse, quamvis secundum
institutionem principum non temere eam dare pro-
posuisses. Esse autem Harpocran νομοῦ Μεμφιτικοῦ
indico tibi. Rogo ergo, indulgentissime imperator,
ut mihi ad Pompeium Plantam, praefectum Aegypti,
amicum tuum, sicut promisisti, epistulam mittas.

Obviam iturus, quo maturius, domine, exoptatis-
simi adventus tui gaudio frui possim, rogo, permittas mihi quam longissime occurrere tibi.

## XI

### C. PLINIUS TRAIANO IMPERATORI

PROXIMA infirmitas mea, domine, obligavit me
Postumio Marino medico; cui parem gratiam referre
beneficio tuo possum, si precibus meis ex consuetudine bonitatis tuae indulseris. Rogo ergo,

loyalty towards me, I shall not oppose your erecting my statue in the place you mention; though in general I am extremely chary of allowing such marks of honour.

## X

### To the Emperor Trajan

I CANNOT express, Sir, the pleasure your letter gave me, by which I am informed that you have made my physician Harpocras a citizen of Alexandria; notwithstanding your resolution to follow the maxim of your predecessors in this point, by being extremely cautious in granting that privilege. Agreeably to your directions, I acquaint you that Harpocras belongs to the nome of Memphis. I intreat you then, most gracious Emperor, to send me as you promised a letter to your good friend, Pompeius Planta, governor of Egypt.

As I purpose (in order to have the earliest enjoyment of your presence, so ardently wished for here) [a] to come to meet you; I beg, Sir, you would permit me to extend my journey as far as possible.

## XI

### To the Emperor Trajan

I WAS greatly obliged, Sir, in my late indisposition, to Posthumius Marinus, my physician; and I can only make him a suitable return by the assistance of the gracious indulgence which you are wont to shew to my petition. I intreat you then to confer Roman

[a] Affairs in Germany had delayed Trajan's return to Rome as Emperor. See x. 1 note.

ut propinquis eius des civitatem, Chrysippo Mithridatis, uxorique Chrysippi Stratonicae Epigoni, item liberis eiusdem Chrysippi, Epigono et Mithridati, ita ut sint in patris potestate, utque iis in libertos servetur ius patronorum. Item rogo, indulgeas ius Quiritium L. Satrio Abascantio et P. Caesio Phosphoro et Anchariae Soteridi; quod a te volentibus patronis peto.

## XII

### C. Plinius Traiano Imperatori

Scio, domine, memoriae tuae, quae est benefaciendi tenacissima, preces nostras inhaerere. Quia tamen in hoc quoque saepe indulsisti, admoneo simul et impense rogo, ut Accium Suram praetura exornare digneris, cum locus vacet. Ad quam spem alioqui quietissimum hortatur et natalium splendor et summa integritas in paupertate et ante omnia felicitas temporum, quae bonam conscientiam civium tuorum ad usum indulgentiae tuae provocat et attollit.

---

*a* An exceptional privilege to the sons, for on Chrysippus gaining the *patria potestas* over them they would normally lose their independent rights, including those over their freedmen. (Hardy.)

citizenship upon the following persons, his relatives; Chrysippus, son of Mithridates, and Stratonica, daughter of Epigonus, who is wife to Chrysippus. I implore likewise the same privilege in favour of Epigonus and Mithridates, the two sons of Chrysippus; but in such manner that they may be under the dominion of their father and yet preserve their right of patronage over their own freedmen.[a] I farther intreat you to grant the full privileges of a Roman to L. Satrius Abascantus, P. Caesius Phosphorus, and Ancharia Soteris. This request I make with the consent of their patrons.

## XII

### To the Emperor Trajan

Though I am well assured, Sir, that you, who never forget any opportunity of exerting your generosity, are not unmindful of the request I lately made you; yet since you have frequently, among many other instances of your indulgence, permitted me to repeat my solicitations to you, I do so now on behalf of Accius Sura; and I earnestly beseech you to honour him with the Praetorship, which is at present vacant. Though his ambition is extremely moderate, yet the quality of his birth, the inflexible integrity which he has shewn in a fortune below mediocrity, and, above all, the happiness of your reign, which emboldens citizens of conscious virtue to claim the indulgence of your favour, prompts him to hope he may experience it in this instance.

# THE LETTERS OF PLINY

## XIII

### C. PLINIUS TRAIANO IMPERATORI

CUM sciam, domine, ad testimonium laudemque morum meorum pertinere tam boni principis iudicio exornari, rogo, dignitati, ad quam me provexit indulgentia tua, vel auguratum vel septemviratum, quia vacant, adicere digneris, ut iure sacerdotii precari deos pro te publice possim, quos nunc precor pietate privata.

## XIV

### C. PLINIUS TRAIANO IMPERATORI

VICTORIAE tuae, optime imperator, maximae, pulcherrimae, antiquissimae et tuo nomine et rei publicae gratulor deosque immortales precor, ut omnes cogitationes tuas tam laetus sequatur eventus, ut virtutibus tantis gloria imperii et novetur et augeatur.

---

*a* The Augurs and the Septemviri formed two of the four great priestly colleges. Pliny received the Augurship (vacant by the death of Julius Frontinus), probably in 103 A.D. *cf.* iv. 8.

# XIII

## To the Emperor Trajan

As I am sensible, Sir, that the highest applause my conduct can receive, is to be distinguished by so excellent a Prince: I beg you would be graciously pleased to add either the office of Augur or Septemvir *a* (both of which are now vacant) to the dignity I already enjoy by your indulgence ; *b* that I may have the satisfaction of publicly offering up those vows for your prosperity, from the duty of my office, which I daily prefer to the Gods in private, from the affection of my heart.

# XIV

## To the Emperor Trajan

I congratulate both you and the public, most excellent Emperor, upon the great and glorious victory you have obtained,*c* so agreeable to the hero-ism of Rome. May the immortal Gods give the same happy success to all your designs, that, under the administration of so many princely virtues, the splendour of the Empire may shine out, not only in its former, but with additional lustre.

*b* The Augurship was usually conferred on consulars ; Pliny had been Consul 100 A.D.
*c* Over the Dacians. See viii. 4. Whether this letter refers to Trajan's first or second campaign is unknown.

## XV

### C. Plinius Traiano Imperatori

Quia confido, domine, ad curam tuam pertinere, nuntio tibi me Ephesum cum omnibus meis ὑπὲρ Μαλέαν navigasse. Quamvis contrariis ventis retentus, nunc destino partim orariis navibus, partim vehiculis provinciam petere. Nam sicut itineri graves aestus, ita continuae navigationi etesiae reluctantur.

## XVI

### Traianus Plinio

Recte renuntiasti, mi Secunde carissime. Pertinet enim ad animum meum, quali itinere *in* [1] provinciam pervenias. Prudenter autem constituis interim navibus, interim vehiculis uti, prout loca suaserint.

## XVII a

### C. Plinius Traiano Imperatori

Sicut saluberrimam navigationem, domine, usque Ephesum expertus ita inde, postquam vehiculis iter facere coepi, gravissimis aestibus atque etiam febri-

[1] in *add. Cat*[2].

## XV

### To the Emperor Trajan

Having safely passed the promontory of Malea, I am arrived at Ephesus with all my train, notwithstanding I was detained for some time by contrary winds; an information, Sir, in which I trust you will think yourself concerned. I design to pursue the remainder of my journey to my province,[a] partly in coasting vessels and partly in post-chaises: for as the excessive heats will prevent my travelling altogether by land, so the Etesian winds, which are now set in, will not permit me to proceed entirely by sea.

## XVI

### Trajan to Pliny

Your communication, my dear Pliny, was extremely proper; as it is much my concern to know in what manner you arrive at your province. You are prudent in arranging to travel either by sea or land, as you shall find most convenient.

## XVII A

### To the Emperor Trajan

As I had a very salubrious voyage to Ephesus, so in travelling post from thence I was extremely incommoded by the heats; they even threw me into a

[a] See Introduction for Pliny's governorship of Bithynia, to which the rest of this book relates.

culis vexatus Pergami substiti. Rursus, cum transissem
in orarias naviculas, contrariis ventis retentus aliquanto
tardius, quam speraveram, id est xv Kal. Octobres,
Bithyniam intravi. Non possum tamen de mora
queri, cum mihi contigerit, quod erat auspicatissimum,
natalem tuum in provincia celebrare. Nunc rei
publicae Prusensium impendia, reditus, debitores
excutio; quod ex ipso tractatu magis ac magis
necessarium intellego. Multae enim pecuniae variis
ex causis a privatis detinentur; praeterea quaedam
minime legitimis sumptibus erogantur. Haec tibi,
domine, in ipso ingressu meo scripsi.


## XVII b

### C. Plinius Traiano Imperatori

Quintodecimo Kalendas Octobres, domine, provinciam intravi, quam in eo obsequio, in ea erga te
fide, quam de genere humano mereris, inveni. Dispice,
domine, an necessarium putes mittere huc mensorem.
Videntur enim non mediocres pecuniae posse revocari
a curatoribus operum, si mensurae fideliter aguntur.
Ita certe prospicio ex ratione Prusensium, quam cum
maxime tracto.

fever, which kept me some time at Pergamum. I then resorted to coasting-vessels; but being detained by contrary winds, I arrived at Bithynia somewhat later than I had hoped, namely on the 17th of September. However, I have no reason to complain of this delay, since it produced me a most auspicious omen—namely, to celebrate your birthday in my province.[a] I am at present engaged in examining into the public finances of the Prusenses, their disbursements, revenues and credits; and the more I look into them, the more I perceive the necessity of my inquiry. Many sums of money are detained in private hands upon various pretences; moreover, some public grants are made for quite illegitimate expenses. This, Sir, I write to you immediately on my arrival.

## XVII b

### TO THE EMPEROR TRAJAN

I ENTERED this province, Sir, on the 17th of September, and found it in those sentiments of obedience and loyalty which you justly merit from all mankind. You will consider, Sir, whether it would not be proper to send hither a surveyor; for it appears that substantial sums of money might be recovered from the contractors for public buildings, if a faithful admeasurement were taken. At least, I am of that opinion, from what I have already seen of the accounts of this city, which I am now in the act of examining.

[a] The reigning Emperor's birthday had always been a public holiday.

## XVIII

### Traianus Plinio

CUPEREM sine querela corpusculi tui et tuorum
pervenire in Bithyniam potuisses, ac simile tibi iter
ab Epheso ei navigationi fuisset, quam expertus usque
illo eras. Quo autem die pervenisses in Bithyniam,
cognovi, Secunde carissime, litteris tuis. Provinciales, credo, prospectum sibi a me intellegent.
Nam et tu dabis operam, ut manifestum sit illis
electum te esse, qui ad eosdem mei loco mittereris.
Rationes autem in primis tibi rerum publicarum
excutiendae sunt; nam et esse eas vexatas satis
constat. Mensores vix etiam iis operibus, quae
aut Romae aut in proximo fiunt, sufficientes habeo;
sed in omni provincia inveniuntur, quibus credi
possit, et ideo non deerunt tibi, modo velis diligenter
excutere.

## XIX

### C. Plinius Traiano Imperatori

ROGO, domine, consilio me regas haesitantem
utrum per publicos civitatum servos, quod usque
adhuc factum, an per milites adservare custodias
debeam. Vereor enim, ne et per servos publicos
parum fideliter custodiantur, et non exiguum militum

---

<sup>a</sup> For the playful use of *corpusculum* cf. vi. 4.
<sup>b</sup> Slaves owned by a state or city wore a sort of livery, had

## XVIII

### Trajan to Pliny

I wish you could have reached Bithynia without any complaint from your *little anatomy*,[a] or that of your train; and that your journey from Ephesus had been as easy as your voyage to that place. I note from your letter, my dear Pliny, what day you reached Bithynia. The people of that province will understand, I believe, that I have their interests at heart. For you will take care to make it clear to them, that you were appointed specially to represent myself. You must pay particular attention to investigating the financial affairs of the towns, which are evidently in confusion. As for surveyors, I have scarce enough for those works which I am carrying on at Rome, and in the neighbourhood; but trustworthy persons of this class may be found in every province, so that you will have no lack of such if you choose to make diligent inquiry.

## XIX

### To the Emperor Trajan

I beg your advice, Sir, on a matter wherein I am greatly doubtful; it is, whether I should have the prisoners guarded by public slaves [b] (as has been hitherto the practice), or by soldiers? On the one hand, I am afraid the public slaves will not perform this duty faithfully; and on the other, that it will

an annual stipend, and were employed as mail-carriers, executioners, attendants at the public baths, libraries, etc.

numerum haec cura distringat. Interim publicis
servis paucos milites addidi. Video tamen periculum esse, ne id ipsum utrisque neglegentiae causa
sit, dum communem culpam hi in illos, illi in hos
regerere posse confidunt.

## XX

### Traianus Plinio

Nihil opus est, mi Secunde carissime, ad con-
tinendas custodias plures commilitones converti.
Perseveremus in ea consuetudine, quae isti provinciae
est, ut per publicos servos custodiantur. Etenim,
ut fideliter hoc faciant, in tua severitate ac diligentia positum est. In primis enim, sicut scribis,
verendum est, ne, si permisceantur servis publicis
milites, mutua inter se fiducia neglegentiores sint.
Sed et illud haereat nobis, quam paucissimos milites
a signis avocandos esse.

## XXI

### C. Plinius Traiano Imperatori

Gabius Bassus, praefectus orae Ponticae, et
reverentissime et officiosissime, domine, venit ad
me et compluribus diebus fuit mecum, quantum

---

<sup>a</sup> An expression avoided as undignified by Augustus and
his immediate successors, but affected by later Emperors,
whose power largely depended on the goodwill of the army.
<sup>b</sup> cf. x. 22.

engage too large a body of the soldiery. In the meanwhile I have joined a few of the latter with the former. I see, however, there is a danger that this plan may occasion negligence on both sides; since each will trust to throwing upon the other the blame attaching to both.

## XX

### TRAJAN TO PLINY

THERE is no occasion, my dear Pliny, to draw off more of my fellow-soldiers [a] to guard the prisoners. Let us rather abide by the custom of your province, and employ the public slaves. Their fidelity in this office depends entirely upon the discipline and care you exercise. It is to be feared, as you observe, that if the soldiers are combined with the public slaves, they will mutually rely on each other, and by that means grow so much the more negligent. But let this be our fixed rule, that as few soldiers as possible should be called away from the colours.[b]

## XXI

### TO THE EMPEROR TRAJAN

GABIUS BASSUS, Prefect of the Pontic shore,[c] visited me in the most respectful and obliging manner, and has been with me, Sir, for several days.

[c] Prefects in the provinces were more or less permanent officials, appointed by the Emperor. Some held civil, others military appointments; among the latter were the Prefects of the Rhine frontier, the Euphrates frontier, and the littoral of the Black Sea.

perspicere potui, vir egregius et indulgentia tua
dignus. Cui ego notum feci praecepisse te, ut
ex cohortibus, quibus me praeesse voluisti, contentus esset beneficiariis decem, equitibus duobus,
centurione uno. Respondit non sufficere sibi hunc
numerum, idque se scripturum tibi. Hoc in causa
fuit, quo minus statim revocandos putarem, quos
habet supra numerum.

## XXII

### Traianus Plinio

Et mihi scripsit Gabius Bassus non sufficere sibi
eum militum numerum, qui ut daretur illi, mandatis
meis complexus sum. Cui quae rescripsissem,[1] ut
notum haberes, his litteris subici iussi. Multum
interest, res poscat an homines imperare latius
velint.[2] Nobis autem utilitas demum spectanda est,
et, quantum fieri potest, curandum, ne milites a
signis absint.

## XXIII

### C. Plinius Traiano Imperatori

Prusenses, domine, balineum habent et sordidum
et vetus. Id itaque indulgentia tua restituere

[1] Cui quae rescripsissem *K*, quid quaeris scripsisse me ? *a*, *B*.
[2] res poscat an homines imperare latius velint *Catan.*, te
poscat an homines in se ut latius velint *a*, *B*, tempus p. an h.
iure uti l. v. *Orell.*

As far as I could observe, he is a person of great merit and worthy of your favour. I acquainted him it was your order that he should retain only ten beneficiary soldiers,ᵃ two troopers, and one centurion, out of the cavalry which you were pleased to assign to my command. He assured me these would not be sufficient for him, and that he would write to you upon this head; for which reason I did not, immediately upon your directions, recall his supernumeraries.

## XXII

### TRAJAN TO PLINY

I HAVE received from Gabius Bassus the letter you mention, acquainting me, that the number of your soldiers I had ordered him was not sufficient: and for your information I have directed my answer to be annexed to this. It is very material to distinguish between what the exigency of affairs requires and what an ambitious desire of extending power may think necessary. As for ourselves, the interest of the public must be our only guide: and it is incumbent upon us to take all possible care, that the soldiers are not absent from their colours.

## XXIII

### TO THE EMPEROR TRAJAN

THE Prusenses, Sir, have an ancient and ruinous bath, which they desire your leave to repair. Upon examining into the condition of it, I find it ought to

ᵃ Privates who were either exempted from fatigue duty, or detailed for some special duty by a superior, were called his *beneficiarii.*

desiderant : ego tamen aestimans novum fieri debere . . . videris mihi desiderio eorum indulgere posse. Erit enim pecunia, ex qua fiat, primum ea, quam revocare a privatis et exigere iam coepi, deinde quam ipsi erogare in oleum soliti parati sunt in opus balinei conferre; quod alioqui et dignitas civitatis et saeculi tui nitor postulat.

## XXIV

### Traianus Plinio

Si instructio novi balinei oneratura vires Prusensium non est, possumus desiderio eorum indulgere, modo ne quid ideo aut intribuatur, aut minus illis in posterum fiat ad necessarias erogationes.

## XXV

### C. Plinius Traiano Imperatori

Servilius Pudens legatus, domine, viii Kal. Decembres Nicomediam venit meque longae exspectationis sollicitudine liberavit.

## XXVI

### C. Plinius Traiano Imperatori

Rosianum Geminum, domine, artissimo vinculo mecum tua in me beneficia iunxerunt. Habui enim

306

be rebuilt; I think therefore you may indulge them in this request, as there will be a sufficient fund for that purpose, partly from those debts which are due from private persons to the public, which I am now calling in, and partly from what they disburse from their treasury towards furnishing the bath with oil, which they are willing to apply to the carrying on of this building: a work which the dignity of the city, and the splendour of your reign seems to demand.

## XXIV

### Trajan to Pliny

If the erecting a public bath will not be too great a charge upon the Prusenses, we may comply with their request: provided, however, that no new tax be levied for this purpose, nor any of those taken off which are applied for necessary purposes.

## XXV

### To the Emperor Trajan

My lieutenant Servilius Pudens came to Nicomedia, Sir, on the 24th of November; and by his arrival freed me, at last, from the solicitude of a very uneasy expectation.

## XXVI

### To the Emperor Trajan

Your generosity to me, Sir, was the occasion of uniting me to Rosianus Geminus, by the strongest

illum quaestorem in consulatu, mei summe ob-
servantissimum expertus. Tantam mihi post consulatum reverentiam praestat, ut publicae necessitu-
dinis pignora privatis cumulet officiis. Rogo ergo,
ut ipse apud te pro dignitate eius precibus meis
faveas, cui et, si quid mihi credis, indulgentiam
tuam dabis. Dabit ipse operam, ut in iis, quae ei
mandaveris, maiora mereatur. Parciorem me in
laudando facit, quod spero tibi et integritatem eius
et probitatem et industriam non solum ex eius
honoribus, quos in urbe sub oculis tuis gessit, verum
etiam ex commilitio esse notissimam. Illud unum,
quod propter caritatem eius nondum mihi videor
satis plene fecisse, etiam atque etiam facio; teque,
domine, rogo, gaudere me exornata quaestoris mei
dignitate, id est per illum mea, quam maturissime
velis.

## XXVII

### C. PLINIUS TRAIANO IMPERATORI

MAXIMUS, libertus et procurator tuus, domine,
praeter decem beneficiarios, quos adsignari a me

ties; for he was my Quaestor when I was Consul. His behaviour to me, during the continuance of our offices, was highly respectful; and he has treated me ever since with so peculiar a regard, that besides the many obligations I owe him upon a public account, I am indebted to him for the strongest pledges of private friendship. I intreat you then to comply with my request for the advancement of one, whom (if my recommendation has any weight) you will even honour with your particular favour; as whatever trust you shall repose in him, he will endeavour to shew himself still deserving of an higher. But I forbear to enter into a more particular detail of his merit; being persuaded, his integrity, his probity, and his vigilance are well known to you, not only from those high posts, which he has exercised in Rome within your immediate inspection; but from his behaviour when he served under you in the field. One thing, however, my affection for him inclines me to think I have not yet sufficiently done; and therefore, Sir, I repeat my entreaties to you, that you will give me the pleasure, as early as possible, of rejoicing in the honourable advancement of my Quaestor; or, in other words, of receiving an addition to my own dignity, in the person of my friend.

## XXVII

### To the Emperor Trajan

I am assured, Sir, by your freedman and receiver-general Maximus, that it is necessary he should have a party of six soldiers assigned to him, over and besides

Gemellino, optimo viro, iussisti, sibi quoque confirmat necessarios esse milites sex. Tres[1] interim, sicut inveneram, in ministerio eius relinquendos existimavi, praesertim cum ad frumentum comparandum iret in Paphlagoniam. Quin etiam tutelae causa, quia desiderabat, addidi duos equites. In futurum quid servari velis, rogo rescribas.

## XXVIII

### Traianus Plinio

Nunc quidem proficiscentem ad comparationem frumentorum Maximum, libertum meum, recte militibus instruxisti. Fungebatur enim et ipse extraordinario munere. Cum ad pristinum actum reversus fuerit, sufficient illi duo a te dati milites et totidem a Virdio Gemellino, procuratore meo, quem adiuvat.

## XXIX

### C. Plinius Traiano Imperatori

Sempronius Caelianus, egregius iuvenis, repertos inter tirones duos servos misit ad me; quorum ego

---

[1] milites sex. Tres *Mommsen*, milites. Ex his interim *a, B, lacunam post* milites *K, post* interim *ind. Müller.*

---

[a] See x. 21, note.

the ten beneficiary soldiers,[a] which by your orders I allotted to the very worthy Gemellinus. Three therefore which I found in his service I thought proper to continue there, especially as he was going into Paphlagonia in order to procure corn. For his better security likewise, and because it was his request, I added two of the horse-guards. But I beg you would inform me in your next despatches, what method you would have me observe for the future in points of this nature.

## XXVIII

### Trajan to Pliny

As my freedman Maximus was going upon an extraordinary commission to procure corn, I approve of your having supplied him with a file of soldiers. But when he shall return to the duties of his former post, I think two from you, and as many from my receiver-general Virdius Gemellinus (to whom he is coadjutor) will be sufficient.

## XXIX

### To the Emperor Trajan

Sempronius Caelianus (whose merit I must always mention with esteem) having discovered two slaves [b] among the recruits has sent them to me. But I

[b] The Roman policy excluded slaves from entering into military service, and it was death if they did so. (Melm.) But in great crises, as after the battle of Cannae, and during the civil wars, slaves were occasionally enlisted.

supplicium distuli, ut te conditorem disciplinae
militaris firmatoremque consulerem de modo poenae.
Ipse enim dubito ob haec maxime, quod, ut iam
dixerant sacramento militari, nondum distributi in
numeros erant. Quid ergo debeam sequi, rogo,
domine, scribas, praesertim cum pertineat ad
exemplum.

## XXX

### TRAIANUS PLINIO

SECUNDUM mandata mea fecit Sempronius Caelianus mittendo ad te eos, de quibus cognosci oportebat,
an capitale supplicium meruisse videantur. Refert
autem, voluntarii se obtulerint an lecti sint vel etiam
vicarii dati. Lecti si sunt, inquisitio peccavit ; si
vicarii dati, penes eos culpa est, qui dederunt ; si ipsi,
cum haberent condicionis suae conscientiam, venerunt, animadvertendum in illos erit. Neque enim
multum interest, quod nondum per numeros distributi sunt. Ille enim dies, quo primum probati sunt,
veritatem ab his originis suae exigit.

deferred passing sentence till I had conferred with you, the glorious founder, and firm support of military discipline, concerning the punishment proper to be inflicted upon them. My principal doubt is, that though they have taken the military oath, they are not yet entered into any particular legion. I beg therefore, Sir, you would let me know what method I shall pursue, especially as it is an affair in which example is concerned.

## XXX

### Trajan to Pliny

SEMPRONIUS CAELIANUS has acted agreeably to my orders, in sending those persons to you for trial, the capital nature of whose offence must be decided by investigation. It is material, in the case in question, to inquire, whether these slaves enlisted themselves voluntarily, or were enrolled by the recruiting officers, or presented as proxies for others. If they were enrolled, the officer is guilty; if they are proxies, the blame rests with those who deputed them; but if, conscious of the legal inabilities of their station, they presented themselves voluntarily, the punishment must fall upon their own heads. That they are not yet entered into any legion makes no great difference in their case; for they ought to have given a true account of themselves immediately, upon their being approved as fit for the service.

## XXXI

### C. PLINIUS TRAIANO IMPERATORI

SALVA magnitudine tua, domine, descendas oportet ad meas curas, cum ius mihi dederis referendi ad te, de quibus dubito. In plerisque civitatibus, maxime Nicomediae et Niceae, quidam vel in opus damnati vel in ludum similiaque his genera poenarum publicorum servorum officio ministerioque funguntur atque etiam ut publici servi annua accipiunt. Quod ego cum audissem, diu multumque haesitavi, quid facere deberem. Nam et reddere poenae post longum tempus plerosque iam senes et, quantum adfirmatur, frugaliter modesteque viventes nimis severum arbitrabar, et in publicis officiis retinere damnatos non satis honestum putabam ; eosdem rursus a republica pasci otiosos inutile, non pasci etiam periculosum existimabam. Necessario ergo rem totam, dum te consulerem, in suspenso reliqui.

Quaeres fortasse, quem ad modum evenerit, ut poenis, in quas dati erant, exsolverentur ; et ego quaesivi, sed nihil comperi, quod adfirmare tibi possim.

---

<sup>a</sup> x. 19, note.

## XXXI

### To the Emperor Trajan

As I have your permission, Sir, to address myself to
you in all my doubts, you will not esteem it below your
dignity to descend to those affairs, which concern
the administration of my post. I find there are in
several cities, particularly those of Nicomedia and
Nicea, certain persons who take upon themselves to
act as public slaves,[a] and receive an annual stipend
accordingly; notwithstanding they have been condemned either to the mines, the public games or
other punishments of like nature. Having received
information of this abuse, I have been long debating
with myself how I should act. On the one hand, to
send them back again after a long interval to their
respective punishments, (many of them being now
grown old, and behaving, as I am assured, with
sobriety and modesty,) would, I thought, be proceeding against them too severely; on the other, to
retain convicts in the public service, seemed not
altogether decent. I considered at the same time,
to support these people in idleness, would be an
useless expense to the public; and to leave them to
starve, would be dangerous. I was obliged therefore
to suspend the determination of this matter, till I
could consult with you.

You will be desirous, perhaps, to be informed,
how it happened that these persons escaped the
punishments to which they were condemned. This
inquiry I have also made myself, but cannot return
you any satisfactory answer. The records of their

Ut decreta, quibus damnati erant, proferebantur, ita
nulla monumenta, quibus liberati probarentur.
Erant tamen, qui dicerent deprecantes iussu
proconsulum legatorumve dimissos. Addebat
fidem, quod credibile erat neminem hoc ausum
sine auctore.

## XXXII

### Traianus Plinio

Meminerimus idcirco te in istam provinciam missum,
quoniam multa in ea emendanda apparuerint. Erit
autem vel hoc maxime corrigendum, quod, qui
damnati ad poenam erant, non modo ea sine auctore,
ut scribis, liberati sunt, sed etiam in condicionem
proborum ministrorum retrahuntur. Qui igitur
intra hos proximos decem annos damnati nec ullo
idoneo auctore liberati sunt, hos oportebit poenae
suae reddi; si qui vetustiores invenientur et senes
ante annos decem damnati, distribuamus illos in ea
ministeria, quae non longe a poena sint. Solent enim
eius modi ad balineum, ad purgationes cloacarum,
item munitiones viarum et vicorum dari.

sentence were indeed produced; but no record of their ever having been reversed. It was asserted, however, that these people were released upon their petition to the proconsuls, or their lieutenants; which seems likely enough to be the truth, as it is improbable any person should have dared to set them at liberty without authority.

## XXXII

### Trajan To Pliny

WE are to remember that you were sent into Bithynia for the particular purpose of correcting those many abuses with which it appeared to be over-run. Now none stands more in need of reformation, than that convicts should not only be set at liberty (as your letter informs me) without authority; but actually restored to the station of respectable officials. Those therefore among them who have been convicted within these ten years, and whose sentence has not been reversed by proper authority, must be sent back again to their respective punishments: but where more than ten years have elapsed since their conviction, and they are grown old and infirm, let them be distributed in such employments as approach penal servitude; that is, either to attend upon the public baths, cleanse the common sewers, or repair the streets and highways, the usual offices to which such persons are assigned.

## XXXIII

### C. Plinius Traiano Imperatori

Cum diversam partem provinciae circumirem, Nicomediae vastissimum incendium multas privatorum domos et duo publica opera quamquam via interiacente, Gerusian et Iseon, absumpsit. Est autem latius sparsum primum violentia venti, deinde inertia hominum, quos[1] satis constat otiosos et immobiles tanti mali spectatores perstitisse; et alioqui nullus usquam in publico sipho, nulla hama, nullum denique instrumentum ad incendia compescenda. Et haec quidem, ut iam praecepi, parabuntur. Tu, domine, dispice, an instituendum putes collegium fabrorum dumtaxat hominum CL. Ego attendam, ne quis nisi faber recipiatur, neve iure concesso in aliud utatur; nec erit difficile custodire tam paucos.

## XXXIV

### Traianus Plinio

Tibi quidem secundum exempla complurium in mentem venit posse collegium fabrorum apud Nicomedenses constitui. Sed meminerimus provin-

---

[1] quos *Rittershusius*, quod *a.*

## XXXIII

### To the Emperor Trajan

While I was making a progress in a different part of the province, a prodigious fire broke out at Nicomedia, which not only consumed several private houses, but also two public buildings, the old men's hospice [a] and the temple of Isis, though they stood on contrary sides of the street. The occasion of its spreading thus far was partly owing to the violence of the wind, and partly to the indolence of the people, who, I am well assured, stood fixed and idle spectators of this terrible calamity. And at any rate, the city was not provided either with a single engine or bucket or any one instrument proper to extinguish fires; these however will be got ready, as I have already ordered. Pray determine, Sir, whether you think it well to institute a guild of fire-men, not to exceed one hundred and fifty members. I will take care none but those of that calling shall be admitted into it; and that the privileges granted them shall not be diverted to any other purpose. As they will be so few, it will be easy enough to keep them under proper regulation.

## XXXIV

### Trajan to Pliny

You are of opinion it would be proper to constitute a guild of fire-men in Nicomedia, agreeably to what has been practised in several other places. But it

[a] Several cities are known to have had these institutions, which provided common meals and a common resort for aged citizens elected to membership.

ciam istam et praecipue eas civitates eius modi
factionibus esse vexatas. Quodcumque nomen ex
quacumque causa dederimus iis, qui in idem contracti
fuerint hetaeriae aeque brevi [1] fient. Satius itaque
est comparari ea, quae ad coercendos ignes auxilio
esse possint, admonerique dominos praediorum, ut et
ipsi inhibeant, ac, si res poposcerit, accursu populi
ad hoc uti.

## XXXV

### C. Plinius Traiano Imperatori

Solemnia vota pro incolumitate tua, qua publica
salus continetur, et suscipimus, domine, pariter et
solvimus, precati deos ut velint ea semper solvi
semperque signari.

## XXXVI

### Traianus Plinio

Et solvisse vos cum provincialibus dis immortalibus vota pro mea salute et incolumitate et nuncupasse libenter, mi Secunde carissime, cognovi ex
litteris tuis.

---

[1] aeque brevi *Lightfoot*, quae breves *a*, *B*.

---

[a] Nicomedia and, probably, Nicaea, her rival.
[b] This had happened in the case of many of the trade-
guilds at Rome.   Our own Trades Unions supply parallels.

is to be remembered that this sort of societies have greatly disturbed the peace of your province in general, and of those cities <sup>a</sup> in particular. Whatever title we give them, and whatever our object in giving it, men who are banded together for a common end will all the same become a political association before long.<sup>b</sup> It will therefore be better to provide suitable means for extinguishing fires, and enjoin owners of house-property to employ these themselves, calling in the help of the populace when necessary.

## XXXV

### To the Emperor Trajan

We have offered,<sup>c</sup> Sir, and acquitted, our annual vows for your safety, in which that of the State is included ; imploring the Gods to grant us ever thus to pay, and thus to confirm them.

## XXXVI

### Trajan to Pliny

I was gratified, my dear Pliny, to learn by your letter, that you, together with the provincials, have both paid and renewed your vows to the immortal Gods, for my health and safety.

---

<sup>c</sup> *suscipere vota* = to undertake vows (for the coming year) ; *vota solvere* = to pay vows (for the past year). The ceremony referred to was performed on the Capitol, in the various camps, and in the provinces, on the 3rd January. (Hardy.)

# THE LETTERS OF PLINY

## XXXVII

### C. Plinius Traiano Imperatori

In aquae ductum, domine, Nicomedenses impen-
derunt sestertium [$\overline{XXX}$] $\overline{CCCXXIX}$, qui imperfectus
adhuc relictus ac etiam destructus est: rursus in
alium ductum erogata sunt cc.  Hoc quoque relicto
novo impendio est opus, ut aquam habeant, qui
tantam pecuniam male perdiderunt.  Ipse perveni
ad fontem purissimum, ex quo videtur aqua debere
perduci, sicut initio tentatum erat, arcuato opere, ne
tantum ad plana civitatis et humilia perveniat.
Manent adhuc paucissimi arcus; possunt et erigi
quidam lapide quadrato, qui ex superiore opere
detractus est; aliqua pars, ut mihi videtur, testaceo
opere agenda erit; id enim et facilius et vilius.  Et
in primis necessarium est mitti a te vel aquilegem
vel architectum, ne rursus eveniat, quod accidit.
Ego illud unum adfirmo, et utilitatem operis et
pulchritudinem saeculo tuo esse dignissimam.

---

<sup>a</sup> About £27,000.
<sup>b</sup> The *Pont de Gard* near Nîmes (*Nemausus*) is a magnifi-
cent specimen of these overground aqueducts.

## XXXVII

### To the Emperor Trajan

THE citizens of Nicomedia, Sir, have expended three million three hundred and twenty-nine thousand sesterces *a* on an aqueduct; but they abandoned it unfinished, and it has actually been pulled down. They made a grant of two hundred thousand sesterces for another aqueduct, but this likewise is discontinued; so that after having thrown away an immense sum they must incur fresh expense in order to be accommodated with water. I have personally visited a most limpid spring from whence the water may be conveyed over arches *b* (as was done in their first design), so as not to reach only the level and low parts of the city. There are but very few arches remaining; others can be erected with the square blocks of stone which have been pulled down from the former work; some part, I think, may be built of brick, *c* as that will be the easier and cheaper method. But first, to prevent another failure, it will be necessary for you to send here an inspector of aqueducts or an engineer. I will venture to affirm one thing—the beauty and usefulness of the work will be entirely worthy of your reign.

*c opus testaceum,* "brickwork," was only used as facing to a concrete core, as was also the *lapis quadratus* just mentioned. (Hardy.)

## XXXVIII

### Traianus Plinio

Curandum est, ut aqua in Nicomedensem civitatem perducatur. Vere credo te ea, qua debebis, diligentia hoc opus aggressurum. Sed medius fidius ad eandem diligentiam tuam pertinet inquirere, quorum vitio ad hoc tempus tantam pecuniam Nicomedenses perdiderint, ne, cum inter se gratificantur, et inchoaverint aquaeductus et reliquerint. Quid itaque compereris, perfer in notitiam meam.

## XXXIX

### C. Plinius Traiano Imperatori

Theatrum, domine, Nicaeae maxima iam parte constructum, imperfectum tamen, sestertium, ut audio (neque enim ratio operis [1] excussa est) amplius centies hausit, vereor ne frustra. Ingentibus enim rimis desedit [2] et hiat, sive in causa solum humidum et molle, sive lapis ipse gracilis et putris; dignum est certe deliberatione, sitne faciendum an sit relinquendum an etiam destruendum. Nam fulturae ac substructiones, quibus subinde suscipitur, non tam firmae mihi quam sumptuosae videntur. Huic theatro ex privatorum pollicitationibus multa deben-

---

[1] operis *Müller*, plus *a*.
[2] desedit *Hardy ex Bodl.* descendit *a*, discedit *Gruter*.

## XXXVIII

### Trajan to Pliny

Care must be taken to supply the city of Nicomedia with water—you will, I am persuaded, set about the work with all due diligence. But it is most certainly no less incumbent upon you to ascertain whose fault it is that the Nicomedians have up to the present squandered such large sums. They must not be suffered to commence and then abandon aqueducts by a system of collusion. You will let me know the result of your inquiry.

## XXXIX

### To the Emperor Trajan

The citizens of Nicaea, Sir, have built the greater part of a theatre which, though it is not yet finished, has already exhausted, as I hear said (for the account has not yet been audited) above ten millions of sesterces; and, I fear, to no purpose. For either from the damp and yielding nature of the ground, or that the stones themselves were thin and friable, the building is sinking and displaying enormous cracks. The question certainly deserves consideration, whether it should be completed, or abandoned, or even pulled down. For the buttresses and bases upon which it is here and there supported, appear to me more expensive than solid. Several private persons have undertaken to build parts of this theatre at their own expense, some

tur ut basilicae circa, ut porticus supra caveam. Quae
nunc omnia differuntur, cessante eo quod ante
peragendum est.

Iidem Nicaeenses gymnasium incendio amissum
ante adventum meum restituere coeperunt longe
numerosius laxiusque, quam fuerat, et iam aliquantum
erogaverunt, periculum est, ne parum utiliter;
incompositum enim et sparsum est. Praeterea
architectus sane aemulus eius, a quo opus inchoatum
est, adfirmat parietes quamquam viginti et duos
pedes latos imposita onera sustinere non posse, quia
sint caemento medii farti nec testaceo opere
praecincti.

Claudiopolitani quoque in depresso loco, imminente
etiam monte ingens balineum defodiunt magis quam
aedificant, et quidem ex ea pecunia, quam buleutae
additi beneficio tuo aut iam obtulerunt ob introitum
aut nobis exigentibus conferent. Ergo, cum timeam,
ne illic publica pecunia, hic, quod est omni pecunia
pretiosius, munus tuum male collocetur, cogor
petere a te, non solum ob theatrum, verum etiam
ob haec balinea mittas architectum dispecturum,
utrum sit utilius post sumptum, qui factus est, quoquo

---

*a* "The word *Cavea* in the original comprehends more than
what we call the *Pit* in our theatres, as it means the whole
space in which the spectators sat." (Melm.) "The *cavea* is
the interior of the semi-circular part of the theatre, the rows
of seats (*cunei*) rising out behind one another from the
orchestra at the bottom to the external wall of the theatre
at the top. . . At the top there was often a double row of

engaging to erect the adjacent basilicas, others the gallery above the pit[a]: all of which are now postponed as the principal fabric is at a stand.

The citizens are also rebuilding, upon a larger scale, the Gymnasium, which was burnt down before my arrival in the province. They have already voted funds for the purpose, which are likely to be wasted, for the structure is ill-planned and rambling. Besides, the present architect (who, it must be owned, is a rival to the one first employed) asserts that the walls, though they are twenty-two feet thick, are not strong enough to support the super-structure, as their core is merely rubble, nor are they faced with brickwork

Furthermore, the people of Claudiopolis are sinking (for I cannot call it building) a large public bath in a hollow at the very foot of a hill, and are appro-priating for this work the fees which those extra members you were pleased to add to their senate paid on their admission, or are now paying on my demand.[b] Lest, therefore, the public money in one place, and in the other (what is infinitely more valuable than any pecuniary consideration) your benefaction, should be misapplied, I am obliged to desire you would send hither an architect to inspect not only the theatre but the bath, and decide whether, after so much money has already been

columns extending all round the *cavea* and forming a kind of ambulatory. . . This is the *porticus* alluded to." (Hardy.)

[b] In Bithynia those *elected* to the local senates paid no entrance fee, but those admitted on the Emperor's nomination paid either one or two thousand denarii, according to circum-stances.

327

modo consummare opera, ut inchoata sunt, an, quae
videntur emendanda, corrigere, quae transferenda,
transferre, ne, dum servare volumus, quod impensum
est, male impendamus, quod addendum est.


## XL

### Traianus Plinio

Quid oporteat fieri circa theatrum, quod inchoatum
apud Nicaeenses est, in re praesenti optime deliberabis
et constitues.   Mihi sufficiet indicari, cui sententiae
accesseris.   Tunc autem a privatis exigi opera tibi
curae sit, cum theatrum, propter quod illa promissa
sunt, factum erit.   Gymnasiis indulgent Graeculi ;
ideo forsitan Nicaeenses maiore animo constructionem
eius aggressi sunt. Sed oportet illos eo contentos esse,
quod possit illis sufficere.

Quid Claudiopolitanis circa balineum, quod parum,
ut scribis, idoneo loco inchoaverunt, suadendum sit,
tu constitues.   Architecti tibi deesse non possunt.
Nulla provincia est, quae non peritos et ingeniosos
homines habeat ; modo ne existimes brevius esse ab
urbe mitti, cum ex Graecia etiam ad nos venire soliti
sunt.

laid out, it will be better to finish them as best we may upon the present plan, or to make improvements and alterations where they are required. Otherwise we may throw away our future outlay by endeavouring not to lose what we have already expended.

## XL

### TRAJAN TO PLINY

You, who are upon the spot, will best be able to consider and determine what is proper to be done concerning the theatre, which the Nicaeans have begun; as for myself, it will be sufficient if you let me know your decision. It will be time enough for you to exact fulfilment of private undertakings with regard to parts of the theatre, when the main building is finished. These paltry Greeks, I know, have a foible for Gymnasia; hence, perhaps, the citizens of Nicaea have been somewhat too ambitious in planning one; but they must be contented with such a one as will be sufficient to answer their occasions.

You must decide for yourself how best to advise the Claudiopolitani with reference to their bath, which they have placed, it seems, in a very improper situation. As there is no province that is not furnished with architects of skill and ingenuity, you cannot possibly be in want of one; pray do not imagine it is your quickest way to get them from Rome, for it is usually from Greece that they come hither.

## XLI

### C. PLINIUS TRAIANO IMPERATORI

INTUENTI mihi et fortunae tuae et animi magnitudinem convenientissimum videtur demonstrare opera non minus aeternitate tua quam gloria digna quantumque pulchritudinis tantum utilitatis habitura. Est in Nicomedensium finibus amplissimus lacus. Per hunc marmora, fructus, ligna, materiae et sumptu modico et labore usque ad viam navibus, inde magno labore, maiore impendio vehiculis ad mare devehuntur.[1] Itaque mari committere cupiunt. Hoc opus multas manus poscit ; at hae porro non desunt. Nam et in agris magna copia est hominum et maxima in civitate, certaque spes omnes libentissime aggressuros opus omnibus fructuosum

Superest, ut tu libratorem vel architectum, si tibi videbitur, mittas, qui diligenter exploret, sitne lacus altior mari, quem artifices regionis huius quadraginta cubitis altiorem esse contendunt. Ego per eadem loca invenio fossam a rege percussam, sed incertum, utrum ad colligendum humorem circumiacentium agrorum an ad committendum flumini lacum ; est enim imperfecta. Hoc quoque dubium, intercepto

---

[1] devehuntur . . . *lacunam indic. Müller.*

## XLI

### To the Emperor Trajan

When I reflect upon your exalted station, and the greatness of your mind, it seems most fitting to point out to you some works worthy alike of your immortality and your fame, and no less useful than magnificent. Bordering upon the territories of the city of Nicomedia is a most extensive lake; over which marbles, produce, timber and commodities are easily and cheaply transported to the high road; but from thence, are conveyed in carriages to the sea-side, at great charge and labour. Accordingly, they desire to connect this lake with the sea. To carry out this work will require, 'tis true, many hands; but these again cannot be scarce, for the country, and particularly the city, is exceedingly populous; and one may assuredly hope that everybody will readily engage in a work which will be of universal benefit.

It only remains then to send hither, if you shall think proper, a surveyor or an architect, in order to examine whether the lake lies above the level of the sea; the mechanics of this province being of opinion that the former is higher by forty cubits. I find there is in the neighbourhood of this place a large canal, which was cut by one of the kings of this country; but as it is left unfinished, it is uncertain whether it was for the purpose of draining the adjacent lands, or of connecting the lake and the river. It is equally doubtful, too, whether the death of the king, or the despair of being able to

rege mortalitate an desperato operis effectu. Sed
hoc ipso (feres enim me ambitiosum pro tua gloria)
incitor et accendor, ut cupiam peragi a te, quae
tantum coeperant reges.

## XLII

### Traianus Plinio

POTEST nos sollicitare lacus iste, ut committere illum
mari velimus; sed plane explorandum est diligenter,
ne, si demissus[1] in mare fuerit, totus effluat, certe
quantum aquarum et unde accipiat. Poteris a Calpurnio Macro petere libratorem, et ego hinc aliquem
tibi peritum eiusmodi operum mittam.

## XLIII

### C. Plinius Traiano Imperatori

REQUIRENTI mihi Byzantiorum rei publicae impendia,
quae maxima fecit, indicatum est, domine, legatum ad
te salutandum annis omnibus cum psephismate mitti,
eique dari nummorum duodena milia. Memor ergo
propositi tui legatum quidem retinendum, psephisma

---

[1] demissus *Catan.*, immissus *a*, *B*, dimissus *Av.*

---

*a* Legate of Lower Moesia, 112 A.D.  *cf.* letters 61, 67 of
this Book.  Letter 18 of Bk V. is addressed to him.

accomplish the design, prevented the completion of it. If the latter was the reason, I am so much the more impelled to desire ardently (you will forgive, I know, my being ambitious for your fame) that you may have the glory of executing, what kings could only attempt.

## XLII

### Trajan to Pliny

The scheme you propose of opening a communication between the lake and the sea, may, perhaps, tempt me to come into it. But you must first carefully ascertain what quantity of water your lake contains, and from whence it is supplied; lest by letting it into the sea, it should be totally exhausted. You may apply to Calpurnius Macer [a] for a surveyor; I will also send you from hence some person skilled in works of this nature.

## XLIII

### To the Emperor Trajan

Upon examining the public expenses of the Byzantines (which I find are extremely great), I was informed, Sir, that they send an envoy every year to salute you with a complimentary decree, and allow him the sum of twelve thousand sesterces. Mindful of your intentions,[b] I thought proper to send the decree without the envoy, that, at the same time

[b] *i.e.* that Pliny should enforce economy on the provincials; *cf.* x. 18, 38.

autem mittendum putavi, ut simul et sumptus
levaretur, et impleretur publicum officium. Eidem
civitati imputata sunt terna milia, quae viatici nomine
annua dabantur legato eunti ad eum, qui Moesiae
praeest, publice salutandum. Haec ego in posterum
circumcidenda existimavi. Te, domine, rogo, ut,
quid sentias, rescribendo aut consilium meum con-
firmare aut errorem emendare digneris.

## XLIV

### Traianus Plinio

Optime fecisti, Secunde carissime, duodena ista
Byzantiis, quae ad salutandum me in legatum im-
pendebantur, remittendo. Fungetur his partibus,
etsi solum eorum psephisma per te missum fuerit.
Ignoscet illis et Moesiae praeses, si minus illum
sumptuose coluerint.

## XLV

### C. Plinius Traiano Imperatori

Diplomata, domine, quorum dies praeterita, an
omnino observari et quam diu velis, rogo scribas,

---

*a* Calpurnius Macer. See x. 42 note.
*b* Orders, signed by the Emperor, to use the imperial post-
ing system, by which official correspondence and travelling
officials were conveyed between Rome and the provinces.

they discharged their public duty to you, they might be eased as regards the cost. This city is likewise charged with the sum of three thousand sesterces as travelling allowance of an envoy, whom they annually send to compliment the governor of Moesia; this expense I judged it right to retrench for the future. I beg, Sir, you would do me the honour either to confirm my judgement, or correct my error in these points, by letting me know your sentiments.

## XLIV

### TRAJAN TO PLINY

I WELL approve, my dear Pliny, of your having remitted to the Byzantines the twelve thousand sesterces which they allowed the envoy commissioned to salute me. I shall esteem their duty as sufficiently paid, though I only receive the act of their senate through your hands. The governor of Moesia[a] must likewise excuse them, if they compliment him at a less expense.

## XLV

### To THE EMPEROR TRAJAN

I BEG, Sir, you would settle a doubt I have concerning your passports[b]; whether you think proper that those whose dates are expired shall remain valid,

"These diplomata at a later time were granted only by the Emperors, but at this period apparently the provincial governors were provided with blank forms which they could fill in and assign." (Hardy.)

meque haesitatione liberes. Vereor enim, ne in alterutram partem ignorantia lapsus aut illicita confirmem aut necessaria impediam.

## XLVI

### Traianus Plinio

Diplomata, quorum praeteritus est dies, in usu esse non debent; ideo inter prima iniungo mihi, ut per omnes provincias ante mittam nova diplomata, quam desiderari possint.

## XLVII

### C. Plinius Traiano Imperatori

Cum vellem Apameae, domine, cognoscere publicos debitores et reditum et impendia, responsum est mihi cupere quidem universos, ut a me rationes coloniae legerentur, numquam tamen esse lectas ab ullo proconsulum; habuisse privilegium et vetustissimum morem arbitrio suo rem publicam administrare. Exegi, ut, quae dicebant, quaeque recitabant, libello complecterentur; quem tibi, qualem acceperam, misi, quamvis intellegerem pleraque ex illo ad id, de quo quaeritur, non pertinere. Te rogo, ut mihi praecipere[1] digneris, quid me putes observare debere. Vereor enim, ne aut excessisse aut non implesse officii mei partes videar.

[1] praecipere, *Av., Bipons, K, Muell.*, praeire, *Ba, Hard., Kukula.*

and how long? For I am apprehensive I may through ignorance fall into one of two errors, and either confirm instruments which are illegal, or obstruct those which are necessary.

## XLVI

### TRAJAN TO PLINY

PASSPORTS whose dates are expired must by no means be made use of. For which reason it is a principal rule with me, to send out fresh passports to all the provinces before there can be any shortage of them.

## XLVII

### TO THE EMPEROR TRAJAN

UPON my desiring, Sir, to examine the public loans, revenues and expenditure of Apamea, the citizens replied they were all extremely willing I should inspect the accounts of the colony, but nevertheless no Proconsul had ever yet perused them, as they had a privilege (and that of very ancient date) of administering their commonwealth in the manner they thought proper. I required them to draw up a memorial of their assertions, together with the authorities they cited, which I transmit to you exactly as I received it; though I am sensible it contains several things foreign to the question. I beg you would honour me with your commands, how I am to act in this affair; for I would not willingly be thought either to exceed or fall short of my commission.

## XLVIII

### Traianus Plinio

Libellus Apameorum, quem epistulae tuae iunxeras, remisit mihi necessitatem perpendendi, qualia
essent, propter quae videri volunt eos, qui pro
consulibus hanc provinciam obtinuerunt, abstinuisse
inspectione rationum suarum, cum, ipse [1] ut eas
inspiceres, non recusaverint. Remuneranda est
igitur probitas eorum, ut iam nunc sciant hoc, quod
inspecturus es, ex mea voluntate salvis, quae habent,
privilegiis esse facturum.

## XLIX

### C. Plinius Traiano Imperatori

Ante adventum meum, domine, Nicomedenses
priori foro novum adicere coeperunt, cuius in angulo
est aedes vetustissima Matris Magnae aut reficienda
aut transferenda ob hoc praecipue, quod est multo
depressior opere eo, quod cum maxime surgit. Ego
cum quaererem, num esset aliqua lex dicta templo,
cognovi alium hic, alium apud nos esse morem
dedicationis. Dispice ergo, domine, an putes aedem,
cui nulla lex dicta est, salva religione posse transferri.
Alioqui commodissimum est, si religio non impedit.

[1] ipse ut eas inspic. *Hardy,* cum ipse . . . non recusave-
rim *Av.,* cum ipsum te ut eas inspic. non recusaverint *a.*

---

[a] The Phrygian Goddess Cybele.
[b] The pontifices on consecrating a temple drew up a *lex
dedicationis* or *lex templi,* defining its precincts, its rights,
its ritual, and the administration of its revenues. (Hardy.)

## XLVIII

### Trajan to Pliny

THE memorial of the Apameans which you annexed to your letter has saved me the necessity of considering the reasons they allege, why the former Proconsuls forbore to inspect their accounts: since they do not refuse to permit *your* examination. Their integrity deserves to be rewarded; and they must be assured for the present that you are to make your inquiry at my personal wish, and with a full reserve to their privileges.

## XLIX

### To the Emperor Trajan

THE Nicomedians, Sir, before my arrival, had begun to build a new Forum contiguous to their former, in a corner of which stands an ancient temple dedicated to the Great Mother.[a] This fabric must either be rebuilt or removed; and for this reason chiefly, because it stands on a much lower level than the lofty building now being erected. Upon inquiry whether this temple had been dedicated under charter,[b] I was informed that their manner of dedication differs from ours. You will be pleased therefore, Sir, to consider whether a temple which has no charter of dedication, may be removed, consistently with the claims of religion; for if there is no objection from that quarter, there is none on the side of inconvenience.

## L

### Traianus Plinio

Potes, mi Secunde carissime, sine sollicitudine religionis, si loci positio videtur hoc desiderare, aedem Matris Deum transferre in eam, quae est accommodatior; nec te moveat, quod lex dedicationis nulla reperitur, cum solum peregrinae civitatis capax non sit dedicationis, quae fit nostro iure.

## LI

### C. Plinius Traiano Imperatori

Difficile est, domine, exprimere verbis, quantam perceperim laetitiam, quod et mihi et socrui meae praestitisti, ut adfinem eius,[1] Caelium Clementem in hanc provinciam transferres. Ex illo enim mensuram beneficii tui penitus intellego, cum tam plenam indulgentiam cum tota domo mea experiar, cui referre gratiam parem ne audeo quidem, quamvis maxime debeam. Itaque ad vota confugio deosque precor, ut iis, quae in me adsidue confers, non indignus existimer.

---

[1] adfinem eius *Beroaldus*, ad finem eius *Av.*, *a*, ad finem consulatus *Catan.*

## L

### TRAJAN TO PLINY

You may without religious scruple, my dear Pliny, if the site requires it, remove the temple of the Mother of the Gods to a more convenient spot. That you can find no charter of dedication, need not influence you ; for the ground of a foreign city is not capable of receiving that kind of consecration which is conferred by our laws.

## LI

### TO THE EMPEROR TRAJAN

It is not easy, Sir, to express the joy I received, when I heard you had, in compliance with the request of my mother-in-law [a] and myself, granted her kinsman Caelius Clemens the Proconsulship of this province after the expiration of his Consular office ; as it is from thence I learn the full extent of your beneficence towards me, which thus graciously spreads itself through my whole family. I dare not pretend to make an equal return to those obligations, I so justly owe you. I can only therefore have recourse to vows, and ardently implore the Gods that I may not be found unworthy of those favours, which you are continually bestowing upon me.

[a] Pompeia Celerina, i. 4, iii. 19, xvi. 10.

# THE LETTERS OF PLINY

## LII

### C. Plinius Traiano Imperatori

Diem, domine, quo servasti imperium, dum
suscipis, quanta mereris laetitia, celebravimus precati
deos, ut te generi humano, cuius tutela et securitas
saluti tuae innisa est, incolumem florentemque prae-
starent. Praeivimus et commilitonibus ius iurandum
more solemni praestantibus et provincialibus, qui
eadem certarunt pietate, iurantibus.

## LIII

### Traianus Plinio

Quanta religione ac laetitia commilitones cum
provincialibus te praeeunte diem imperii mei cele-
braverint, libenter, mi Secunde carissime, cognovi ex
litteris tuis.

## LIV

### C. Plinius Traiano Imperatori

Pecuniae publicae, domine, providentia tua et
ministerio nostro et iam exactae sunt et exiguntur:
quae vereor ne otiosae iaceant. Nam et praediorum comparandorum aut nulla aut rarissima occa-

342

## LII

### To the Emperor Trajan

We have celebrated, Sir, (with those sentiments of joy your virtues justly merit,) the day of your accession, when, at the same time that you accepted, you saved the empire. And we sincerely implored the Gods to preserve you in health and prosperity, as it is upon your welfare that the security and repose of mankind depend. I have administered the oath of allegiance to my fellow-soldiers in the usual form, the people of the province emulously expressing their affection to you by taking the same oath.

## LIII

### Trajan to Pliny

Your letter, my dear Pliny, was extremely acceptable, as it gave me an account how religiously and joyfully my fellow-soldiers and the provincials solemnized the day of my accession to the empire, under your presidency.

## LIV

### To the Emperor Trajan

The money owing to the public, by the prudence, Sir, of your counsels, and the care of my administration, is either actually paid in, or now recovering; but I am afraid it must lie unemployed. For as on one side, there are few or no opportunities of purchasing land, so on the other, one cannot meet

sio est; nec inveniuntur, qui velint debere rei
publicae, praesertim duodenis assibus,[1] quanti a
privatis mutuantur. Dispice ergo, domine, numquid
minuendam usuram ac per hoc idoneos debitores
invitandos putes, et, si ne sic quidem reperiuntur,
distribuendum inter decuriones pecuniam, ita ut
recte rei publicae caveant; quod quamquam invitis
recusantibus minus acerbum erit leviore usura
constituta.

## LV

### Traianus Plinio

Et ipse non aliud remedium dispicio, mi Secunde
carissime, quam ut quantitas usurarum minuatur,
quo facilius pecuniae publicae collocentur. Modum
eius ex copia eorum, qui mutuabuntur, tu constitues.
Invitos ad accipiendum compellere, quod fortassis
ipsis otiosum futurum sit, non est ex iustitia nostro-
rum temporum.

[1] duodenis assibus *deleri volunt Ernestius et Hard.*, usuris
assibus *Salmasius et Gronovius.*

[a] The reason why they did not choose to borrow of the

with any person who is willing to borrow of the municipality (especially at the interest of 12 *per cent.*) when they can raise money upon the same terms from private hands.[a] You will consider then, Sir, whether it may not be advisable, in order to invite responsible persons to borrow this money, to lower the interest; or if that scheme should not succeed, to parcel it out among the town-councillors, upon their giving sufficient security to the public. And though they should not be willing to receive it, yet as the rate of interest will be abated, the hardship will be so much the less.


## LV

### TRAJAN TO PLINY

LIKE you, my dear Pliny, I see no other method of facilitating the placing out of the public money, than by lowering the interest; the amount of which reduction you will determine according to the number of the borrowers. But to compel persons to receive it, who are not disposed to do so, when possibly they themselves may have no opportunity of employing it, is by no means consistent with the justice of my government.

public at the same rate of interest which they paid to private persons, was because in the former instance they were obliged to give security (Melm.); and the state was a more formidable creditor than individuals.

## LVI

### C. Plinius Traiano Imperatori

Summas, domine, gratias ago, qui inter maximas occupationes in[1] iis, de quibus te consului, me quoque regere dignatus es; quod nunc quoque facias rogo. Adiit enim me quidam indicavitque adversarios suos a Servilio Calvo, clarissimo viro, in triennium relegatos in provincia morari. Illi contra ab eodem se restitutos adfirmaverunt edictumque recitaverunt. Qua causa necessarium credidi rem integram ad te referre. Nam sicut mandatis tuis cautum est, ne restituam ab alio aut a me relegatos, ita de iis, quos alius relegaverit et restituerit, nihil comprehensum est.

Ideo tu, domine, consulendus fuisti, quid observare me velles tam hercule de his quam de illis, qui in perpetuum relegati nec restituti in provincia deprehenduntur. Nam haec quoque species incidit in cognitionem meam. Est enim adductus ad me in perpetuum relegatus Iulio Basso proconsule. Ego, quia sciebam acta Bassi rescissa datumque a senatu ius omnibus, de quibus ille aliquid constituisset, ex

---

[1] in add. Gierig, Ernesti, K.

---

[a] Proconsul of Bithynia 108–110 A.D.
[b] Proconsul 98 A.D. See IV. 9, VI. 29.

## LVI

### To the Emperor Trajan

I RETURN you my highest acknowledgements, Sir, that among the many important occupations in which you are engaged, you have condescended to direct me also on those points wherein I have consulted you: a favour which I must now again beseech you to grant me. A certain person came before me with a complaint, that his adversaries, who had been banished for three years by Servilius Calvus,[a] a man of senatorial rank, still remained in the province: they, on the contrary, affirmed that Calvus had restored them again to their country, and produced his edict to to that purpose. I thought it necessary, therefore, to refer the whole affair to you. For as I have your express orders not to restore any person who has been sentenced to banishment either by myself or others; so I have no directions with respect to those who, having been banished by some of my predecessors in this government, have by them also been restored.

I am obliged then, to beg you would inform me, Sir, what method I should observe, as well with regard to these, as to others, who, having been condemned to perpetual banishment and never restored, are found in the province; for cases of that nature have likewise fallen under my cognizance. A person was brought before me who had been sentenced to perpetual exile by the Proconsul Julius Bassus[b]; but knowing that the decrees of Bassus had been rescinded, and that the Senate had granted a new trial to all those who had come under his

347

integro agendi dumtaxat per biennium, interrogavi
hunc, quem relegaverat, an adiisset docuissetque
proconsulem. Negavit.

Per quod effectum est, ut te consulerem, redden-
dum eum poenae suae an gravius aliquid et quid
potissimum constituendum putares et in hunc et in
eos, si qui forte in simili condicione invenirentur.
Decretum Calvi et edictum, item decretum Bassi his
litteris subieci.

## LVII

### Traianus Plinio

Quid in persona eorum statuendum sit, qui a
P. Servilio Calvo proconsule in triennium relegati et
mox eiusdem edicto restituti in provincia reman-
serunt, proxime tibi rescribam, cum causas huius
facti a Calvo requisiero. Qui a Iulio Basso in perpetuum relegatus est, cum per biennium agendi
facultatem habuerit, si existimabat se iniuria relega-
tum, neque id fecerit atque in provincia morari per-
severaverit, vinctus mitti ad praefectos praetorii mei
debet. Neque enim sufficit, eum poenae suae restitui,
quam contumacia elusit.

---

<sup>a</sup> *i.e.* the Proconsul of 99 or 100.
<sup>b</sup> Not to be tried by them, but to remain in their custody
pending the emperor's decision on the case. Thus St. Paul

sentence, provided they appealed within the space of
two years, I inquired of this man whom he had
banished whether he had acquainted the Proconsul [a]
with his case? He replied he had not.

I beg then you would inform me whether you
would have him sent back again into exile; or
whether you think some more severe, and what kind
of punishment, should be inflicted upon him, and
such others who may hereafter be found to lie under
the same delinquency. I have annexed to my
letter the decree of Calvus, and the edict by which
the persons mentioned above were restored, as also
the decree of Bassus.

## LVII

### Trajan to Pliny

I will let you know my determination concerning
those exiles which were banished for three years by
the proconsul P. Servilius Calvus, and afterwards
restored to the province by his edict, when I shall
have informed myself from him of the reasons of this
proceeding. With respect to that person who was
sentenced to perpetual banishment by Julius Bassus,
yet continued to remain in the province, without
making his appeal if he thought himself aggrieved,
(though he had two years given him for that purpose,)
I would have him sent in chains to my Praetorian
prefects [b]; for only to remand him back to a punishment, which he has contumaciously eluded, will by
no means be sufficient.

was kept at Rome by the Praetorian Guard; *Philippians*,
i. 13. (Hardy.)

## LVIII

### C. Plinius Traiano Imperatori

Cum citarem iudices, domine, conventum inchoaturus, Flavius Archippus vacationem petere coepit ut philosophus. Fuerunt, qui dicerent non liberandum eum iudicandi necessitate, sed omnino tollendum de iudicum numero reddendumque poenae, quam fractis vinculis evasisset. Recitata est sententia Velii Pauli proconsulis, qua probabatur Archippus crimine falsi damnatus in metallum. Ille nihil proferebat, quo restitutum se doceret; adlegabat tamen pro restitutione et libellum a se Domitiano datum et epistulas eius ad honorem suum pertinentes et decretum Prusensium. Addebat his et tuas litteras scriptas sibi, addebat et patris tui edictum et epistulam, quibus confirmasset beneficia a Domitiano data. Itaque, quamvis eidem talia crimina applicarentur, nihil decernendum putavi, donec te consulerem de eo, quod mihi constitutione tua dignum videbatur. Ea, quae sunt utrimque recitata, his litteris subieci.

---

*a* They probably decreed him a statue, *cf.* Letter LX. (Hardy.)

## LVIII

### To the Emperor Trajan

When I cited the jurors, Sir, to attend me at a sessions which I was going to hold, Flavius Archippus clair ed the privilege of being excused, as exercising the profession of a philosopher. It was alleged by some who were present, that he ought not so much to be excused from that office as struck out of the roll of jurors, and remanded back to the punishment from which he had escaped by breaking his chains. At the same time a sentence of the Proconsul Velius Paullus was read, by which it appeared that Archippus had been condemned to the mines for forgery. He had nothing to produce in proof that this sentence had ever been reversed. He adduced, however, as implying his restitution, a petition which he presented to Domitian, together with honorific letters from that Prince, and a decree of the Prusensians.[a] To these he subjoined a letter which he had received from you; as also an edict and a letter of your august father confirming the grants which had been made to him by Domitian. For these reasons, notwithstanding such crimes were laid to his charge, I did not think proper to determine any thing concerning him, without first consulting with you in the affair, which seems to merit your personal decision. I have transmitted to you, with this letter, the documents put in by both parties

# THE LETTERS OF PLINY

## Epistula Domitiani ad Terentium Maximum

Flavius Archippus philosophus impetravit a me, ut agrum ei ad c̄[1] circa Prusiadam, patriam suam, emi iuberem,[2] cuius reditu suos alere posset. Quod ei praestari volo. Summam expensam liberalitati meae feres.

## Eiusdem ad L. Appium Maximum

Archippum philosophum, bonum virum et professione sua etiam moribus[3] respondentem, commendatum habeas velim, mi Maxime, et plenam ei humanitatem tuam praestes in iis, quae verecunde a te desideraverit

## Edictum Divi Nervae

Quaedam sine dubio, Quirites, ipsa felicitas temporum edicit, nec spectandus est in iis bonus princeps, quibus illum intellegi satis est, cum hoc sibi quisque civium meorum spondere possit, me securitatem omnium quieti meae praetulisse, ut et libenter nova beneficia conferrem, et ante me concessa servarem. Ne tamen aliquam gaudiis publicis afferat haesitationem vel eorum, qui impetraverunt, diffidentia,

---

[1] ut agrum ei ad c̄ *Hardy, ex marg. B,* ut agr. ei DC *a,* ut agr. ei adderem *Av.*

[2] suam emi iuberem *a, B,* suam tam uberem *Av.*

[3] moribus *Ritterhusius,* maioribus, *a, Av.*

---

[a] Apparently manager of the Imperial domain in Bithynia.

[b] Proconsul of Bithynia under Domitian.

# BOOK X. lviii

### DOMITIAN'S LETTER TO TERENTIUS MAXIMUS [a]

FLAVIUS ARCHIPPUS the philosopher has prevailed with me to give an order that 100,000 sesterces be laid out in purchasing him an estate near Prusa, his native place, sufficient to support his family. Let this be accordingly done; and place the sum expended to the article of my benefactions.

### FROM THE SAME, TO L. APPIUS MAXIMUS [b]

I RECOMMEND, my dear Maximus, to your protection, that worthy philosopher Archippus, a person whose morals are agreeable to his profession; and I would have you accede with your utmost courtesy to his modest requests.

### THE EDICT OF THE EMPEROR NERVA

THERE are some points, no doubt, Quirites, concerning which the happy tenor of my government itself issues an edict [c]; and a good prince need not be narrowly scrutinized in matters wherein his intention cannot but be clearly understood. Every citizen may rest assured, even without a reminder, that I gave up my private repose to the security of the public in order to dispense new benefits, and confirm those of my predecessor. But lest the memory of him [d] who made these grants, or the diffidence of those who received them, should cast

---

[c] The edicts of each Emperor became *ipso facto* invalid at his death; and after Titus, a new Emperor usually confirmed by edict the benefactions of his predecessor. See Hardy's note.          [d] Domitian.

vel eius memoria, qui praestitit; necessarium pariter
credidi ac laetum, obviam dubitantibus indulgentiam
meam mittere. Nolo existimet quisquam, quae alio
Principe vel privatim vel publice consecutus *sit*,
ideo saltem a me rescindi, ut potius mihi debeat.
Sint rata et certa,[1] nec gratulatio ullius instau-
ratis eget precibus, [et qui non habent, me,] quem
fortuna imperii vultu meliore respexit. Me novis
beneficiis vacare patiantur: et ea demum sciant
roganda esse, quae non habent.

## Epistula Eiusdem ad Tullium Iustum

Cum rerum omnium ordinatio, quae prioribus
temporibus inchoatae consummatae sunt, observanda
sit, tum epistulis etiam Domitiani standum est.

## LIX

### C. Plinius Traiano Imperatori

Flavius Archippus per salutem tuam aeternita-
temque petit a me, ut libellum, quem mihi dedit,
mitterem tibi. Quod ego sic roganti praestandum
putavi, ita tamen, ut missurum me notum accu-
satrici eius facerem, a qua et ipsa acceptum libellum his epistulis iunxi, quo facilius velut audita
utraque parte dispiceres, quid statuendum putares.

---

[1] sint rata et certa *Beroaldus, Hard.*, si ingrata et c. *Av.*,
si enim grata et c. *a*, sint si rata, et c. *B, Kukula.*

any misgiving over public joy, I thought it as necessary as agreeable to obviate these doubts, by a special mark of my indulgence. I would have no one think that I shall rescind either the public or private benefactions of a former prince, in order to gain credit by restoring them. They shall be fully ratified; and let no one, on whom the Fortune of the Empire has smiled, think his happiness in need of fresh petitions. Rather let them leave me leisure to bestow new benefits; under the assurance, that I need only be solicited for those which have not already been obtained.

### From the same, to Tullius Justus

As in all matters, whether begun or accomplished, the rules laid down in the last reign are to be observed, so even the letters of Domitian must be held binding upon us.

## LIX

### To the Emperor Trajan

Flavius Archippus has conjured me by your prosperity and immortal glory, that I would transmit to you the memorial which he presented to me. I thought I might grant a request conceived in such terms, provided I acquainted his prosecutrix [a] with this my intention, from whom I have also received a memorial on her part. I have annexed it to my letter; that by hearing each side, you may more easily perceive what to determine in this affair.

[a] Furia Prima, see next Letter.

## LX

### Traianus Plinio

Potuit quidem ignorasse Domitianus, in quo statu
esset Archippus, cum tam multa ad honorem eius
pertinentia scriberet; sed meae naturae accom-
modatius est credere etiam statui eius subventum
interventu principis, praesertim cum etiam statuarum
ei honor toties decretus sit ab iis, qui *non*[1] ignorabant,
quid de illo Paulus proconsul pronuntiasset. Quae
tamen, mi Secunde carissime, non eo pertinent, ut,
si quid illi novi criminis obicitur, minus de eo audien-
dum putes. Libellos Furiae Primae accusatricis,
item ipsius Archippi, quos alteri epistulae tuae
iunxeras, legi.

## LXI

### C. Plinius Traiano Imperatori

Tu quidem, domine, providentissime vereris, ne
commissus flumini atque ita mari lacus effluat; sed
ego in re praesenti invenisse videor, quem ad modum
huic periculo occurrerem. Potest enim lacus fossa
usque ad flumen adduci nec tamen in flumen emitti,
sed relicto quasi margine contineri pariter et dirimi.

---

[1] non *add. Ernestius.*

*a sc.* the Prusensians. See note on Letter LVIII.

## LX

### TRAJAN TO PLINY

It is possible Domitian might be ignorant of the position of Archippus when he wrote letters so much to that philosopher's honour. However, it is more agreeable to my disposition to suppose that Prince's intervention actually restored him to his former situation; especially since he so often had even the honour of a statue decreed to him by those [a] who could not be ignorant of the sentence which the Proconsul Paulus pronounced upon him. But I do not mean to intimate by this, my dear Pliny, that if any new charge should be brought against him, you should be less disposed to hear his accusers. I have examined the memorial of his prosecutrix, Furia Prima, as also that of Archippus himself, which you sent with your former letter.

## LXI

### TO THE EMPEROR TRAJAN

It is with great foresight, Sir, you are apprehensive that the lake [b] may be exhausted by being connected with the river and consequently with the sea; but, being on the spot, I think I have found a method to obviate that risk. For the lake may be brought close to the river by a canal without opening directly into it; a sort of border being left between them to form at once a bulwark and a division.

[b] See x. 41, 42.

Sic consequemur, ut nec vacuetur [1] flumini mixtus et
sit perinde ac si misceatur. Erit enim facile per
illam brevissimam terram, quae interiacebit, advecta
fossa onera transponere in flumen.

Quod ita fiet, si necessitas coget, et spero, non
coget. Est enim et lacus ipse satis altus et nunc
in contrariam partem flumen emittit, quod inter-
clusum inde et, quo volumus, aversum, sine ullo
detrimento lacus tantum aquae, quantum nunc portat,
effundet. Praeterea per id spatium, per quod fossa
facienda est, incidunt rivi; qui si diligenter colligan-
tur, augebunt illud, quod lacus dederit. Enimvero,
si placeat fossam longius ducere et artius [2] pressam
mari aequare nec in flumen, sed in ipsum mare
emittere, repercussus maris servabit et reprimet,
quidquid e lacu veniet.

Quorum si nihil nobis loci natura praestaret,
expeditum tamen erat cataractis aquae cursum
temperare. Verum et haec et alia multo sagacius
conquiret explorabitque librator, quem plane, domine,
debes mittere, ut polliceris. Est enim res digna et
magnitudine tua et cura. Ego interim Calpurnio

[1] vacuetur *Madv. adv.* iii. 216, vacuo videatur *a, Av.*,
vicino videatur *Catan.*
[2] artius *vulg.*, altius *Gierig, Madv.*

[a] Pliny means, of course, that the outflow of the lake
through his canal will be compensated for by blocking up

By this means we shall not only secure the lake from being drained by union with the river, but all the same purposes will be answered as if they were united; for it will be extremely easy to convey over that little intervening ridge whatever burdens shall be brought down by the canal.

This is a scheme which may be pursued, if it should be found necessary; but I hope there will be no occasion to put it into practice. For the lake itself is pretty deep, and as it is, a river runs out of it on the opposite side; by damming this up, and diverting it in whatever direction we please, we can ensure its sending out the same quantity of water as it now conveys, without any diminution of the lake.[a] Besides, there are several little brooks along the proposed course of the canal which, if carefully collected, will augment the supply of water from the lake. But if we should rather approve of the canal's being extended farther, and cut narrower,[b] so as to reach sea-level, and run not into the river but direct into the sea, the reflux of the tide will make good and check the discharge from the lake.

After all, if the nature of the place should not admit of any of these schemes, the course of the water may be easily regulated by sluices. These, however, and other particulars, will be more skilfully examined into by the engineer, whom, agreeably to your promise, I am sure you will send; for indeed, Sir, it is an enterprise well worthy of your attention and magnificence. In the meanwhile I have wrote

this river; but he oddly speaks as if the new outflow would be the river itself, diverted into a new channel.
[b] *i.e.* "to minimise the quantity of water contained by its greater length." (Hardy.)

Marco, clarissimo viro, auctore te scripsi, ut libratorem quam maxime idoneum mitteret.

## LXII

### TRAIANUS PLINIO

MANIFESTUM est, mi Secunde carissime, nec prudentiam nec diligentiam tibi defuisse circa istum lacum, cum tam multa provisa habeas, per quae nec periclitetur exhauriri et magis in usus nobis futurus sit. Elige igitur id, quod praecipue res ipsa suaserit. Calpurnium Macrum credo facturum, ut te libratore instruat, neque enim provinciae istae his artificibus carent.

## LXIII

### C. PLINIUS TRAIANO IMPERATORI

SCRIPSIT mihi, domine, Lycormas, libertus tuus, ut, si qua legatio a Bosporo venisset urbem petitura, usque in adventum suum retineretur. Et legatio quidem dumtaxat in eam civitatem, in qua ipse sum, nulla adhuc venit; sed venit tabellarius Sauromatae regis quem ego,[1] usus opportunitate, quam mihi casus obtulerat, cum tabellario, qui Lycormam ex itinere

---

[1] Sauromatae regis quem ego *Schaefer, KII.*, *Müll.*, *Kukula*, cuius ego *Âv.*, quem ego *a, KI., Hard.*

---

[a] See x. 42.     [b] *sc.* Nicaea; *cf.* x. 67.
[c] Hardy has shown that *Sauromatae* does not refer to a

to the illustrious Calpurnius Macer,<sup>a</sup> in pursuance of your orders, to send me a proper engineer for this occasion.

## LXII

### TRAJAN TO PLINY

IT is evident, my dear Pliny, that neither your prudence nor your care have been wanting in this affair of the lake, since you have provided so many expedients both against the hazard of its being drained away, and to make it of more general benefit to us. Select, then, whichever scheme is recommended by circumstances. Calpurnius Macer will do his best, no doubt, to supply you with an engineer ; and artists of that kind are not wanting in the provinces near you.

## LXIII

### TO THE EMPEROR TRAJAN

I RECEIVED, Sir, a despatch from your freedman Lycormas, desiring me, if any embassy from the Bosporus should come hither in the way to Rome, that I would detain it till his arrival. None has yet arrived ; at least in the city where I am.<sup>b</sup> But a courier passing through this place from King Sauromates,<sup>c</sup> I lay hold of that opportunity which accidentally offers itself, of sending with him the courier who brought Lycormas' despatch ; that you

problematical king of the Sauromatae (Sarmatians), but to the Bosporan King Sauromates, who reigned from 92 or 93 A.D. till 124 A.D.

praecessit, mittendum putavi, ut possis ex Lycormae
et ex regis epistulis pariter cognoscere, quae fortasse
pariter scire debes.

## LXIV

### C. PLINIUS TRAIANO IMPERATORI

REX Sauromates scripsit mihi esse quaedam, quae
deberes quam maturissime scire. Qua ex causa
festinationem tabellarii, quem ad te cum epistulis
misit, diplomate adiuvi.

## LXV

### C. PLINIUS TRAIANO IMPERATORI

MAGNA, domine, et ad totam provinciam pertinens
quaestio est de condicione et alimentis eorum, quos
vocant θρεπτούς. In qua ego, auditis constitutioni-
bus principum quia nihil inveniebam aut proprium
aut universale, quod ad Bithynos ferretur, consulendum te existimavi, quid observari velles, neque enim
putavi, posse me in eo, quod auctoritatem tuam
posceret, exemplo esse contentum.

Recitabatur autem apud me edictum, quod dice-
batur divi Augusti, ad Asiam[1] pertinens; recitatae

[1] Asiam *Hard.*, Anniam *vulg.*, Achaiam *Momm.*

[a] *i.e.* whether they were legally slaves, and, if not,
whether those who had reared them could claim to recover
the cost of their upbringing.

may learn simultaneously from the letter of Lycormas and the letter of the King, matters which perhaps you ought to be informed of at one and the same time.

## LXIV

### To the Emperor Trajan

King Sauromates has written to me that certain affairs have happened which require your immediate knowledge. I have therefore assisted the courier whom he dispatched with a letter to you, to arrive more speedily, by granting him an order to employ the public post.

## LXV

### To the Emperor Trajan

A very considerable question, Sir, in which the whole province is interested, has been lately started, concerning the state and maintenance [a] of what are called *foundlings*. I have examined the rulings of former Princes upon this head, but not finding any thing in them either particular or general relating to the Bithynians, I thought it necessary to apply to you for your directions. For in a point which requires the special interposition of your authority, I could not content myself with following precedents.

An edict of the Emperor Augustus (as pretended) was read to me, concerning Asia [b]; also a letter from

[b] *i.e.* the Roman province so called.

et epistulae divi Vespasiani ad Lacedaemonios et divi Titi ad eosdem, dein ad Achaeos : et Domitiani ad Avidium Nigrinum et Armenium Brocchum proconsules, item ad Lacedaemonios ; quae ideo tibi non misi, quia et parum emendata et quaedam non certae fidei videbantur, et quia vera et emendata in scriniis tuis esse credebam.

## LXVI

### Traianus Plinio

Quaestio ista, quae pertinet ad eos, qui liberi nati expositi, deinde sublati a quibusdam et in servitute educati sunt, saepe tractata est, nec quicquam invenitur in commentariis eorum principum, qui ante me fuerunt, quod ad omnes provincias sit constitutum. Epistulae sane sunt Domitiani ad Avidium Nigrinum et Armenium Brocchum, quae fortasse debeant observari ; sed inter[1] eas provincias, de quibus rescripsit, non[2] est Bithynia ; et ideo nec adsertionem denegandam iis, qui ex eius modi causa in libertatem vindicabuntur, puto, neque ipsam libertatem redimendam pretio alimentorum.

[1] inter *a, Av..* intra *K.*     [2] non *om. Av., add. a.*

Vespasian to the Lacedaemonians, and another from Titus to the same, with one likewise from him to the Achaeans. Also a letter from Domitian to the Proconsuls Avidius Nigrinus and Armenius Brocchus, and another to the Lacedaemonians: but I have not transmitted them to you, as well because they were ill-copied (and some of them, too, of doubtful authority) as because I imagine the true copies are preserved in your Record Office.[a]

## LXVI

### TRAJAN TO PLINY

THE question concerning free-born persons who have been exposed as infants and reared in slavery by those who took them up, has been frequently discussed; but I do not find in the archives of the Princes my predecessors, any general regulation upon this head, extending to all the provinces. There are, indeed, letters of Domitian to Avidius Nigrinus and Armenius Brocchus, which perhaps ought to be observed; but Bithynia is not comprehended in the provinces therein mentioned. I am of opinion therefore, that those who desire emancipation upon this ground should not be debarred from publicly asserting their freedom, nor be obliged to purchase it by repaying the cost of their maintenance.

[a] "Under the empire, the *scrinia* . . . were the official bureaux where the public archives were kept." (Hardy.)

## LXVII

### C. Plinius Traiano Imperatori

Legato Sauromatae regis, cum sua sponte Niceae,
ubi me invenerat, biduo substitisset, longiorem
moram faciendam, domine, non putavi; primum
quod incertum adhuc erat, quando libertus tuus
Lycormas venturus esset, deinde quod ipse proficisce-
bar in diversam provinciae partem ita officii necessitate exigente. Haec in notitiam tuam perferenda
existimavi, quia proxime scripseram petiisse Lycormam, ut legationem, si qua venisset a Bosporo,
usque in adventum suum retinerem. Quod diutius
faciendi nulla mihi probabilis ratio occurrit; praesertim cum epistulae Lycormae, quas detinere, ut
ante praedixi, nolui, aliquot diebus hunc legatum
antecessurae viderentur.

## LXVIII

### C. Plinius Traiano Imperatori

Petentibus quibusdam, ut sibi reliquias suorum,
aut propter iniuriam vetustatis aut propter fluminis
incursum aliaque his similia quaecumque secundum
exemplum proconsulum transferre permitterem, quia
sciebam in urbe nostra ex eius modi causis collegium
pontificum adiri solere, te, domine, maximum pontifi-
cem consulendum putavi, quid observare me velis.

---

<sup>a</sup> The *pontifices* were the highest of the four great sacer-
dotal colleges. From the time of Augustus, their president
(*Pontifex Maximus*) was the reigning Emperor.

## LXVII

### To the Emperor Trajan

The ambassador from King Sauromates having voluntarily stayed two days at Nicaea, where he found me, I thought it best, Sir, not to detain him longer : firstly, because it was quite uncertain when your freedman Lycormas would arrive, and secondly, official duties obliged me to set out for a different part of the province. Of this I thought it necessary that you should be informed, because I lately acquainted you in a letter, that Lycormas had desired if any embassy should come this way from Bosporus, that I would detain it till his arrival. But I see no valid reason for doing so any longer, especially as the despatches from Lycormas which (as I mentioned before) I was not willing to detain, would probably reach you some days sooner than this ambassador.

## LXVIII

### To the Emperor Trajan

Having been petitioned by some persons to grant them the liberty (agreeably to the practice of Proconsuls) of removing the relics of their deceased relations, upon the suggestion, that either their monuments were decayed by age, or ruined by the inundations of the river, or for other reasons of the same kind ; I thought proper, Sir, knowing that it is usual at Rome to consult the pontifical college [a] on such matters, to ask you, as the sovereign of that sacred order, what course you would have me follow.

## LXIX

### Traianus Plinio

Durum est iniungere necessitatem provincialibus
pontificum adeundorum, si reliquias suorum propter
aliquas iustas causas transferre ex loco in alium
locum velint. Sequenda ergo potius tibi exempla
sunt eorum, qui isti provinciae praefuerunt, et ex
causa cuique ita aut permittendum, aut negandum.

## LXX

### C. Plinius Traiano Imperatori

Quaerenti mihi, domine, Prusae ubi posset balineum, quod indulsisti, fieri, placuit locus, in quo
fuit aliquando domus, ut audio, pulchra, nunc de-
formis ruinis. Per hoc enim consequemur, ut
foedissima facies civitatis ornetur, atque etiam ut
ipsa civitas amplietur, nec ulla aedificia tollantur,
sed, quae sunt vetustate sublapsa, relaxentur[1] in
melius. Est autem huius domus condicio talis:
legaverat eam Claudius Polyaenus Claudio Caesari,
iusseratque in peristylio templum ei fieri, reliqua ex
domo locari. Ex ea reditum aliquamdiu civitas

---

[1] relaxentur *K*, *Hard.*, reparentur *a*.

[a] x. 24.

## LXIX

### Trajan to Pliny

It will be a hardship upon the provincials to oblige them to address themselves to the college of Pontiffs, whenever they have just reasons for removing the ashes of their ancestors. In this case therefore it will be better you should follow the example of the governors your predecessors, and grant or deny them this liberty as you shall see reasonable.

## LXX

### To the Emperor Trajan

I have inquired, Sir, at Prusa, for a proper site on which to erect the bath you were pleased to allow that city to build; [a] and I have found one to my satisfaction. It was formerly occupied by a dwelling-house—beautiful, I am told, which is now a hideous ruin. By fixing upon that spot, we shall gain the advantage of ornamenting the city in a part which at present is exceedingly deformed, and actually make it more spacious without pulling down any buildings, but merely by advantageously opening out the ruins time has made. There are some circumstances attending this structure, of which it is proper I should inform you. One Claudius Polyaenus bequeathed it to the Emperor Claudius Caesar with direction that a temple should be erected to that Prince in the piazza, and that the remainder of the house should be let. The

369

percepit; deinde paulatim partim spoliata, partim
neglecta cum peristylio domus tota collapsa est, ac
iam paene nihil ex ea nisi solum superest; quod tu,
domine, sive donaveris civitati sive venire iusseris,
propter opportunitatem loci pro summo munere
accipiet.

Ego, si permiseris, cogito in area vacua balineum
collocare, eum autem locum, in quo aedificia fuerunt,
exedra et porticibus amplecti atque tibi consecrare,
cuius beneficio elegans opus dignumque nomine tuo
fiet. Exemplar testamenti, quamquam mendosum,
misi tibi; ex quo cognosces multa Polyaenum in
eiusdem domus ornatum reliquisse, quae, ut domus
ipsa, perierunt, a me tamen, in quantum potuerit,
requirentur.

## LXXI

### Traianus Plinio

Possumus apud Prusenses area ista cum domo
collapsa, quam vacare scribis, ad exstructionem
balinei uti. Illud tamen parum expressisti, an aedes
in peristylio Claudio facta esset. Nam si facta est,
licet collapsa sit, religio eius occupavit solum.

city received the rents for a considerable time;
but partly by its having been plundered, and partly
by its being neglected, the whole house together
with the piazza is entirely gone to ruin, and there is
now scarce anything remaining of it, but the ground
upon which it stood. If you shall think proper, Sir,
either to give or sell this spot of ground to the city,
as it lies so conveniently for their purpose, they
will receive it as the highest mark of your favour.

I intend, with your permission, to place the bath
in the vacant space; and to extend a range of
colonnades, together with alcoves, on that part where
the former edifice stood. This new fabric I design
to dedicate to you, by whose bounty it will rise with
all the elegance and magnificence worthy of your
glorious name. I have sent you a copy of the will
by which, though it is not very correct, you will see
that Polyaenus left large sums for the ornament of
this house; but those also are lost with all the rest;
I will however make the strictest inquiry after them
that I am able.

## LXXI

### Trajan to Pliny

I HAVE no objection to the Prusenses making use
of the vacant space together with the ruined house,
which you say is untenanted, for the situation of
their bath. But it is not sufficiently clear by your
letter, whether the temple in the piazza was actually
erected to Claudius or not: for if it were, even
if it be now in ruins, the site is preoccupate to
his worship.

# THE LETTERS OF PLINY

## LXXII

### C. Plinius Traiano Imperatori

Postulantibus quibusdam, ut de agnoscendis liberis restituendisque natalibus et secundum epistulam Domitiani scriptam Minicio Rufo et secundum exempla proconsulum ipse cognoscerem, respexi ad senatus consultum pertinens ad eadem genera causarum, quod de his tantum provinciis loquitur, quibus proconsules praesunt; ideoque rem integram distuli, dum tu, domine, praeceperis, quid observare me velis.

## LXXIII

### Traianus Plinio

Si mihi senatus consultum miseris, quod haesitationem tibi fecit, aestimabo, an debeas cognoscere de agnoscendis liberis et natalibus suis restituendis.

---

*a i.e.* by the husband of their mother, if she was suspected of unfaithfulness.

*b i.e.* granting the rights of a freeborn citizen to those of servile birth. "The phrase was based on the theory that the original condition of men was one of freedom." Hardy.

## LXXII

### To the Emperor Trajan

I HAVE been pressed by certain persons to take upon myself the cognizance of cases relating to the acknowledgement of children[a] and the restitution of birthright,[b] in accordance with a letter of Domitian's to Minicius Rufus, and the practice of former proconsuls. But upon referring to a decree of the Senate concerning cases of this nature, I find it only mentions the Proconsular provinces.[c] I therefore, Sir, defer intermeddling in this affair, till I shall receive your commands how you would have me act.

## LXXIII

### Trajan to Pliny

IF you will send me the decree of the Senate, which occasions your doubt, I shall be able to judge, whether you ought to take upon yourself the cognizance of causes relating to paternity, and restitution of birth-right.

[a] *i.e.* the senatorial provinces, the governor of which enjoyed the title of pro-consul. Though Bithynia was still a senatorial province, Pliny had been sent to govern it as the Emperor's Legate (see Introduction), and hence scrupled to assume Pro-consular rights.

## LXXIV

### C. PLINIUS TRAIANO IMPERATORI

APULEIUS, domine, miles, qui est in statione
Nicomedensi, scripsit mihi quendam nomine Cal-
lidromum, cum detineretur a Maximo et Dionysio
pistoribus, quibus operas suas locaverat, confugisse
ad tuam statuam perductumque ad magistratus
indicasse, servisse aliquando Laberio Maximo cap-
tumque a Susago in Moesia et a Decibalo muneri
missum Pacoro, Parthiae regi, pluribusque annis in
ministerio eius fuisse, deinde fugisse atque ita in
Nicomediam pervenisse.

Quem ego perductum ad me, cum eadem narrasset,
mittendum ad te putavi ; quod paulo tardius feci,
dum requiro gemmam, quam sibi habentem imaginem
Pacori, et quibus insignibus [1] ornatus fuisset, sub-
tractam indicabat. Volui enim hanc quoque, si
inveniri potuisset, simul mittere, sicut glebulam
misi, quam se ex Parthico metallo attulisse dicebat.
Signata est annulo meo, cuius est aposphragisma,
quadriga.

[1] insignibus *add. Catan.*

---

[a] Statues of the emperors, even during their lifetime, had
the same rights of sanctuary attached to them as had certain
altars and statues of the gods.

## LXXIV

### To the Emperor Trajan

I received a letter, Sir, from Apuleius, a soldier now in garrison at Nicomedia, informing me that one Callidromus on being detained by Maximus and Dionysius, bakers to whom he had hired himself, fled for refuge to your statue [a]; that being brought before a magistrate, he declared he was formerly slave to Laberius Maximus [b]; but being taken prisoner by Susagus in Moesia,[c] he was sent as a present to Pacorus king of Parthia, in whose service he continued several years, from whence he made his escape, and came to Nicomedia.

When he was examined before me, he repeated this account; so that I thought it best to send him to you. But I deferred his journey while I had search made for a gem which he said had been stolen from him, upon which was engraven the figure of Pacorus in his royal habit; for I was desirous (if it could have been found) of sending this curiosity to you along with the man himself, as I am now sending a small ingot of gold, which he says he brought with him from the Parthian mines. I have fixed my seal to it, the impression of which is, a chariot drawn by four horses.

[b] One of Trajan's generals in the Dacian war.
[c] A general, or ally, of Decebalus the Dacian King.

## LXXV

### C. PLINIUS TRAIANO IMPERATORI

IULIUS, domine, Largus ex Ponto nondum mihi
visus ac ne auditus quidem (scilicet iudicio tuo
credidit) dispensationem quandam mihi erga te pietatis suae ministeriumque mandavit. Rogavit enim
testamento, ut hereditatem suam adirem cernerem-
que ac deinde perceptis quinquaginta milibus nummum reliquum omne Heracleotarum et Tianorum
civitatibus redderem, ita ut esset arbitrii mei, utrum
opera facienda, quae honori tuo consecrarentur,
putarem an instituendos quinquennales agonas, qui
Traiani appellentur. Quod in notitiam tuam per-
ferendum existimavi ob hoc maxime, ut dispiceres,
quid eligere debeam.

## LXXVI

### TRAIANUS PLINIO

IULIUS LARGUS fidem tuam, quasi te bene nosset,
elegit. Quid ergo potissimum ad perpetuitatem
memoriae eius faciat, secundum cuiusque loci condicionem ipse dispice, et quod optimum existimaveris,
sequere.

## LXXV

### To the Emperor Trajan

Julius Largus, Sir, of Pontus, though I never yet saw, nor indeed, even heard of him (to be sure, he relied on your testimonial [a]), has intrusted me with the administration, so to speak, of his loyal sentiments towards you. He has desired me in his will to take formal possession of his estate, and, after deducting 50,000 sesterces for my own use, to make over the remainder to the cities of Heraclea and Tium, conditionally upon their either erecting some public edifice in your honour, or instituting Athletic games, to be celebrated every five years, and called *Trajan's games*, according as I shall determine. Of this I thought it necessary to acquaint you; and for this reason chiefly, that you may decide which alternative I should choose.

## LXXVI

### Trajan to Pliny

By the confidence Julius Largus has reposed in you, one would imagine he had known you well. You will consider then what will most tend to the perpetuating of his memory, according to the circumstance of the respective places; and pursue whatever course you shall think most proper.

[a] *i.e.* the appointment of Pliny to Bithynia. For *iudicium* in this sense *cf.* x. 4. *ut gloriari . . . iudiciis tuis possim.* (Hardy.)

## LXXVII

### C. PLINIUS TRAIANO IMPERATORI

PROVIDENTISSIME, domine, fecisti, quod praecepisti
Calpurnio Macro, clarissimo viro, ut legionarium
centurionem Byzantium mitteret. Dispice, an etiam
Iuliopolitanis simili ratione consulendum putes,
quorum civitas, cum sit perexigua, onera maxima
sustinet tantoque graviores iniurias, quanto est
infirmior, patitur. Quidquid autem Iuliopolitanis
praestiteris, id etiam toti provinciae proderit. Sunt
enim in capite Bithyniae plurimisque per eam com-
meantibus transitum praebent.

## LXXVIII

### TRAIANUS PLINIO

EA condicio est civitatis Byzantiorum confluente
undique in eam commeantium turba, ut secundum
consuetudinem praecedentium temporum honoribus
eius praesidio centurionis legionarii consulendum
habuerimus. Si [1] Iuliopolitanis succurrendum eodem
modo putaverimus, onerabimus nos exemplo. Plures
enim tanto magis eadem requirent, quanto infirmiores
erunt. Tibi eam fiduciam diligentiae habeo, ut
credam te omni ratione id acturum, ne sint obnoxii

---

[1] si *om. a, Av.*

## LXXVII

### To the Emperor Trajan

You acted agreeably, Sir, to your consummate prudence, when you commanded the illustrious Calpurnius Macer [a] to send a legionary centurion [b] to Byzantium. Pray, consider whether the city of Juliopolis does not deserve the same regard, which though it is extremely small, sustains very great burthens, and is so much the more exposed to injuries, as it is less capable of resisting them. Whatever benefits you shall confer upon that city, will in effect be advantageous to the whole province: for it is situated at the entrance of Bithynia, and is the town through which all who travel into that province generally pass.

## LXXVIII

### Trajan to Pliny

The circumstances of the city of Byzantium are such, by the great confluence of travellers to it, that I have thought proper to aid the magistrates with a legionary centurion's guard as has been customary in former reigns. But if we should assist the city of Juliopolis in the same manner, we should burden ourselves with a precedent; for other towns will request the same aid, and the more readily, the weaker they are. I have so much confidence in your activity, as to believe you will omit no method

[a] See x. 42.
[b] i.e. a detachment of legionaries under a centurion. (Hardy.)

iniuriis. Si qui autem se contra disciplinam meam gesserint, statim coerceantur; aut, si plus admiserint, quam ut in re praesenti satis puniantur, si milites erunt, legatis eorum, quod[1] deprehenderis, notum facies aut, si in urbem versus venturi erunt, mihi scribes.

## LXXIX

### C. PLINIUS TRAIANO IMPERATORI

CAUTUM est, domine, Pompeia lege, quae Bithynis data est, ne quis capiat magistratum neve sit in senatu minor annorum triginta. Eadem lege comprehensum est, ut, qui ceperint magistratum, sint in senatu. Secutum est dein edictum divi Augusti, quo permisit minores magistratus ab annis duobus et viginti capere. Quaeritur ergo, an, qui minor triginta annorum gessit magistratus, possit a censoribus in senatum legi et, si potest, an ii quoque, qui non gesserint, possint per eandem interpretationem ab ea aetate senatores legi, a qua illis magistratum gerere permissum est; quod alioqui factitatum adhuc et esse necessarium dicitur, quia sit aliquanto melius honestorum hominum liberos quam e plebe in curiam admitti.

---

[1] quod *Rittershusius*, quae *a*, *Av.*

---

[a] After subjugating Mithridates of Pontus (65 B.C.), when Bithynia was made a Roman province. A kind of constitution (*lex provinciae*) for each province thus acquired by

of protecting the town from injuries. Any breaches of public order as by me established, are to be instantly suppressed ; or, should the offence be too serious for summary chastisement, if the culprits are soldiers, you will report the misdemeanour to their officers ; but if they are persons who are returning to Rome, inform me by letter.

## LXXIX

### To the Emperor Trajan

It is enacted, Sir, by the provincial code which Pompey drew up for Bithynia,[a] that no person shall exercise any magistracy, or be admitted into the senate, under the age of thirty. By the same law it is provided, that those who have held a magistracy shall be senators of course. Subsequently, however, an edict of the Emperor Augustus permitted minor offices to be held at the age of twenty-two. The question therefore is, whether those who have held office before the age of thirty, may be legally admitted into the senate by the Censors, and if so, whether by the same kind of construction they may be admitted senators, at the age when they are allowed to be magistrates, though they have not actually borne any office. A custom, it seems, which has hitherto been observed, and is said to be necessary, as it is a good deal better that persons of noble birth should be admitted into the senate, than those of plebeian rank.

conquest was framed by the victorious general in conjunction with ten commissioners of senatorial rank sent from Rome for the purpose, and was known by his name.

Ego a destinatis censoribus, quid sentirem, interrogatus eos quidem, qui minores triginta annis gessissent magistratum, putabam posse in senatum et secundum edictum Augusti et secundum legem Pompeiam legi, quoniam Augustus gerere magistratus minoribus annis triginta permisisset, lex senatorem esse voluisset, qui gessisset magistratum. De iis autem, qui non gessissent, quamvis essent aetatis eiusdem cuius illi, quibus gerere permissum est, haesitabam ; per quod effectum est, ut te, domine, consulerem, quid observari velles. Capita legis, tum edictum Augusti, litteris subieci.

## LXXX

### Traianus Plinio

Interpretationi tuae, mi Secunde carissime, idem existimo hactenus, edicto divi Augusti novatam esse legem Pompeiam ut magistratum quidem capere possint ii, qui non minores duorum et viginti annorum essent, et, qui cepissent, in senatum cuiusque civitatis pervenirent Ceterum non capto magistratu eos, qui minores triginta annorum sint, quia magistratum capere possint, in curiam etiam loci cuiusque non existimo legi posse.

The Censors elect having desired my sentiments upon this point, I was of opinion that, taking the law of Pompey and the edict of Augustus together, those who had held a magistracy before the age of thirty, might be admitted into the senate; because the edict allows the office of magistrate to be undertaken before thirty; and the law declares, that whoever has been a magistrate, has a right to be a senator. But with respect to those who never held a magistracy, though they were of the age required for that purpose, I had some doubt; and therefore, Sir, I apply to you for your directions. I have annexed to this letter sections of the law, together with the edict of Augustus.

## LXXX

### TRAJAN TO PLINY

I AGREE with you, my dear Pliny, in your construction; and am of opinion that the law of Pompey is so far repealed by the edict of the Emperor Augustus, that those persons who are not less than twenty-two years of age may hold the office of magistrate, and when they have, may be received into the senate of their respective cities. But I think those who are under thirty years of age, and have not held the office of magistrate, cannot, upon pretence that in point of years they might have done so, claim a place in the senate of their several communities.

# THE LETTERS OF PLINY

## LXXXI

### C. Plinius Traiano Imperatori

Cum Prusae ad Olympum, domine, publicis
negotiis intra hospitium eodem die exiturus vacarem,
Asclepiades magistratus indicavit appellatum me a
Claudio Eumolpo. Cum Cocceianus Dion in bule
adsignari civitati opus, cuius curam egerat, vellet,
tum Eumolpus adsistens Flavio Archippo dixit
exigendam esse a Dione rationem operis ante quam
rei publicae traderetur, quod aliter fecisset, ac
debuisset. Adiecit etiam esse in eodem opere
positam tuam statuam et corpora sepultorum, uxoris
Dionis, et filii ; postulavitque, ut cognoscerem pro
tribunali.

Quod cum ego me protinus facturum dilaturumque
profectionem dixissem, ut longiorem diem ad instru-
endam causam darem, utque in alia civitate cognoscerem, petiit. Ego me auditurum Niceae respondi.
Ubi cum consedissem[1] cogniturus, idem Eumolpus,
tamquam adhuc parum instructus, dilationem petere
coepit, contra Dion, ut audiretur, exigere. Dicta
sunt utrimque multa etiam de causa. Ego cum
dandam dilationem et te[2] consulendum existimarem

[1] Ubi cum consedissem *Orelli*, ubi consedissem *Av.*, ubi
cum sedissem *a*.     [2] te *om. a, Av.*

---

[a] Dio, surnamed Chrysostom, rhetorician and philosopher,

384

## LXXXI

### To the Emperor Trajan

WHILST I was dispatching some public affairs, Sir, in the official lodgings at Prusa near Olympus, with an intention of leaving that city the same day, I learned from the magistrate Asclepiades that Claudius Eumolpus had appealed to me. Cocceianus Dio,[a] it seems, at a meeting of the senate desired that a public edifice, which had been erected under his charge, might be handed over to the city in form. But Eumolpus, acting for Flavius Archippus, insisted that Dio should render an account of the expenses of this work, before it was assigned to the corporation; suggesting that he had not properly executed his commission. He added that your statue had been placed in the said building, although the bodies of Dio's wife and son are interred there, and petitioned that I would hold a judicial inquiry on the matter.

Upon my complying, and offering to defer my journey, he desired a later day in order to prepare the cause, and that I would try it in some other city. I appointed the city of Nicaea; but when I took my seat, Eumolpus, on the plea of not being yet sufficiently instructed, requested a further adjournment; Dio, on the contrary, insisted that the cause should be heard then and there. When this point and also the merits of the cause had been argued at length on both sides, I decided to grant the adjournment and meanwhile to advise with you in

was a native of Prusa. Sojourning at Rome, he became an intimate friend of the Emperor Nerva.

in re ad exemplum pertinenti, dixi utrique parti,
ut postulationum suarum libellos darent. Volebam
enim te ipsorum potissimum verbis ea, quae erant
proposita, cognoscere. Et Dion quidem se daturum
dixit et Eumolpus respondit complexurum se libello,
quae reipublicae peteret, ceterum, quod ad sepultos
pertineret, non accusatorem se, sed advocatum Flavi
Archippi, cuius mandata pertulisset. Archippus, cui
Eumolpus sicut Prusiade adsistebat, dixit se libellum
daturum. At[1] nec Eumolpus nec Archippus quam
plurimis diebus exspectati, adhuc mihi libellos dederunt ; Dion dedit, quem huic epistulae iunxi.

Ipse in re praesenti fui et vidi tuam quoque
statuam in bibliotheca positam, id autem, in quo
dicuntur sepulti filius et uxor Dionis, in area collo-
catum, quae porticibus includitur. Te, domine, rogo,
ut me in hoc praecipue genere cognitionis regere
digneris, cum alioqui magna sit exspectatio, ut
necesse est in ea re, quae et in confessum venit et
exemplis defenditur, deliberare.

## LXXXII

### Traianus Plinio

Potuisti non haerere, mi Secunde carissime,
circa id de quo me consulendum existimasti, cum
propositum meum optime nosses non ex metu

---

[1] at *Schaefer,* ita *a, Av.*

---

[a] *i.e.* of the emperor's statue being in the same building
with dead bodies.

an affair which would set up a precedent. Accordingly, I directed both parties to give in a memorial of their respective demands; for I wished you to judge the statements of both from their own words. This Dio promised to do; and Eumolpus engaged to draw up a memorial on the claims of the town. But he added, that he made no personal accusation with respect to the sepulchres, being merely the advocate of Archippus, whose instructions he had laid before me. Archippus, however, for whom Eumolpus was counsel here, as at Prusa, undertook to present a memorial. But neither Eumolpus nor Archippus, though I have waited many days, have yet sent me their memorials; Dio has sent me his, and I have annexed it to this letter.

I have visited the spot myself where I saw your statue placed in a library; the alleged burial-place of Dio's wife and son is in a courtyard which is enclosed with a colonnade. I intreat, Sir, you would deign to direct me in such an inquiry above all others, as it is one to which the world is greatly attentive. And, indeed, it highly deserves a very mature deliberation, since the fact[a] is not only acknowledged, but defended by many examples.

## LXXXII

### Trajan to Pliny

As you well know, my dear Pliny, it is the fixed maxim of my government not to create an awe of my person by severe and rigorous measures and by construing every slight offence into an act of treason,

nec terrore hominum aut criminibus maiestatis reverentiam nomini meo acquiri. Omissa ergo ea quaestione, quam non admitterem, etiamsi exemplis adiuvaretur, ratio totius operis effecti sub cura Cocceiani Dionis excutiatur, cum et utilitas civitatis exigat, nec aut recuset Dion aut debeat recusare.

## LXXXIII

### C. PLINIUS TRAIANO IMPERATORI

ROGATUS, domine, a Nicaeensibus publice per ea, quae mihi et sunt et debent esse sanctissima, id est per aeternitatem tuam salutemque, ut preces suas ad te perferrem, fas non putavi negare acceptumque ab his libellum huic epistulae iunxi.

## LXXXIV

### TRAIANUS PLINIO

NICAEENSIBUS, qui intestatorum civium suorum concessam vindicationem bonorum a divo Augusto adfirmant, debebis vacare contractis omnibus personis ad idem negotium pertinentibus adhibitis Virdio Gemellino et Epimacho, liberto meo, procuratoribus, ut, aestimatis etiam iis, quae contra dicuntur, quod optimum credideritis, statuatis.

there was no occasion for you to hesitate a moment upon the point, concerning which you thought proper to consult me. Without entering therefore into that question, (to which I would by no means give any attention, though there were ever so many instances of the same kind,) I recommend to your care the examination of Dio's accounts relating to the public works which he has finished; as it is a case in which the interest of the city is concerned, and as Dio neither ought, nor indeed does refuse, to submit to the inquiry.

## LXXXIII

### To the Emperor Trajan

THE Nicaeans having conjured me, Sir, by (what is, and ought to be, most sacred to me) your prosperity and immortal glory, to present to you their petition; I did not think myself at liberty to refuse them: I have therefore enclosed it in this letter.

## LXXXIV

### Trajan to Pliny

THE Nicaeans, I find, claim a right by an edict of Augustus to the estate of every citizen who dies intestate. You will therefore summon the several parties interested in this question, and with the assistance of Epimachus and Virdius Gemellinus, my Procurators (having duly weighed every argument that shall be alleged against the claim), determine as shall appear most reasonable.

## LXXXV

### C. PLINIUS TRAIANO IMPERATORI

MAXIMUM, libertum et procuratorem tuum,
domine, per omne tempus, quo fuimus una, probum et industrium et diligentem ac sicut rei tuae
amantissimum ita disciplinae tenacissimum expertus
libenter apud te testimonio prosequor ea fide, quam
tibi debeo.

## LXXXVI A

### C. PLINIUS TRAIANO IMPERATORI

GABIUM BASSUM, domine, praefectum orae Ponticae, integrum, probum, industrium, atque inter
ista reverentissimum mei expertus voto pariter et
suffragio prosequor ea fide, quam tibi debeo.

## LXXXVI B

### C. PLINIUS TRAIANO IMPERATORI

FABIUM VALENTEM instructum commilitio tuo valde
probo, cuius disciplinae debet quod indulgentia tua
dignus est.   Apud me et milites et pagani, a quibus
iustitia eius et humanitas inspecta est, certatim ei
qua privatim qua publice testimonia pertribuerunt
Quod in notitiam tuam perfero ea fide quam tibi
debeo.

## LXXXV

### To the Emperor Trajan

Your freedman and procurator, Maximus, behaved, Sir, during all the time we were together, with great probity, care and diligence : as one strongly attached to your interest, and strictly observant of discipline. This testimony I willingly give him : and I do it with all the fidelity I owe you.

## LXXXVI A

### To the Emperor Trajan

After having experienced, Sir, in Gabius Bassus, Prefect of the Pontic shore, the greatest integrity, honour and vigilance, as well as the most particular respect to myself, I cannot refuse him my best wishes and suffrage ; and I give them to him with all that fidelity which is due to you.

## LXXXVI B

### To the Emperor Trajan

I warmly recommend Fabius Valens, who learned a soldier's duty under you ; to which training it is owing that he merits the honour of your favour. The soldiery and the people here, who have had full experience of his justice and humanity, endeavour to rival each other in that glorious testimony they give of him, as well in public as in private ; and I notify this with all the sincerity you have a right to expect from me.

# THE LETTERS OF PLINY

## LXXXVII

### C. PLINIUS TRAIANO IMPERATORI

NYMPHIDIUM LUPUM, domine, primipilarem com-
militonem habui, cum ipse tribunus essem, ille
praefectus. Inde familiariter diligere coepi. Crevit
postea caritas ipsa mutuae vetustate amicitiae.
Itaque et quieti eius inieci manum et exegi, ut me
in Bithynia consilio instrueret. Quod ille amicissime
et otii et senectutis ratione postposita et iam fecit et
facturus est. Quibus ex causis necessitudines eius
inter meas numero, filium in primis, Nymphidium
Lupum, iuvenem probum, industrium et egregio
patre dignissimum, suffecturum indulgentiae tuae,
sicut primis eius experimentis cognoscere potes, cum
praefectus cohortis plenissimum testimonium meruerit Iuli Ferocis et Fusci Salinatoris, clarissimorum
virorum. Meum gaudium, domine, meam gratulationem filii honores continebis.[1]

---

[1] continebis *Catan.*, continerent *Av.*, a.

---

*a i.e.* (probably) of the camp, not of a cohort, like his son.
(see below). "Since the time of Domitian each legion had
a separate camp, and accordingly a separate *praefectu*

## LXXXVII

### To the Emperor Trajan

Nymphidius Lupus, Sir, formerly a chief centurion, was my comrade in arms; he was prefect <sup>a</sup> at the same time that I was military tribune: and it was from thence my affection for him began. A long acquaintance hath since mutually endeared and strengthened our friendship. For this reason I did violence to his repose, and insisted upon his attending me in Bithynia, as my assessor in council. He most readily granted me this proof of his friendship; and without any regard to the plea of age, or the ease of retirement, he has shared with me the fatigue of business; and upon all occasions is still ready to give me his assistance. I look upon his relations therefore as my own; in which number Nymphidius Lupus, his son, claims my particular notice. He is a youth of great merit and indefatigable application; and in every view of his character, well worthy of so excellent a father. That he is equal to any honour you shall think proper to confer upon him, the early proof he gave of his qualifications will easily convince you; as his conduct as prefect of a cohort gained him the full applause of those most illustrious personages, Julius Ferox, and Fuscus Salinator. And I will add, Sir, that any increase of dignity which he shall receive, will be an occasion of particular congratulation to myself.

*castrorum* . . . usually appointed from the *primipilares*." (Hardy.)

## LXXXVIII

### C. Plinius Traiano Imperatori

Opto, domine, et hunc natalem et plurimos alios quam felicissimos agas aeternaque laude florentem virtutis tuae gloriam et incolumis et fortis aliis super alia operibus augeas.

## LXXXIX

### Traianus Plinio

Agnosco vota tua, mi Secunde carissime, quibus precaris, ut plurimos et felicissimos natales florente statu rei publicae nostrae agam.

## XC

### C. Plinius Traiano Imperatori

Sinopenses, domine, aqua deficiuntur; quae videtur et bona et copiosa ab sextodecimo miliario posse perduci. Est tamen statim ab capite paulo amplius mille passibus locus suspectus et mollis, quem ego interim explorari modico impendio iussi, an recipere et sustinere opus possit. Pecunia curantibus nobis contracta non deerit, si tu, domine, hoc genus operis et salubritati et amoenitati valde sitientis coloniae indulseris.

## LXXXVIII

### To the Emperor Trajan

May this and many succeeding birthdays be attended, Sir, with the highest felicity to you; and may you, in the midst of an uninterrupted course of health and prosperity, be still adding to the increase of that immortal glory which your virtues justly merit.

## LXXXIX

### Trajan to Pliny

Your wishes, my dear Pliny, for my enjoyment of many happy birthdays amidst the glory and prosperity of the republic, were extremely agreeable to me.

## XC

### To the Emperor Trajan

The city of Sinope is ill supplied, Sir, with water, which, however, may be brought thither from about sixteen miles' distance in great plenty and perfection. The ground indeed, near the source of this spring, is for something more than a mile of a very suspicious and marshy nature; but I have directed an examination to be made (which will be done at a small expense) whether it is capable of bearing any superstructure. I have taken care to provide a sufficient fund for this purpose, if you shall approve, Sir, of a work so conducive to the health and amenity of this colony, greatly distressed by a scarcity of water.

## XCI

### Traianus Plinio

Ut coepisti, Secunde carissime, explora diligenter,
an locus ille, quem suspectum habes, sustinere opus
aquae ductus possit. Neque enim dubitandum puto,
quin aqua perducenda sit in coloniam Sinopensem,
si modo et viribus suis ipsa id adsequi potest, cum
plurimum ea res et salubritati et voluptati eius
collatura sit.

## XCII

### C. Plinius Traiano Imperatori

Amisenorum civitas et libera et foederata beneficio
indulgentiae tuae legibus suis utitur. In hac datum
mihi publice libellum ad eranos pertinentem his
litteris subieci, ut tu, domine, dispiceres, quid et
quatenus aut permittendum aut prohibendum
putares.

## XCIII

### Traianus Plinio

Amisenos, quorum libellum epistulae tuae iunxeras,
si legibus istorum, quibus de officio foederis utuntur,
concessum est eranum habere, possumus, quo minus
habeant, non impedire, eo facilius, si tali collatione,
non ad turbas et illicitos coetus, sed ad sustinendam
tenuiorum inopiam utuntur. In ceteris civitatibus,
quae nostro iure obstrictae sunt, res huius modi pro-
hibenda est.

## XCI

### Trajan to Pliny

I would have you proceed, my dear Pliny, in carefully examining, whether the ground you suspect is firm enough to support an aqueduct. For I have no manner of doubt that it is proper the city of Sinope should be supplied with water; provided their finances will bear the expense of a work so conducive to their health and pleasure.

## XCII

### To the Emperor Trajan

The free and confederate [a] city of Amisus enjoys, by your indulgence, the privilege of its own laws. A memorial being presented to me there concerning mutual benefit societies, I have enclosed it in this letter that you may consider, Sir, whether, and how far, these meetings are to be permitted or prohibited.

## XCIII

### Trajan to Pliny

With regard to the Amisenians, whose petition you had attached to your letter, if a benefit society be agreeable to the laws which they enjoy under the terms of the treaty, we cannot oppose it; especially if these contributions are employed, not for the purposes of riot and faction, but for the support of the indigent. In other cities, however, which are subject to our laws, I would have all societies of this nature prohibited.

[a] *civitas foederata* was one whose autonomy was secured to it by formal treaty.

## XCIV

### C. Plinius Traiano Imperatori

Suetonium Tranquillum, probissimum, honestissimum, eruditissimum virum, et mores eius secutus et
studia iampridem, domine, in contubernium assump-
si, tantoque magis diligere coepi, quanto hunc
propius inspexi. Huic ius trium liberorum necessarium faciunt duae causae ; nam et iudicia amicorum
promeretur et parum felix matrimonium expertus est
impetrandumque a bonitate tua per nos habet, quod
illi fortunae malignitas denegavit. Scio, domine,
quantum beneficium petam, sed peto a te, cuius in
omnibus desideriis meis plenissimam indulgentiam
experior. Potes autem colligere, quanto opere
cupiam, quod non rogarem absens, si mediocriter
cuperem.

## XCV

### Traianus Plinio

Quam parce haec beneficia tribuam, utique, mi Secunde carissime, haeret tibi, cum etiam in senatu

---

* ii. 13, note.

## XCIV

### To the Emperor Trajan

Suetonius Tranquillus, Sir, is a person of great merit and learning, as well as of noble birth. I was so much pleased with his turn and manners, that I long since made him one of my intimates; and my affection for him still increased the more I discovered of his character. Two reasons concur to make the privilege which the law grants to those who have three children,[a] extremely necessary to him; he is legatee to several of his friends,[b] and has had ill success in his marriage. Those advantages therefore which nature has denied to him, he hopes to obtain from your goodness, by means of my intercession. I am thoroughly sensible, Sir, of the value of the favour I am asking; but I know I am making this request to one whose gracious compliance with all my desires I have amply experienced. How passionately I wish to obtain this favour, you will judge by my thus requesting it in my absence, which I should not have done, had it been a point wherein I am only commonly solicitous.

## XCV

### Trajan to Pliny

You cannot but know, my dear Pliny, how reserved I am in granting favours of this kind, having frequently declared in the senate, that I had not ex-

---

[b] By the *Lex Papia Poppaea* (vii. 16, note) childless persons forfeited one half of every legacy they received.

adfirmare soleam non excessisse me numerum, quem apud amplissimum ordinem suffecturum mihi professus sum. Tuo tamen desiderio subscripsi et dedisse me ius trium liberorum Suetonio Tranquillo ea condicione, qua adsuevi, referri in commentarios meos iussi.

## XCVI

### C. Plinius Traiano Imperatori

Solemne est mihi, domine, omnia, de quibus dubito, ad te referre. Quis enim potest melius vel cunctationem meam regere, vel ignorantiam instruere? Cognitionibus de Christianis interfui numquam. Ideo nescio, quid et quatenus aut puniri soleat, aut quaeri. Nec mediocriter haesitavi, sitne aliquod discrimen aetatum, an quamlibet teneri nihil a robustioribus differant, detur paenitentiae venia, an ei, qui omnino Christianus fuit, desisse non prosit, nomen ipsum, etiamsi flagitiis careat, an flagitia cohaerentia nomini puniantur.

Interim in iis, qui ad me tamquam Christiani deferebantur, hunc sum secutus modum. Interrogavi ipsos, an essent Christiani. Confitentes iterum ac tertio interrogavi supplicium minatus. Perseverantes duci iussi. Neque enim dubitabam, qualecunque esset, quod faterentur, pertinaciam certe et

ceeded the number which I assured that illustrious order I would be contented with. I have yielded, however, to your request; and have directed an article to be inserted in my register, that I have conferred upon Tranquillus, on my usual conditions, the privilege which the law grants to those who have three children.

## XCVI

### To the Emperor Trajan

It is a rule, Sir, which I inviolably observe, to refer myself to you in all my doubts; for who is more capable of guiding my uncertainty or informing my ignorance? Having never been present at any trials of the Christians, I am unacquainted with the method and limits to be observed either in examining or punishing them. Whether any difference is to be made on account of age, or no distinction allowed between the youngest and the adult; whether repentance admits to a pardon, or if a man has been once a Christian it avails him nothing to recant; whether the mere profession of Christianity, albeit without crimes, or only the crimes associated therewith are punishable—in all these points I am greatly doubtful.

In the meanwhile, the method i have observed towards those who have been denounced to me as Christians is this: I interrogated them whether they were Christians; if they confessed it I repeated the question twice again, adding the threat of capital punishment; if they still persevered, I ordered them to be executed. For whatever the nature of their creed might be, I could at least feel no doubt that

inflexibilem obstinationem debere puniri. Fuerunt alii similis amentiae ; quos, quia cives Romani erant, adnotavi in urbem remittendos.

Mox ipso tractatu, ut fieri solet, diffundente se crimine plures species inciderunt. Propositus est libellus sine auctore multorum nomina continens. Qui negabant se esse Christianos aut fuisse, cum praeeunte me deos appellarent, et imagini tuae, quam propter hoc iusseram cum simulacris numinum adferri, ture ac vino supplicarent, praeterea maledicerent Christo, quorum nihil posse cogi dicuntur, qui sunt re vera Christiani, dimittendos esse putavi. Alii ab indice nominati esse se Christianos dixerunt et mox negaverunt ; fuisse quidem, sed desiisse, quidam ante triennium, quidam ante plures annos, non nemo etiam ante viginti quinque.[1] Omnes et imaginem tuam deorumque simulacra venerati sunt : et Christo maledixerunt.

Adfirmabant autem hanc fuisse summam vel culpae suae vel erroris, quod essent soliti stato die ante lucem convenire carmenque Christo quasi deo dicere secum invicem seque sacramento non in scelus aliquod obstringere, sed ne furta, ne latrocinia, ne adulteria committerent, ne fidem fallerent, ne

---

[1] viginti quinque *Rittershusius*, quoque *a*, *Av*.

*a* Except by special delegation of the Emperor's own jurisdiction, no provincial governor had power to inflict the death

contumacy and inflexible obstinacy deserved chastisement. There were others also possessed with the
same infatuation, but being citizens of Rome,[a] I
directed them to be carried thither.

These accusations spread (as is usually the case)
from the mere fact of the matter being investigated
and several forms of the mischief came to light.
A placard was put up, without any signature, accusing
a large number of persons by name. Those who
denied they were, or had ever been, Christians,
who repeated after me an invocation to the Gods,
and offered adoration, with wine and frankincense,
to your image, which I had ordered to be brought for
that purpose, together with those of the Gods, and
who finally cursed Christ—none of which acts, it is
said, those who are really Christians can be forced
into performing—these I thought it proper to
discharge. Others who were named by that informer at first confessed themselves Christians, and
then denied it; true, they had been of that persuasion
but they had quitted it, some three years, others
many years, and a few as much as twenty-five years
ago. They all worshipped your statue and the images
of the Gods, and cursed Christ.

They affirmed, however, the whole of their guilt,
or their error, was, that they were in the habit of
meeting on a certain fixed day before it was light,
when they sang in alternate verses a hymn to
Christ, as to a god, and bound themselves by a
solemn oath, not to any wicked deeds, but never
to commit any fraud, theft or adultery, never to
falsify their word, nor deny a trust when they

penalty on a Roman citizen, but must allow him to take his
trial at Rome. cf. St. Paul's "appeal to Caesar," Acts xxv. 11.

depositum appellati abnegarent. Quibus peractis
morem sibi discedendi fuisse rursusque coeundi ad
capiendum cibum, promiscuum tamen et innoxium ;
quod ipsum facere desiisse post edictum meum, quo
secundum mandata tua hetaerias esse vetueram. Quo
magis necessarium credidi ex duabus ancillis, quae
ministrae dicebantur, quid esset veri et per tormenta
quaerere. Sed nihil aliud inveni, quam supersti-
tionem pravam, immodicam.

Ideo dilata cognitione ad consulendum te decurri.
Visa est enim mihi res digna consultatione, maxime
propter periclitantium numerum. Multi enim
omnis aetatis, omnis ordinis, utriusque sexus etiam,
vocantur in periculum et vocabuntur. Neque enim
civitates tantum, sed vicos etiam atque agros
superstitionis istius contagio pervagata est ; quae
videtur sisti et corrigi posse. Certe satis constat,
prope iam desolata templa coepisse celebrari, et sacra
solemnia diu intermissa repeti : passimque venire
victimas, quarum adhuc rarissimus emptor invenie-
batur. Ex quo facile est opinari, quae turba hominum
emendari possit, si fiat paenitentiae locus.

should be called upon to deliver it up; after which it was their custom to separate, and then re-assemble to partake of food—but food of an ordinary and innocent kind.[a] Even this practice, however, they had abandoned after the publication of my edict, by which, according to your orders, I had forbidden political associations.[b] I judged it so much the more necessary to extract the real truth, with the assistance of torture, from two female slaves, who were styled *deaconesses*: but I could discover nothing more than depraved and excessive superstition.

I therefore adjourned the proceedings, and betook myself at once to your counsel. For the matter seemed to me well worth referring to you,—especially considering the numbers endangered. Persons of all ranks and ages, and of both sexes are, and will be, involved in the prosecution. For this contagious superstition is not confined to the cities only, but has spread through the villages and rural districts; it seems possible, however, to check and cure it. 'Tis certain at least that the temples, which had been almost deserted, begin now to be frequented; and the sacred festivals, after a long intermission, are again revived; while there is a general demand for sacrificial animals, which for some time past have met with but few purchasers. From hence it is easy to imagine what multitudes may be reclaimed from this error, if a door be left open to repentance.

[a] Like the medieval Jews, the early Christians were suspected of ritually murdering children, and even of drinking their blood at these " love feasts."
[b] On *hetaeriae* see x. 33 note.

## XCVII

### Traianus Plinio

Actum quem debuisti, mi Secunde, in excutiendis causis eorum, qui Christiani ad te delati fuerant, secutus es. Neque enim in universum aliquid, quod quasi certam formam habeat, constitui potest. Conquirendi non sunt; si deferantur et arguantur, puniendi sunt, ita tamen, ut, qui negaverit se Christianum esse idque re ipsa manifestum fecerit, id est supplicando diis nostris, quamvis suspectus in praeteritum fuerit, veniam ex paenitentia impetret. Sine auctore vero propositi libelli nullo crimine locum habere debent. Nam et pessimi exempli, nec nostri saeculi est.

## XCVIII

### C. Plinius Traiano Imperatori

Amastrianorum civitas, domine, et elegans et ornata habet inter praecipua opera pulcherrimam eandemque longissimam plateam; cuius a latere per spatium omne porrigitur nomine quidem flumen, re vera cloaca foedissima; quae sicut turpis et immundissima aspectu, ita pestilens est odore taeterrimo. Quibus ex causis non minus salubritatis quam decoris

## XCVII

### TRAJAN TO PLINY

THE method you have pursued, my dear Pliny, in sifting the cases of those denounced to you as Christians is extremely proper. It is not possible to lay down any general rule which can be applied as the fixed standard in all cases of this nature. No search should be made for these people; when they are denounced and found guilty they must be punished; with the restriction, however, that when the party denies himself to be a Christian, and shall give proof that he is not (that is, by adoring our Gods) he shall be pardoned on the ground of repentance, even though he may have formerly incurred suspicion. Informations without the accuser's name subscribed must not be admitted in evidence against anyone, as it is introducing a very dangerous precedent, and by no means agreeable to the spirit of the age.

## XCVIII

### TO THE EMPEROR TRAJAN

THE elegant and beautiful city of Amastris, Sir, has among other capital buildings a most noble and extensive piazza. On one entire side of this structure runs what is called indeed a river, but in fact is no other than a vile common sewer, extremely offensive to the eye, and at the same time very unwholesome by its noxious smell. It will be advantageous therefore in point of health, as well as

interest eam contegi ; quod fiet, si permiseris, curantibus nobis, ne desit quoque pecunia operi tam magno, quam necessario.

## XCIX

### Traianus Plinio

Rationis est, mi Secunde carissime, contegi aquam istam, quae per civitatem Amastrianorum fluit, si intecta salubritati obest. Pecunia ne huic operi desit, curaturum te secundum diligentiam tuam certum habeo.

## C

### C. Plinius Traiano Imperatori

Vota, domine, priorum annorum nuncupata alacres laetique persolvimus novaque rursus certante [1] commilitonum et provincialium pietate, suscepimus precati deos, ut te remque publicam florentem et incolumem ea benignitate servarent, quam super magnas plurimasque virtutes praecipua sanctitate, obsequio,[2] deorum honore meruisti.

[1] certante *Cellarius*, curante *a*, *Av.*
[2] obsequio *Beroaldus*, obsequi *a*, *Av.*

ornament, to have it covered; which shall be done, with your permission : as I will take care, on my part, that money be not wanting for executing so noble and necessary a work.

## XCIX

### Trajan to Pliny

It is highly reasonable, my dear Pliny, if the water which runs through the city of Amastris is prejudicial to the health of the inhabitants while open, that it should be covered. I am well assured you will, with your usual application, take care that the money necessary for this work shall not be wanting.

## C

### To the Emperor Trajan

We have paid, Sir, with great joy and alacrity, the vows which we offered up for you the last year; and have again publicly renewed them, the army and provincials vying with each other in demonstrations of loyalty. We implored the Gods to preserve you and the commonwealth in safety and prosperity, with that peculiar favour, which not only your other many and great virtues, but particularly your distinguished piety and reverence of them, deserve.

## CI

### Traianus Plinio

Solvisse vota dis immortalibus te praeeunte pro mea incolumitate commilitones cum provincialibus laetissimo consensu et in futurum nuncupasse libenter, mi Secunde carissime, cognovi litteris tuis.

## CII

### C. Plinius Traiano Imperatori

Diem, quo in te[1] tutela generis humani felicissima successione translata est, debita religione celebravimus commendantes dis imperii tui auctoribus et vota publica et gaudia.

## CIII

### Traianus Plinio

Diem imperii mei debita laetitia et religione a commilitonibus et provincialibus praeeunte te celebratum libenter, mi Secunde carissime, cognovi litteris tuis.

[1] quo in te *B*, in quem α.

## CI

### TRAJAN TO PLINY

IT was very agreeable to me, my dear Pliny, to learn by your letter, that the army and the provincials seconded you with great joy and unanimity in those vows which you paid and renewed to the immortal Gods for my welfare.

## CII

### TO THE EMPEROR TRAJAN

WE have celebrated, with all the devotion we ought, the day in which, by a very happy succession, the protection of mankind was transferred to you; commending to the Gods, from whom you received the empire, our public vows and congratulations.

## CIII

### TRAJAN TO PLINY

I WAS extremely well pleased to be informed by your letter, my dear Pliny, that you had, at the head of the soldiers and the provincials, solemnized my accession to the empire, with all due joy and devotion.

## CIV

### C. PLINIUS TRAIANO IMPERATORI

VALERIUS, domine, Paulinus, excepto uno[1] ius Latinorum suorum mihi reliquit; ex quibus rogo tribus interim ius Quiritium des. Vereor enim, ne sit immodicum pro omnibus pariter invocare indulgentiam tuam, qua debeo tanto modestius uti, quanto pleniorem experior. Sunt autem, pro quibus peto, C. Valerius Astraeus, C. Valerius Dionysius, C. Valerius Aper.

## CV

### TRAIANUS PLINIO

CUM honestissime iis, qui apud fidem tuam a Valerio Paulino depositi sunt, consultum velis, matura per me. Iis interim, quibus nunc petisti, dedisse me ius Quiritium referri in commentarios meos iussi idem facturus in ceteris, pro quibus petieris.

---

[1] excepto uno *Bipons*; excepto [Paulino] uno *a*; excepto Paul. *Av.*, *Müller*.

---

[a] Lit. "his Latini." By a law passed 19 A.D., freedmen over thirty years old who were formally manumitted by

# BOOK X. civ.—cv

## CIV

### To the Emperor Trajan

Valerius Paulinus, Sir, having left me his right
of patronage over all his freedmen,[a] except one, I
intreat you to grant full Roman citizenship to three
of them. To desire you to extend this favour to
them all, would, I fear, be too unreasonable a trespass
upon your indulgence; which, as I have amply
experienced, I ought to be so much the more
cautious in troubling. The persons for whom I
make this request are, C. Valerius Astraeus, C.
Valerius Dionysius, and C. Valerius Aper.

## CV

### Trajan to Pliny

As it is very generous of you to consult the
interest of those whom Valerius Paulinus has con-
fided to your trust, I cannot but encourage your
good intentions. I have meanwhile given full
Roman citizenship to those persons for whom you
requested it, and have directed the grant to be
registered: I am ready to do the same for the rest,
whenever you shall desire me.

Roman citizens, became full citizens themselves; failing any
one of these three conditions they gained only the partial
citizenship known as the "Latin" franchise, and were
called *Latini Juniani* from the title of the law in question
(*lex Junia Norbana*).

413

## CVI

### C. Plinius Traiano Imperatori

Rogatus, domine, a P. Accio Aquila, centurione cohortis sextae equestris, ut mitterem tibi libellum, per quem indulgentiam pro statu filiae suae implorat, durum putavi negare, cum scirem, quantam soleres militum precibus patientiam humanitatemque praestare.

## CVII

### Traianus Plinio

Libellum P. Accii Aquilae, centurionis cohortis sextae equestris, quem misisti, legi; cuius precibus motus dedi filiae eius civitatem Romanam. Libellum rescripti, quem illi redderes, misi tibi.

## CVIII

### C. Plinius Traiano Imperatori

Quid habere iuris velis et Bithynas et Ponticas civitates in exigendis pecuniis, quae illis vel ex locationibus vel ex venditionibus aliisve causis debeantur, rogo, domine, rescribas. Ego inveni

## CVI

### To the Emperor Trajan

P. Accius Aquila, centurion of the sixth equestrian cohort, requested me, Sir, to transmit his petition to you concerning the status of his daughter.[a] I thought it would be unkind to refuse him this good office, knowing, as I do, with what patience and humanity you receive the petitions of the soldiers.

## CVII

### Trajan to Pliny

I have read the petition of P. Accius Aquila, centurion of the sixth equestrian cohort, which you sent to me; and in compliance with his request, I have given his daughter the freedom of the city of Rome. I send you at the same time the patent, which you will deliver to him.

## CVIII

### To the Emperor Trajan

I beg, Sir, you would inform me what rights you wish assigned to the cities of Bithynia and Pontus with regard to recovering their debts, either for rent, or goods sold, or upon any other consideration. I

[a] Accius was an alien who had received Roman citizenship, but under conditions which left his daughter an alien. See Hardy's note.

a plerisque proconsulibus concessam eis protopraxian,
eamque pro lege valuisse. Existimo tamen tua
providentia constituendum aliquid et sanciendum,
per quod utilitatibus eorum in perpetuum consulatur.
Nam, quae sunt ab aliis instituta, sint licet sapienter
indulta, brevia tamen et infirma sunt, nisi illis tua
contingat auctoritas.

## CIX

### Traianus Plinio

Quo iure uti debeant Bithynae vel Ponticae
civitates in iis pecuniis, quae ex quaque causa rei
publicae debebuntur, ex lege cuiusque animadvertendum est. Nam, sive habent privilegium, quo
ceteris creditoribus anteponantur, custodiendum est,
sive non habent, in iniuriam privatorum id dari a me
non oportebit.

## CX

### C. Plinius Traiano Imperatori

Ecdicus, domine, Amisenorum civitatis petebat
apud me a Iulio Pisone denariorum circiter XL milia
donata ei publice ante XX annos bule et ecclesia

find they have a privilege granted to them by several Proconsuls, of being preferred to other creditors; and this custom has prevailed, as if it had been established by law. Your prudence, I imagine, will think it necessary to enact some settled rule, by which their advantage may always be secured. For the ordinances of others, however wisely conceded, are but feeble and temporary expedients, unless confirmed by your authority.

## CIX

### Trajan to Pliny

THE rule by which the cities either of Pontus or Bithynia are to be governed, in the recovery of debts of whatever kind, due to their several communities, must be determined agreeably to their respective laws. Where any of them enjoy the privilege of being preferred to other creditors, it must be observed; but, where no such privilege prevails, it is not just I should establish one, in prejudice of private property.

## CX

### To the Emperor Trajan

THE solicitor to the treasury[a] of the city of Amisus laid a claim, Sir, before me against Julius Piso of about 40,000 denarii, which were given him by the public above twenty years ago, with the

[a] "The *ecdicus* was a public prosecutor in financial matters. We only know of the title in connection with Asia Minor." (Hardy.)

417

consentiente utebaturque mandatis tuis, quibus eius
modi donationes vetantur. Piso contra plurima se
in rempublicam contulisse ac prope totas facultates
erogasse dicebat. Addebat etiam temporis spatium
postulabatque, ne id, quod pro multis et olim accepisset, cum eversione reliquae dignitatis reddere
cogeretur. Quibus ex causis integram cognitionem
differendam existimavi, ut te, domine, consulerem
quid sequendum putares.

## CXI

### TRAIANUS PLINIO

SICUT largitiones ex publico fieri mandata pro-
hibent, ita, ne multorum securitas subruatur, factas
ante aliquantum temporis retractari atque in irritum
vindicari non oportet. Quidquid ergo ex hac causa
actum ante viginti annos erit, omittamus. Non
minus enim hominibus cuiusque loci, quam pecuniae
publicae consultum volo.

consent of the general council and assembly of the city; and he founded his demand upon certain of your edicts by which donations of this kind are prohibited. Piso, on the other hand, asserted that he had conferred large sums of money upon the community, and, indeed, had expended that way almost his whole estate. He insisted upon the length of time which had intervened since this donation, and hoped that he should not be compelled, to the ruin of the remainder of his fortunes, to refund a sum, which had been granted him long since, in return for many good offices he had done to the city. For this reason, Sir, I thought it necessary to suspend giving any judgement in this cause, till I shall receive your directions.

## CXI

### TRAJAN TO PLINY

THOUGH by my edicts I have ordained, that no largesses shall be given out of the public money; yet, that numberless private persons may not be disturbed in the secure possession of their fortunes, those donations which have been made long since, ought not to be called in question or revoked. We will not, therefore, inquire into any thing that has been transacted in this affair so long ago as twenty years; for I would be no less attentive to secure the repose of every private man, than the treasure of every public community.

## CXII

### C. Plinius Traiano Imperatori

Lex Pompeia, domine, qua Bithyni et Pontici
utuntur, eos, qui in bulen a censoribus leguntur,
dare pecuniam non iubet ; sed ii, quos indulgentia
tua quibusdam civitatibus super legitimum numerum
adicere permisit, et singula milia denariorum et bina
intulerunt. Anicius deinde Maximus proconsul eos
etiam, qui a censoribus legerentur, dumtaxat in
paucissimis civitatibus aliud aliis iussit inferre.
Superest ergo, ut ipse dispicias, an in omnibus
civitatibus certum aliquid omnes, qui deinde buleutae
leguntur, debeant pro introitu dare. Nam quod in
perpetuum mansurum est, a te constitui decet, cuius
factis dictisque debetur aeternitas.

## CXIII

### Traianus Plinio

Honorarium decurionatus omnes, qui in quaque
civitate Bithyniae decuriones fiunt, inferre debeant
necne, in universum a me non potest statui. Id ergo
quod semper tutissimum est, sequendam cuiusque

# CXII

## To the Emperor Trajan

THE Pompeian law, Sir, which is observed in
Pontus and Bithynia, does not direct that any
money should be given by those who are elected
into the public council by the Censors. It has
however been usual for such members as have been
admitted into those assemblies, in pursuance of the
privilege which you were pleased to grant to some
particular cities, of receiving above their legal
number, to pay one or two thousand denarii.
Subsequent to this, the Proconsul Anicius Maximus
ordained (though indeed his edict extended to some
few cities only) that those who were elected by the
Censors should also pay into the treasury a certain
sum, which varied in different places. It remains,
therefore, for your consideration whether it would
not be proper for all the cities to settle a certain sum
for each member, who is elected into the council, to
pay upon his entrance; for it well becomes you,
whose every word and action deserves immortality,
to give laws that shall for ever be permanent.

# CXIII

## Trajan to Pliny

I CAN give no general directions applicable to all
the cities of Bithynia, whether those who are made
members of their respective councils shall pay an
honorary fee upon their admittance, or not. It
seems best therefore, in this case (what indeed upon

civitatis legem puto ; scilicet adversus eos, qui inviti
fiunt decuriones, id existimo acturos, ut erogatio
ceteris praeferatur.

## CXIV

### C. PLINIUS TRAIANO IMPERATORI

LEGE, domine, Pompeia, permissum Bithynicis
civitatibus adscribere sibi, quos vellent, cives, dum
ne quem earum civitatum[1] quae sunt in Bithynia.
Eadem lege sancitur, quibus de causis e senatu censoribus eiciantur. Inde me quidam ex censoribus
consulendum putaverunt, an eicere deberent eum,
qui esset alterius civitatis. Ego, quia lex sicut
adscribi civem alienum vetabat, ita eici e senatu ob
hanc causam non iubebat, praeterea quia ab aliquibus
adfirmabatur mihi, in omni civitate plurimos esse
buleutas ex aliis civitatibus, futurumque ut multi
homines multaeque civitates concuterentur ea parte
legis, quae iampridem consensu quodam exolevisset,
necessarium existimavi consulere te, quid servandum
putares. Capita legis his litteris subieci.

---

[1] dum ne quem earum civ., *B*, dum neque merum civ., *Av.*

* lxxix. note

all occasions is the safest way), to leave each city to
its respective laws. But I think, however, that the
Censors ought to set the sum lower to those who are
chosen into the senate contrary to their inclinations,
than to the rest.

## CXIV

### To the Emperor Trajan

The Pompeian law,[a] Sir, allows the Bithynians to
give the freedom of their respective cities to whatever persons they think proper, provided they do
not already belong to any of the cities of this
province.[b] The same law specifies the particular
causes for which the Censors may expel any member
of the senate. Certain of the Censors accordingly
have desired my sentiments, whether they ought to
expel a member if he should happen to be a citizen
of another Bithynian state. But I thought it
necessary to receive your instructions in this case;
not only because the law, though it forbids such
persons to be admitted citizens, does not direct a
senator to be expelled for the same reason, but
because I am informed that there are in every city
several members of their senate who are in these
circumstances. If therefore this clause of the law,
which seems to be antiquated by a long custom to
the contrary, should be enforced, many cities, as well
as private persons, will be thrown into great confusion.
I have subjoined the heads of this law to my letter.

[b] The rule that a man could not be citizen of more than
one city was often contravened in practice, and difficulties
and confusion necessarily resulted.

## CXV

### TRAIANUS PLINIO

MERITO haesisti, Secunde carissime, quid a te
responderi oporteret censoribus consulentibus, an
legerent in senatum aliarum civitatium, eiusdem
tamen provinciae cives. Nam et legis auctoritas et
longa consuetudo usurpata contra legem in diversum
movere te potuit. Mihi hoc temperamentum eius
placuit, ut ex praeterito nihil novaremus, sed mane-
rent quamvis contra legem adsciti quarumcunque
civitatium cives, in futurum autem lex Pompeia ob-
servaretur; cuius vim si retro quoque velimus custodire, multa necesse est perturbari.

## CXVI

### C. PLINIUS TRAIANO IMPERATORI

QUI virilem togam sumunt vel nuptias faciunt vel
ineunt magistratum vel opus publicum dedicant,
solent totam bulen atque etiam e plebe non exiguum
numerum vocare binosque denarios vel singulos dare.
Quod an celebrandum et quatenus putes, rogo
scribas. Ipse enim sicut arbitror, praesertim ex

# BOOK X. cxv.–cxvi

## CXV

### Trajan to Pliny

You might very reasonably, my dear Pliny, be doubtful what decision to give to the inquiry of the Censors; whether they might elect into the senate citizens of other cities though of the same province? The authority of law on one side, and long custom prevailing against it on the other, might well throw you into a state of suspense. The proper mean to observe in this case, will be, to make no change in what is past, but to suffer those senators who are already elected, though contrary to law, to keep their seats, to whatever city they may belong; in all future elections, however, to pursue the directions of the Pompeian law: for to extend its influence backwards, must necessarily introduce great confusion.

## CXVI

### To the Emperor Trajan

It is customary here upon any person's taking the manly robe,[a] solemnizing his marriage, entering upon the office of a magistrate, or dedicating any public work, to invite the whole senate, together with a considerable part of the commonalty, and distribute to each of the company one or two denarii. I beg you would inform me, whether you think proper this ceremony should be observed, and if so, within what limits. For myself, though I am of opinion that

[a] i. 9, note.

425

solemnibus causis, concedendas iussisti invitationes,[1]
ita vereor, ne ii, qui mille homines, interdum etiam
plures vocant, modum excedere et in speciem
dianomes incidere videantur.

## CXVII

### TRAIANUS PLINIO

MERITO vereris, ne in speciem dianomes incidat
invitatio, quae et in numero modum excedit et
quasi per corpora, non viritim singulos ex notitia ad
solemnes sportulas contrahit. Sed ego ideo prudentiam tuam elegi, ut formandis istius provinciae
moribus ipse moderareris et ea constituas, quae ad
perpetuam eius provinciae quietem essent profutura.

## CXVIII

### C. PLINIUS TRAIANO IMPERATORI

ATHLETAE, domine, ea, quae pro iselasticis certaminibus constituisti, deberi sibi putant statim ex

---

[1] concedendas iussisti invitationes *Hardy*, concedendum
iussisti B, *Budaeus*, concedendum iussi invit. *a*, concedendas
esse invit. *Orelli*.

---

*a* *dianome* (Gr. διανομή, "distribution") here means "distribution of bribes," such as was made by candidates through
their agents.
*b* Iselastic (Gr. εἰσελαστικός, "of entry") games were those
which entitled the victors to make a triumphal entry into

426

upon some occasions, especially those of public festivals, this kind of invitations may be permitted; yet when they are carried so far as to draw together a thousand persons and sometimes more, it is going, I fear, beyond a reasonable number, and has something the appearance of ambitious largesses.[a]

## CXVII

### TRAJAN TO PLINY

IT is with justice you apprehend, that these public invitations, which extend to an unreasonable number of people, and where the dole is distributed, not singly to a few acquaintances, but as it were to whole collective bodies, may be turned to turbulent purposes of ambition. But I made choice of your prudence, expressly that you might take your own measures for regulating the manner and settling the peace of this province.

## CXVIII

### TO THE EMPEROR TRAJAN

THE Athletic victors, Sir, in the iselastic games,[b] think they ought to receive the pension you have established for the conquerors at those combats from their native city, in a chariot of state, which was driven through a breach in the walls made for the occasion. These honours were originally confined to victors at the four great Hellenic games (the Olympic, Pythian, Isthmian, Nemean); but in Imperial times it appears that any games could become, or cease to be, iselastic at the Emperor's pleasure. Iselastic victors had always received a pension, or free maintenance, for life from their cities; Trajan had increased these (probably daily) allowances. (Hardy.)

eo die, quo sunt coronati ; nihil enim referre, quando sint patriam invecti, sed quando certamine vicerint, ex quo invehi possint. Ego contrascribo [1] 'iselastici nomine' ita ut [2] vehementer addubitem, an sit potius id tempus, quo εἰσήλασαν, intuendum. Iidem obsonia petunt pro eo agone, qui a te iselasticus factus est, quamvis vicerint, ante quam fieret. Aiunt enim congruens esse, sicut non detur sibi pro iis certaminibus, quae esse iselastica, postquam vicerunt, desierunt, ita pro iis dari, quae esse coeperunt. Hic quoque non mediocriter haereo, ne cuiusquam retro habeatur ratio, dandumque, quod tunc, cum vincerent, non debebatur. Rogo ergo, ut dubitationem meam regere, id est beneficia tua interpretari, ipse digneris.

## CXIX

### Traianus Plinio

Iselasticum tunc primum mihi videtur incipere deberi, cum quis in civitatem suam ipse εἰσήλασεν. Obsonia eorum certaminum, quae iselastica esse placuit mihi, si ante iselastica non fuerunt, retro non

---

[1] Ego contrascribo 'iselastici nomine' *Orelli, ex a, Av.*, Ego contra scribo is. nom.

[2] ita ut *Beroaldus*, itaque eorum *a, Av.*

the day they are crowned: for it is not at all material, they say, when they may be triumphantly conducted into their city, but when they merit that honour by their conquest. I habitually countersign the drafts for payment with the words "under the head of iselastic money," so that I am strongly inclined to believe that the time of their public entry is to be alone considered. They likewise petition to be allowed the pension you give at those combats which you have made iselastic, though they were conquerors before that establishment took place: for it is but reasonable, they assert, that they should receive their rewards in this case, as they are deprived of them at those games which have been divested of the honour of being iselastic, since their victories. But I am extremely doubtful, whether a retrospect should be admitted in this case, and a reward given to which they had no right at the time they gained the victory. I beg therefore you would be pleased to direct my judgement in these points, by explaining the intention of your own benefactions.

## CXIX

### Trajan to Pliny

The reward proposed to the conqueror in the iselastic games, is not, I think due till he makes his public entry into his city. Nor at those combats which I have thought proper to make iselastic, ought pensions to be extended backwards to those

debentur. Nec proficere pro desiderio athletarum
potest quod eorum quae postea iselastica non esse
constitui, quam vicerant[1] accipere desierunt. Mutata enim condicione certaminum nihilo minus,
quae ante perceperant, non revocantur.

## CXX

### C. PLINIUS TRAIANO IMPERATORI

USQUE in hoc tempus, domine, neque cuiquam
diplomata commodavi neque in rem ullam nisi tuam
misi. Quam perpetuam servationem meam quaedam
necessitas rupit. Uxori enim meae audita morte avi
volenti ad amitam suam excurrere usum eorum
negare durum putavi, cum talis officii gratia in
celeritate consisteret, sciremque te rationem itineris
probaturum, cuius causa erat pietas. Haec scripsi,
quia mihi parum gratus tibi fore videbar, si dissimu-
lassem inter alia beneficia hoc unum me debere
indulgentiae tuae, quod fiducia eius quasi consulto te
non dubitavi facere, quem si consuluissem, sero
fecissem.

[1] quod eorum quae postea iselastica non esse constitui, quam
vicerant *Schaefer*, quid eorum q. p. is. non lege const., quam
qui ierant *a*.

who conquered there before that alteration took place. Nor is it a point in their favour that they have ceased to receive the emolument for those games which subsequent to their victories I have ordained are not to be iselastic; since, notwithstanding any change which has been made relating to these games, they are not called upon to return the recompense which they received prior to such alteration.

## CXX

### To the Emperor Trajan

I HAVE never, Sir, accommodated any person with an order for post chaises,[a] or dispatched a courier provided with one, except upon your affairs. I find myself however at present under a sort of necessity of breaking through this fixed rule. My wife having received an account of her grandfather's[b] death, and being desirous to wait upon her aunt[c] with all possible expedition, I thought it would be unkind to deny her the use of this privilege; as the grace of so tender an office consists in the early discharge of it, and as I well knew a journey which was founded in filial piety, could not fail of your approbation. I have informed you of this, as I should think myself highly ungrateful, were I to dissemble, that among other great obligations which I owe to your indulgence, I have this in particular, that in confidence of your favour I have ventured to do without consulting you, what would have been too late had I waited for your consent.

[a] x. 45.    [b] Fabatus.    [c] Hispulla.

## CXXI

### Traianus Plinio

Merito habuisti, Secunde carissime, fiduciam animi mei. Nec dubitandum fuisset, si exspectasses, donec me consuleres, an iter uxoris tuae diplomatibus, quae officio tuo dedi, adiuvandum esset, usum eorum intentioni non profuisse, cum apud amitam suam uxor tua deberet etiam celeritate gratiam adventus sui augere.

## CXXI

### Trajan to Pliny

You did me justice, my dear Pliny, by confiding in my affection towards you. Without doubt, if you had waited for my consent to forward your wife in her journey by means of those warrants which I have intrusted to your care, the use of them would not have answered your purpose; since it was proper this visit to her aunt should have the additional recommendation, of being paid with all possible expedition.

# BIOGRAPHICAL INDEX

## OF NOTABLE PERSONS ADDRESSED OR MENTIONED BY PLINY

ARRIA THE ELDER (III. 16; VI. 24), wife to Caecina Paetus, crowned an heroic life by showing her condemned husband how to die, A.D. 42 (*see* III. 16, note). Her daughter,

ARRIA THE YOUNGER (III. 11, 16; VII. 19; IX. 13), was already married to Thrasea Paetus at the time of her mother's death, which she wished to emulate twenty-four years later, when Thrasea was condemned for treason to Nero (66 A.D.). But he persuaded her to live for the sake of their daughter Fannia (*q.v.*). Banished by Domitian, Arria returned with the other political exiles on Nerva's accession (96 A.D.). Her death occurred some time before that of Fannia (VII. 19), but the date is unknown.

ARULENUS RUSTICUS, L. JUNIUS (I. 5, 14; III. 11; V. 1; IX. 29), first showed his fiery spirit when as a young man (*flagrans iuvenis cupidine laudis*, Tacitus, *Ann.* XVI. 26), being tribune of the plebs, he would have vetoed the Senate's condemnation of Thrasea Paetus, but for Thrasea's earnest representation that he would only throw away his own life by ineffectually interposing (66 A.D.). Praetor under Vitellius in 69 A.D., he was among the envoys sent by the Senate to meet Vespasian's troops; and was wounded by them while

unsuccessfully making overtures for peace (I. 5; Tac. *Hist.* III. 80). Quiescent under Vespasian and Titus, he could not brook in silence the tyranny of Domitian; he published a panegyric upon Thrasea Paetus and Helvidius Priscus which led to his execution for treason, 93 A.D. His book was publicly burned by order of the Senate (*scilicet illo igne vocem populi Romani et libertatem senatus et conscientiam generis humani aboleri arbitrabantur*, Tac. *Agric.* 2). Rusticus was doubly suspect as a disciple of Stoicism, which was supposed to foster revolutionary principles; and Suetonius (*Dom.* 10) connects his condemnation with Domitian's expulsion of all philosophers from Rome.

CORNUTUS TERTULLUS, C. JULIUS (II. 11, 12; IV. 17; V. 14; VII. 21, 31; IX. 13), Pliny's colleague in the prefecture of the treasury and in the consulship, was his senior by about twenty years. Pliny loved and revered him, and their official relations were the happiest possible (V. 14). Cornutus was given the curatorship of the Aemilian Way while Pliny was holding that of the Tiber (V. 14); later he successively governed four provinces, the second being Bithynia, where he apparently succeeded Pliny on the latter's death.

435

# BIOGRAPHICAL INDEX

Augurs. Among other high offices, he was propraetor of Britain in 75-78 A.D.; his conduct in this arduous post is praised by Tacitus (*Agric.* 17). His treatise on Strategy, another on the aqueducts of Rome, and fragments of a third on field-surveying, are still extant.

LICINIUS SURA (IV. 30; VII. 27), a native of Spain, became the trusted friend and counsellor of Trajan, whom Nerva is said to have adopted partly on Sura's advice. The success of Trajan's Dacian campaigns was largely owing to his services as chief of the staff, which the Emperor repaid with many high honours. Hadrian, who was Sura's *quaestor* during those campaigns, gained Trajan's favour through his influence; so that Sura may be said to have made two emperors. Trajan erected a statue to him after his death.

MAURICUS, JUNIUS (I. 5, 14; II. 18; III. 11; IV. 22; VI. 14), was brother to Arulenus Rusticus, and exiled in the year of his execution (93 A.D.). Recalled by Nerva, he was *persona grata* with that Emperor and with Trajan; but no more is known of his later life. He showed the bold, uncompromising character, which Pliny illustrates by two anecdotes (IV. 22), at an early age; first by reproving public lawlessness under Galba (Plutarch, *Galba* 8), and again, on Vespasian's accession, by seeking to prosecute the informers of Nero's time. Pliny addresses three letters (I. 14; II. 18; VI. 14) to Mauricus, who evidently treated him as a valued friend of the family.

METTIUS CARUS (I. 5; VII. 19, 27), pilloried for ever as the typical informer by Tacitus, Martial and Juvenal, is said by the scholiast on the last-named to

have been a dwarf, and a favourite freedman of Nero. Herennius Senecio was one of his victims under Domitian; Pliny might have been another, but for the tyrant's death (VII. 27). His end is unknown; the statement of the scholiast on Juvenal that he was himself informed against, and put to death, being invalidated by a manifest anachronism. One hopes it is so far true, that Carus did finally pay the just penalty of his crimes.

PISO, L. CALPURNIUS (III. 7), consul with Nero 57 A.D., was proconsul of Africa when killed there by Valerius Festus, 70 A.D. (*see* FESTUS). His father (" L. Piso," III. 7), consul 27 A.D., had likewise been proconsul of Africa; his grandfather was Cn. Calp. Piso, the enemy and alleged murderer of Germanicus.

PISO (L. Calp. Piso Licinianus) (II. 20), was adopted as heir by Galba on his accession, and murdered with him five days afterwards (Jan. 15, 69 A.D.). His wife, Verania, the lady pestered by Regulus (II. 20) bought her husband's head from the assassins.

PLINIUS SECUNDUS, C., THE ELDER (I. 19; III. 5; V. 8; VI. 16), our Pliny's uncle and adoptive father (see *Introd.*), was born in the middle of the reign of Tiberius and perished, a martyr to scientific curiosity, in the great eruption of Vesuvius, August 79 A.D. (VI. 16). Though his life was passed in active civil and military service in almost every province of the empire, he was the most learned man and prolific writer of his day. His voluminous works (III. 5) are lost, with the exception of his *Natural History* in thirty-seven books—" a priceless storehouse of information on every

# BIOGRAPHICAL INDEX

branch of natural science as known to the ancient world " (Mackail).

POMPEIUS FALCO, Q. (I. 23 ; IV. 27 ; VII. 22 ; IX. 15), son-in-law to Q. Sosius Senecio, had a distinguished official career under Trajan, Hadrian, and Antoninus Pius, holding several of the most important provincial governor-ships besides other high positions.

QUINTILIANUS (M. FABIUS) (II. 14 ; VI. 6, 32), was born at Calagurris, a small town of Hispania Tarraconensis, where he taught rhetoric after studying it at Rome under Domitius Afer, and became known to Galba, then proconsul of that province. On Galba being declared Emperor (68 A.D.), Quintilian accompanied him to Rome, and was made a public teacher of rhetoric, an appointment which he held for about twenty years of fame and prosperity. He died, apparently, either shortly before, or not long after, Domitian, who made him tutor to his two grand-nephews, and gave him consular ank. His great work, the *Institutio Oratoria*, appeared about 93 A.D. and " at once became the final and standard treatise on the theory and practice of Latin oratory " (Mackail).

REGULUS, M. AQUILIUS (I. 5, 20 ; II. 11, 20 ; IV. 2, 7 ; VI. 2), became notorious as an informer in the two last years of Nero, when the consulars M. Licinius Crassus Frugi and Q. Sulpicius Camerinus Peticus were executed on charges brought by him. According to Pliny (I. 5) he played an equally infamous part, though more covertly, under Domitian ; but his having virulently attacked the memory of Rusticus and Senecio seems to have been the head and front of his offending. Pliny's contem-

plated prosecution of him after Domitian's death was not carried out, whether owing to Nerva's policy of letting bygones be bygones, or because Pliny's adviser (I. 5) saw that the case against Regulus would not really hold water. Notwithstanding Pliny's ridicule, he makes it clear that Regulus was an able and eloquent advocate. Martial praises his oratory as highly as he does Pliny's, ranking both with Cicero's (Epp. IV. 16 ; v. 28, 63 ; VI. 64). Regulus died early in Trajan's reign (VI. 2), not unregretted by his old adversary.

RUSTICUS, see ARULENUS.

SENECIO, HERENNIUS, see HEREN-NIUS.

SENECIO, Q. SOSIUS (I. 13 ; IV. 4), was twice consul under Trajan, who honoured him with a statue ; but his more enduring monument is the dedication to him by Plutarch of the *Lives*. He was son-in-law to Julius Frontinus and father-in-law to Pompeius Falco.

SEPTICIUS CLARUS, C. (I. 1, 15 ; II. 9 ; VII. 28 ; VIII. 1), is only memorable as having received the dedication of two famous works. Pliny addressed to him the introductory letter (I. 1) prefixed to the first Book ; and while he was Praetorian Prefect under Hadrian, Suetonius dedicated to him his *Lives of the Twelve Caesars* (120 A.D.). Like Suetonius, who was then Hadrian's secretary, Septicius lost his office the following year, and for the same reason (see SUETONIUS).

SUETONIUS TRANQUILLUS, C. (I. 18, 24 ; III. 8 ; V. 10 ; IX. 34 ; X. 94, 95), son of an officer of the Thirteenth Legion, was born not long before 75 A.D. As a young man he practised at the bar and became an intimate friend of Pliny, his senior by

438

# BIOGRAPHICAL INDEX

some twelve years, whose influence secured him a military tribuneship (III. 8) and the *ius trium liberorum* (X. 94, 95). Suetonius was later one of Hadrian's private secretaries, but lost office and Imperial favour in 121 A.D. by failing in respect towards the Empress Sabina, and devoted the last forty years of his life to writing voluminously on grammar, rhetoric, antiquities, and the natural sciences. His works are almost entirely lost with the fortunate exception of his *Lives of the Twelve Caesars*—a *chronique scandaleuse*, but also an inestimable mine of personal detail about the early Emperors. The *Lives* can hardly have been the work referred to by Pliny in v. 10 as long overdue, since they were not published until 120 A.D.

TACITUS, CORNELIUS (I. 6; II. 1, 11; IV. 13, 15; VI. 9, 16, 20; VII. 20, 33; VIII. 7; IX. 10, 14, 23), of whose family nothing is known, was born early in Nero's reign, and began his official career, as quaestor, not later than 79 A.D., being then at least twenty-five, and already married to the daughter of Agricola. He was thus some seven years older than Pliny, whose friend and associate he became while both practised at the bar. Praetor under Domitian, 88 A.D., Tacitus rose to the consulship as Nerva's colleague, 97 A.D. In the following year he published that pearl of biographies, the memoir of Agricola, and the treatise *De Origine Situ Moribus ac Populis Germaniae*, the first fruits of his genius, with the exception of an early essay on oratory (*Dialogus de Oratoribus*). Then followed the works that have made him immortal—the *Histories* and the *Annals*, presenting the history of the Roman Empire from the death

of its founder, Augustus, down to that of Domitian. Allusions to current events in the *Annals* show that this, his latest work, was published after 115 A.D., and it seems likely that Tacitus did not long survive that date. At least, he did not live to fulfil his expressed intention of recording the happier times of Nerva and Trajan.

THRASEA PAETUS, P. FANNIUS (III. 16; VI. 29; VII. 19; VIII. 22), a native of Padua, husband of the younger Arria, and father of Fannia, took a leading part in public affairs under Claudius, and under Nero until 63 A.D., when he marked his opposition to Nero by withdrawing altogether from the Senate. Three years later he was condemned for treason, and allowed to forestall execution by suicide (*see* ARRIA and RUSTICUS). Martial (Epp. I. 8) couples Thrasea with Cato as a type of Roman Stoicism.

TRAJAN (Marcus Ulpius Trajanus) (VOL. I.: II.; III. 6; IV. 8; VI. 22, 26, 31; VOL. II.: II. 4, and X. *passim*) *b.* 52, *d.* 117 A.D. A native of Spain, on the death of Nerva became Emperor at the age of forty-four. Equally great as soldier and administrator, he stands highest among the "good Emperors"—Nerva and his four successors, under whom the ancient world enjoyed for eighty-five years the full blessings of the "Pax Romana." On his accession, the assembled populace saw him enter Rome on foot, accompanied only by his wife and some personal friends. Holding economy to be the first condition of good government, he rejected all Imperial pomp, walked about the city unattended, and lived frugally like a private citizen. Thus, without any new taxation, he financed several grand public works, and two great wars. His enormous industry, and minute

# BIOGRAPHICAL INDEX

knowledge of the details of administration throughout the Empire, comes out in his correspondence with Pliny. So does his enlightened view of provincial government. "Interfere as little as possible with local rights and customs," he says in effect; "there must be no waste or jobbery, but otherwise let the municipalities manage their own affairs." As a soldier, Trajan is still more famous. In six years of war he subdued and thoroughly Romanised the Dacians; in three years more he overthrew the great Parthian monarchy, and carried the Roman eagles as far as the Persian Gulf. At his death on his way home from that campaign, he left the Empire at its greatest extent.

VERGINIUS RUFUS (II. 1: v. 3; VI. 10; IX. 19), Pliny's guardian and second father, was the Nestor of his time. Born in the first year of Tiberius (14 A.D.) and dying in the second of Nerva (97 A.D.), he saw eleven wearers of the purple, but he prudently refused for himself in the terrible "Year of Four Emperors" (68–69 A.D.). In that year, as Legate of Upper Germany, he crushed the formidable revolt of Julius Vindex, governor of Gallia Lugdunensis, by the decisive battle of Besançon; his victorious army, casting off allegiance to Nero, then vainly urged him to proclaim himself Emperor and lead them into Italy. A few months later, when Galba's "transient and embarrassed phantom" had followed Nero to the shades, Verginius joined forces with Otho against Vitellius: and when the Vitellians won the day at Betriacum, his beaten and desperate soldiers, after once more importuning him to claim the Empire, actually demanded his death from its new master. But Vitellius, to his credit, took pains to save him (Tacitus, *Hist.* II. 68). Having weathered these storms, Verginius lived honoured and prosperous under the three Flavian Emperors; if, as Pliny seems to imply (II. 1), he was suspected and disliked by Vespasian and Domitian, neither attempted to molest him. He was thrice consul; firstly in 63 A.D. under Nero; secondly in 69 A.D. under Otho; thirdly in 97 A.D., the year of his death, when Nerva made him his colleague in that office. Pliny is better inspired than usual when he declares (II. 1) that to have his funeral eulogy pronounced by Tacitus set the coping-stone upon the good luck of Verginius.

# INDEX SIGLORUM

R (Ricc.) codex Ashburnhamensis R. 98 olim Riccardianus.

F codex S. Marci 284

M „ XLVII.36 bibliothecae Mediceo-Laurentanae.

D codex Dresdensis D. 166.

V „ Vaticanus lat. 3864.

B „ Bodleianus.

p editio princeps, 1471.

r „ Romana 1474.

Av. „ Avantii 1502.

Catan. „ Catanaei 1506.

a „ Aldina 1508.

Bip. „ Bipontina, 1789.

K¹ „ Keili 1853.

K² „ „ 1873.

K = K¹ et K².

# INDEX OF NAMES AND PLACES

## A

Abascantus, II. 293.
Accius, (1) I. 369; (2) I. 531; (3) Aquila, II. 415 and n.; (4) Sura, II. 293.
Achaea, Achaeans, II. 169, 365.
Achilles, I. 306, n., 459.
Acilianus, (1) cf. Minicius; (2) I. 149–51.
Acilius, (1) I. 51, 241; (2) Rufus, I. 435, 471.
Acutius Nerva, I. 135.
Acfulanius, cf. Marcellinus.
Aemilian (Way), I. 416, n., 417.
Aeneas, I. 528, n.
Aeschinea, I. 67, 101, 281; II. 239.
Afer, cf. Domitius.
Afranius, cf. Dexter.
Africa, I. 123, 131, 211, 215, 217; II. 69, 251, 277.
Africanus, Julius, II. 17–19.
Alba, I. 203.
Albinus, cf. Lucceius.
Alexandria, Alexandrians, I. 498, n.; II. 285 and n., 291.
Allifanus, Pontus, I. 417, 515; II. 9.
Alsium, I. 463.
Altinum, I. 186, n., 187.
Amastris, II. 407–9.
Ameria, II. 155.
Amisus, II. 397, 417.
Ammius, cf. Flaccus.
Ancharia, cf. Soteris.
Andalusia, cf. Baetica.
Anicius Maximus, II. 421.
Anio, II. 143.
Annianus, I. 149.
Annius, (1) cf. Bassus; (2) Severus, I. 205, 361.
Anteia, (wife of Helvidius 2), II. 199.
Antilochus, I. 306, n.
Antonia Maximilla, II. 283 and n.
Antonius, cf. Arrius.

Antonius, Marcus (orator), I. 435.
Apamea, II. 337–9.
Apennines, I. 377, 381, 387.
Aper, (1) Flavius, I. 415; (2) Valerius, II. 413.
Apollinaris, (1) I. 117; (2) Domitius, II. 203; (3) cf. Sidonius.
Appius Maximus, II. 353.
Apuleius, II. 375.
Aquila, cf. Accius.
Aquilius, cf. Regulus.
Archippus, Flavius, II. 351–7, 385–7.
Arionilla, I. 11.
Aristo, cf. Tituus
Aristogeiton, II. 237.
Ariston, Claudius, I. 523.
Aristophanes, I. 72, n., 73, 498, n.
Armenius, cf. Brocchus.
Arria, (1) wife of Caecina Paetus (B.I.), I. 247–51, 507; (2) wife of Thrasea Paetus, (B.I.), I. 235, 250, n.; II. 197, 188, 203.
Arrianus, (1), I. 3, 123, 135, 443; II. 159; (2) Maturus, I. 187, 287, 309.
Arrius, Antoninus, I. 277, 279, 331, 351, 421.
Artemidorus, I. 233–7.
Artemisius Popilius, II. 243.
Arulenus Rusticus, (B.I.), I. xii, 10, n., 49, 235, 362, n., 363.
Asclepiades, II. 385.
Asia, Roman province, I. 279; II. 155, 363, 417.
Asinius, (1) Baesus, I. 233–5; (2) Gallus, I. 21, 151, 165, 327; II. 153; (3) Gallus (son of Pollio), II. 9, n., 11; (4) Rufus (father of (1)), I. 321–3.
Asudius, cf. Curianus.
Athenodorus, II. 69–73.
Athens, Athenians, Attic, I. 279, 498, n.; II. 65, 69, 71, 168, n., 169, 229, 237–9.

441

# INDEX OF NAMES AND PLACES

# INDEX OF NAMES AND PLACES

# INDEX OF NAMES AND PLACES

# INDEX OF NAMES AND PLACES

445

# INDEX OF NAMES AND PLACES

## M

Macedo, cf. Larcius.

Macedon, II. 168, n.

Macer, cf. Baebius, Calpurnius.

Macrinus, (1) Caecilius, I. 113, 191–3, 143, 183; II. 13, 29, 103; (2) cf. Minicius.

Magnus, cf. Fonteius, Pompeius.

Malea, II. 297.

Mamilianus, II. 215, 231.

Mancia, cf. Curtilius.

Marcellinus, (1) Aefulanus, I. 421; II. 165; (2) Claudius, I. 131; (3) cf. Egnatius.

Marcianus, Flavius, I. 127, 131–3.

Marcus, (1) Freedman of Pliny, II. 105; (2) cf. Antonius.

Marinus, cf. Postumius.

Marius, (1) Caius, II. 105; (2) cf. Priscus.

Mars, II. 25, 234, n.

Marsian, estate, I. 149.

Martial, I. xv, 266, n., 267–9.

Maturus, cf. Arrianus.

Mauricus, Junius, (B.I.), I. 15, 17, 49, 165, 235, 339, 471.

Maximilla, cf. Antonia.

Maximus, (1) I. 143, 461, 465, 535; II. 67, 153, 169, 172, n., 177, 277; (2) a Baker, II. 375; (3) a Freedman of Trajan, II. 300, 311, 391; (4) Messius, I. 263, 345; (5) Valerius, I. 218, n.; (6) Vibius, I. 187; (7) cf. Anicius, Appius, Laberius, Nonius, Terentius.

Melmoth, I. v–vii, and notes *passim*.

Memmius, I. 369.

Memphis, II. 291.

Menander, I. 499.

Messala, I. 369.

Messalinus Catullus, I. 345.

Messius, cf. Maximus.

Metilius, cf. Crispus, Nepos.

Mettius Carus, (B.I.), I. 11; II. 49, 75.

Misias, II. 81.

Milan, I. 307, n., 311, 417, n.; II. 59.

Minerva, I. 19, 269; II. 25.

Minicianus, Cornelius, I. 215, 301; II. 57, 123.

Minicius, (1) Acilianus, I. 49, 51, 53; (2) Fundanus, I. 31, 321–5,

421, 425, 453; daughter of, I. 421–5; (3) Macrinus, I. 49, 51; (4) Rufus, II. 373; (5) cf. Justus.

Misenum, I. 477 ff., 491–7.

Mithridates, II. 293, 380, n.

Mnestheus, I. 400, n.

Modena, I. 417, n.

Modestus, (1) I. 11, 12, n., 13, 15, 17; (2) slave to Sabina, I. 301.

Moesia, II. 232, n., 335, 375.

Montanus, (1) II. 77, 103; (2) cf. Atticinus.

Mummius, I. 204, n.; II. 105.

Murena, (1) I. 67; (2) a Tribune, II. 207.

Musonius, I. 234, n., 235.

Mustius, II. 267.

## N

Naples, I. 207, 211.

Narnia, I. 9.

Naso, Julius, I. 283, 453–7, 463.

Nemausius, (Nimes), II. 322, n.

Nemean Games, II. 427.

Nepos, (1) I. 97, 247, 487, perhaps (3); (2) Cornelius, I. 351, 369; (3) Metilius (or Maecilius), I. 347; (4) cf. Licinius, Varidisius.

Neratius, (1) Marcellus, I. 213; (2) cf. Priscus.

Nero, (1) Emp., I. 11, 90, n., 91, 93, 197, 209, 211, 234, n., 250, n., 369, 375, 525; II. 63, n., 187, n.; (2) Drusus, I. 196, n., 197.

Nerva, (1) Emp., I. xii, xiii, 90 n., 91, 93, 117, 119, 212, n. (?), 291, 293, 307–9, 329, 339, 369; II. 82, n., 83, 89, 126, n., 198, n., 199, 200, n., 209 and n., 274, n., 275, 277 and n., 281, 287, 351–3, 385, n.; (2) cf. Acutius.

Nicaea, II. 315, 320, n., 325, 329, 360, n., 367, 385, 389.

Nicetes, I. 455.

Nicomedia, II. 307, 315, 319, 320, n., 323, 325, 331, 339, 375.

Nigrinus, (1) I. 415, 435; II. 15; (2) cf. Avidius.

Nomenclatores, I. 145, n.

Nominatus, cf. Tuscilius.

Nonianus, I. 47.

Nonius, (1) II. 247; (2) Celer, I. 529; (3) Maximus, I. 335, 373.

446

# INDEX OF NAMES AND PLACES

447

# INDEX OF NAMES AND PLACES

# INDEX OF NAMES AND PLACES

449

# INDEX OF NAMES AND PLACES

PRINTED IN GREAT BRITAIN BY RICHARD CLAY AND COMPANY, LTD.,
BUNGAY, SUFFOLK.

# THE LOEB CLASSICAL LIBRARY

## VOLUMES ALREADY PUBLISHED

### *Latin Authors*

AMMIANUS MARCELLINUS. Translated by J. C. Rolfe. 3 Vols. (*3rd Imp., revised.*)

APULEIUS: THE GOLDEN ASS (METAMORPHOSES). W. Adlington (1566). Revised by S. Gaselee. (*8th Imp.*)

S. AUGUSTINE: CITY OF GOD. 7 Vols. Vol. I. G. E. McCracken.

ST. AUGUSTINE, CONFESSIONS OF. W. Watts (1631). 2 Vols. (Vol. I. 7*th Imp.*, Vol. II. 6*th Imp.*)

ST. AUGUSTINE, SELECT LETTERS. J. H. Baxter. (*2nd Imp.*)

AUSONIUS. H. G. Evelyn White. 2 Vols. (*2nd Imp.*)

BEDE. J. E. King. 2 Vols. (*2nd Imp.*)

BOETHIUS: TRACTS and DE CONSOLATIONE PHILOSOPHIAE. Rev. H. F. Stewart and E. K. Rand. (*6th Imp.*)

CAESAR: ALEXANDRIAN, AFRICAN and SPANISH WARS. A. G. Way.

CAESAR: CIVIL WARS. A. G. Peskett. (*6th Imp* )

CAESAR: GALLIC WAR. H. J. Edwards. (*11th Imp.*)

CATO: DE RE RUSTICA; VARRO: DE RE RUSTICA. H. B. Ash and W. D. Hooper. (*3rd Imp.*)

CATULLUS. F. W. Cornish; TIBULLUS. J. B. Postgate; PERVIGILIUM VENERIS. J. W. Mackail. (*13th Imp.*)

CELSUS: DE MEDICINA. W. G. Spencer. 3 Vols. (Vol. I. 3*rd Imp.* revised, Vols. II. and III. 2*nd Imp.*)

CICERO: BRUTUS, and ORATOR. G. L. Hendrickson and H. M. Hubbell. (*3rd Imp.*)

[CICERO]: AD HERENNIUM. H. Caplan.

CICERO: DE FATO; PARADOXA STOICORUM; DE PARTITIONE ORATORIA. H. Rackham (With De Oratore. Vol. II.) (*2nd Imp.*)

CICERO: DE FINIBUS. H. Rackham. (*4th Imp. revised.*)

CICERO: DE INVENTIONE, etc. H. M. Hubbell.

CICERO: DE NATURA DEORUM and ACADEMICA. H. Rackham. (*3rd Imp.*)

CICERO: DE OFFICIIS. Walter Miller. (*7th Imp.*)

CICERO: DE ORATORE. 2 Vols. E. W. Sutton and H. Rackham. (*2nd Imp.*)

CICERO: DE REPUBLICA and DE LEGIBUS; SOMNIUM SCIPIONIS. Clinton W. Keyes. (*4th Imp.*)

CICERO: DE SENECTUTE, DE AMICITIA, DE DIVINATIONE. W. A. Falconer. (*6th Imp.*)

CICERO: IN CATILINAM, PRO FLACCO, PRO MURENA, PRO SULLA. Louis E. Lord. (*3rd Imp. revised.*)

CICERO: LETTERS TO ATTICUS. E. O. Winstedt. 3 Vols. (Vol. I. 7th *Imp.*, Vols. II. and III. 4th *Imp.*)
CICERO: LETTERS TO HIS FRIENDS. W. Glynn Williams. 3 Vols. (Vols. I. and II. 4th *Imp.*, Vol. III. 2nd *Imp. revised.*)
CICERO: PHILIPPICS. W. C. A. Ker. (4th *Imp. revised.*)
CICERO: PRO ARCHIA, POST REDITUM, DE DOMO, DE HARUSPICUM RESPONSIS, PRO PLANCIO. N. H. Watts. (3rd *Imp.*)
CICERO: PRO CAECINA, PRO LEGE MANILIA, PRO CLUENTIO, PRO RABIRIO. H. Grose Hodge. (3rd *Imp.*)
CICERO: PRO CAELIO, DE PROVINCIIS CONSULARIBUS. PRO BALBO. R. Gardner.
CICERO: PRO MILONE, IN PISONEM, PRO SCAURO, PRO FONTEIO. PRO RABIRIO POSTUMO, PRO MARCELLO, PRO LIGARIO, PRO REGE DEIOTARO. N. H. Watts. (3rd *Imp.*)
CICERO: PRO QUINCTIO, PRO ROSCIO AMERINO, PRO ROSCIO COMOEDO, CONTRA RULLUM. J. H. Freese. (3rd *Imp.*)
CICERO: PRO SESTIO, IN VATINIUM. R. Gardner.
CICERO: TUSCULAN DISPUTATIONS. J. E. King. (4th *Imp.*)
CICERO: VERRINE ORATIONS. L. H. G. Greenwood. 2 Vols. (Vol. I. 3rd *Imp.*, Vol. II. 2nd *Imp.*)
CLAUDIAN. M. Platnauer. 2 Vols. (2nd *Imp.*)
COLUMELLA: DE RE RUSTICA. DE ARBORIBUS. H. B. Ash, E. S. Forster and E. Heffner. 3 Vols. (Vol. I. 2nd *Imp.*)
CURTIUS, Q.: HISTORY OF ALEXANDER. J. C. Rolfe. 2 Vols. (2nd *Imp.*)
FLORUS. E. S. Forster and CORNELIUS NEPOS. J. C. Rolfe. (2nd *Imp.*)
FRONTINUS: STRATAGEMS and AQUEDUCTS. C. E. Bennett and M. B. McElwain. (2nd *Imp.*)
FRONTO: CORRESPONDENCE. C. R. Haines. 2 Vols. (3rd *Imp.*)
GELLIUS, J. C. Rolfe. 3 Vols. (Vol. I. 3rd *Imp.*, Vols. II. and III. 2nd *Imp.*)
HORACE: ODES and EPODES. C. E. Bennett. (14th *Imp. revised.*)
HORACE: SATIRES, EPISTLES, ARS POETICA. H. R. Fairclough. (9th *Imp. revised.*)
JEROME: SELECTED LETTERS. F. A. Wright. (2nd *Imp.*)
JUVENAL and PERSIUS. G. G. Ramsay. (8th *Imp.*)
LIVY. B. O. Foster, F. G. Moore, Evan T. Sage, and A. C. Schlesinger and R. M. Geer (General Index). 14 Vols. (Vol. I. 5th *Imp.*, Vol. V. 4th *Imp.*, Vols. II.–IV., VI. and VII., IX.–XII. 3rd *Imp.*, Vol. VIII., 2nd *Imp. revised.*)
LUCAN. J. D. Duff. (4th *Imp.*)
LUCRETIUS. W. H. D. Rouse. (7th *Imp. revised.*)
MARTIAL. W. C. A. Ker. 2 Vols. (Vol. I. 5th *Imp.*, Vol. II. 4th *Imp. revised.*)
MINOR LATIN POETS: from PUBLILIUS SYRUS to RUTILIUS NAMATIANUS, including GRATTIUS, CALPURNIUS SICULUS, NEMESIANUS, AVIANUS, and others with " Aetna " and the " Phoenix." J. Wight Duff and Arnold M. Duff. (3rd *Imp.*)

2

OVID: THE ART OF LOVE and OTHER POEMS. J. H. Mozley. (4th Imp.)
OVID: FASTI. Sir James G. Frazer. (2nd Imp.)
OVID: HEROIDES and AMORES. Grant Showerman. (7th Imp.)
OVID: METAMORPHOSES. F. J. Miller. 2 Vols. (Vol. I. 11th Imp., Vol. II. 10th Imp.)
OVID: TRISTIA and EX PONTO. A. L. Wheeler. (4th Imp.)
PERSIUS. Cf. JUVENAL.
PETRONIUS. M. Heseltine, SENECA APOCOLOCYNTOSIS. W. H. D. Rouse. (9th Imp. revised.)
PLAUTUS. Paul Nixon. 5 Vols. (Vol. I. 6th Imp., II. 5th Imp., III. 4th Imp., IV. and V. 2nd Imp.)
PLINY: LETTERS. Melmoth's Translation revised by W. M. L. Hutchinson. 2 Vols. (7th Imp.)
PLINY: NATURAL HISTORY. H. Rackham and W. H. S. Jones. 10 Vols. Vols. I.–V. and IX. H. Rackham. Vols. VI. and VII. W. H. S. Jones. (Vol. I. 4th Imp., Vols. II. and III. 3rd Imp., Vol. IV. 2nd Imp.)
PROPERTIUS. H. E. Butler. (7th Imp.)
PRUDENTIUS. H. J. Thomson. 2 Vols.
QUINTILIAN. H. E. Butler. 4 Vols. (Vols. I. and IV. 4th Imp., Vols. II. and III. 3rd Imp.)
REMAINS OF OLD LATIN. E. H. Warmington. 4 vols. Vol. I. (ENNIUS AND CAECILIUS.) Vol. II. (LIVIUS, NAEVIUS, PACUVIUS, ACCIUS.) Vol. III. (LUCILIUS and LAWS OF XII TABLES.) (2nd Imp.) (ARCHAIC INSCRIPTIONS.)
SALLUST. J. C. Rolfe. (4th Imp. revised.)
SCRIPTORES HISTORIAE AUGUSTAE. D. Magie. 3 Vols. (Vol. I. 3rd Imp. revised, Vols. II. and III. 2nd Imp.)
SENECA: APOCOLOCYNTOSIS. Cf. PETRONIUS.
SENECA: EPISTULAE MORALES. R. M. Gummere. 3 Vols. (Vol. I. 4th Imp., Vols. II. and III. 3rd Imp.)
SENECA: MORAL ESSAYS. J. W. Basore. 3 Vols. (Vol. II. 4th Imp., Vols. I. and III. 2nd Imp. revised.)
SENECA: TRAGEDIES. F. J. Miller. 2 Vols. (Vol. I. 4th Imp. Vol. II. 3rd Imp. revised.)
SIDONIUS: POEMS AND LETTERS. W. B. Anderson. 2 Vols. (Vol. I. 2nd Imp.)
SILIUS ITALICUS. J. D. Duff. 2 Vols. (Vol. I. 2nd Imp. Vol. II. 3rd Imp.)
STATIUS. J. H. Mozley. 2 Vols. (2nd Imp.)
SUETONIUS. J. C. Rolfe. 2 Vols. (Vol. I. 7th Imp., Vol. II. 6th Imp. revised.)
TACITUS: DIALOGUES. Sir Wm. Peterson. AGRICOLA and GERMANIA. Maurice Hutton. (7th Imp.)
TACITUS: HISTORIES AND ANNALS. C. H. Moore and J. Jackson. 4 Vols.. (Vols. I. and II. 4th Imp. Vols. III. and IV. 3rd Imp.)
TERENCE. John Sargeaunt. 2 Vols. (Vol. I. 8th Imp., Vol. II. 7th Imp.)
TERTULLIAN: APOLOGIA and DE SPECTACULIS. T. R. Glover. MINUCIUS FELIX. G. H. Rendall. (2nd Imp.)
VALERIUS FLACCUS. J. H. Mozley. (3rd Imp. revised.)

Varro: De Lingua Latina. R. G. Kent. 2 Vols. (*3rd Imp. revised.*)
Velleius Paterculus and Res Gestae Divi Augusti. F. W. Shipley. (*2nd Imp.*)
Virgil. H. R. Fairclough. 2 Vols. (Vol. I. 19*th Imp.*, Vol. II. 14*th Imp. revised.*)
Vitruvius: De Architectura. F. Granger. 2 Vols. (Vol. I. 3*rd Imp.*, Vol. II. 2*nd Imp.*)

## Greek Authors

Achilles Tatius. S. Gaselee. (*2nd Imp.*)
Aelian: On the Nature of Animals. 3 Vols. Vols. I. and II. A. F. Scholfield.
Aeneas Tacticus, Asclepiodotus and Onasander. The Illinois Greek Club. (*2nd Imp.*)
Aeschines. C. D. Adams. (*3rd Imp.*)
Aeschylus. H. Weir Smyth. 2 Vols. (Vol. I. 7*th Imp.*, Vol. II. 6*th Imp. revised.*)
Alciphron, Aelian, Philostratus Letters. A. R. Benner and F. H. Fobes.
Andocides, Antiphon, Cf. Minor Attic Orators.
Apollodorus. Sir James G. Frazer. 2 Vols. (*3rd Imp.*)
Apollonius Rhodius. R. C. Seaton. (*5th Imp.*)
The Apostolic Fathers. Kirsopp Lake. 2 Vols. (Vol. I. 8*th Imp.*, Vol. II. 6*th Imp.*)
Appian: Roman History. Horace White. 4 Vols. (Vol. I. 4*th Imp.*, Vols. II.–IV. 3*rd Imp.*)
Aratus. Cf. Callimachus.
Aristophanes. Benjamin Bickley Rogers. 3 Vols. Verse trans. (*5th Imp.*)
Aristotle: Art of Rhetoric. J. H. Freese. (*3rd Imp.*)
Aristotle: Athenian Constitution, Eudemian Ethics, Vices and Virtues. H. Rackham. (*3rd Imp.*)
Aristotle: Generation of Animals. A. L. Peck. (*2nd Imp.*)
Aristotle: Metaphysics. H. Tredennick. 2 Vols. (4*th Imp.*)
Aristotle: Meteorologica. H. D. P. Lee.
Aristotle: Minor Works. W. S. Hett. On Colours, On Things Heard, On Physiognomies, On Plants, On Marvellous Things Heard, Mechanical Problems, On Indivisible Lines, On Situations and Names of Winds, On Mellissus, Xenophanes, and Gorgias. (*2nd Imp.*)
Aristotle: Nicomachean Ethics. H. Rackham. (6*th Imp. revised.*)
Aristotle: Oeconomica and Magna Moralia. G. C. Armstrong; (with Metaphysics, Vol. II.). (4*th Imp.*)
Aristotle: On the Heavens. W. K. C. Guthrie. (*3rd Imp. revised.*)
Aristotle: On the Soul, Parva Naturalia, On Breath. W. S. Hett. (*2nd Imp. revised.*)

4

ARISTOTLE: ORGANON—Categories, On Interpretation, Prior Analytics. H. P. Cooke and H. Tredennick. (3rd Imp.)
ARISTOTLE: ORGANON—Posterior Analytics, Topics. H. Tredennick and E. S. Forster.
ARISTOTLE: ORGANON—On Sophistical Refutations.
On Coming to be and Passing Away, On the Cosmos. E. S. Forster and D. J. Furley.
ARISTOTLE: PARTS OF ANIMALS. A. L. Peck; MOTION AND PROGRESSION OF ANIMALS. E. S. Forster. (4th Imp. revised.)
ARISTOTLE: PHYSICS. Rev. P. Wicksteed and F. M. Cornford. 2 Vols. (Vol. I. 2nd Imp., Vol. II. 3rd Imp.)
ARISTOTLE: POETICS and LONGINUS. W. Hamilton Fyfe; DEMETRIUS ON STYLE. W. Rhys Roberts. (5th Imp. revised.)
ARISTOTLE: POLITICS. H. Rackham. (4th Imp. revised.)
ARISTOTLE: PROBLEMS. W. S. Hett. 2 Vols. (2nd Imp. revised.)
ARISTOTLE: RHETORICA AD ALEXANDRUM (with PROBLEMS. Vol. II.). H. Rackham.
ARRIAN: HISTORY OF ALEXANDER and INDICA. Rev. E. Iliffe Robson. 2 Vols. (3rd Imp.)
ATHENAEUS: DEIPNOSOPHISTAE. C. B. Gulick. 7 Vols. (Vols. I.–IV., VI. and VII. 2nd Imp., Vol. V. 3rd Imp.)
ST. BASIL: LETTERS. R. J. Deferrari. 4 Vols. (2nd Imp.)
CALLIMACHUS: FRAGMENTS. C. A. Trypanis.
CALLIMACHUS, Hymns and Epigrams, and LYCOPHRON. A. W. Mair; ARATUS. G. R. Mair. (2nd. Imp.)
CLEMENT of ALEXANDRIA. Rev. G. W. Butterworth. (3rd Imp.)
COLLUTHUS. Cf. OPPIAN.
DAPHNIS AND CHLOE. Thornley's Translation revised by J. M. Edmonds; and PARTHENIUS. S. Gaselee. (4th Imp.)
DEMOSTHENES I.: OLYNTHIACS, PHILIPPICS and MINOR ORATIONS. I.–XVII. AND XX. J. H. Vince. (2nd Imp.)
DEMOSTHENES II.: DE CORONA and DE FALSA LEGATIONE. C. A. Vince and J. H. Vince. (3rd Imp. revised.)
DEMOSTHENES III.: MEIDIAS, ANDROTION, ARISTOCRATES, TIMOCRATES and ARISTOGEITON, I. AND II. J. H. Vince (2nd Imp.)
DEMOSTHENES IV.–VI.: PRIVATE ORATIONS and IN NEAERAM. A. T. Murray. (Vol. IV. 3rd Imp., Vols. V. and VI. 2nd Imp.)
DEMOSTHENES VII.: FUNERAL SPEECH, EROTIC ESSAY, EXORDIA and LETTERS. N. W. and N. J. DeWitt.
DIO CASSIUS: ROMAN HISTORY. E. Cary. 9 Vols. (Vols. I. and II. 3rd Imp., Vols. III.–IX. 2nd Imp.)
DIO CHRYSOSTOM. J. W. Cohoon and H. Lamar Crosby. 5 Vols. (Vols. I.–IV. 2nd Imp.)
DIODORUS SICULUS. 12 Vols. Vols. I.–VI. C. H. Oldfather. Vol. VII. C. L. Sherman. Vols. IX. and X. R. M. Geer. Vol. XI. F. Walton. (Vol. I. 3rd Imp., Vols. II.–IV. 2nd Imp.)
DIOGENES LAERTIUS. R. D. Hicks. 2 Vols. (5th Imp.)
DIONYSIUS OF HALICARNASSUS: ROMAN ANTIQUITIES. Spelman's translation revised by E. Cary. 7 Vols. (Vols. I.–V. 2nd Imp.)

5

EPICTETUS. W. A. Oldfather. 2 Vols. (*3rd Imp.*)

EURIPIDES. A. S. Way. 4 Vols. (Vols. I. and IV. *7th Imp.*, Vol. II. *8th Imp.*, Vol. III. *6th Imp.*) Verse trans.

EUSEBIUS: ECCLESIASTICAL HISTORY. Kirsopp Lake and J. E. L. Oulton. 2 Vols. (Vol. I. *3rd Imp.*, Vol. II. *5th Imp.*)

GALEN: ON THE NATURAL FACULTIES. A. J. Brock. (*4th Imp.*)

THE GREEK ANTHOLOGY. W. R. Paton. 5 Vols. (Vols. I.–IV. *5th Imp.*, Vol. V. *3rd Imp.*)

GREEK ELEGY AND IAMBUS with the ANACREONTEA. J. M. Edmonds. 2 Vols. (Vol. I. *3rd Imp.*, Vol. II. *2nd Imp.*)

THE GREEK BUCOLIC POETS (THEOCRITUS, BION, MOSCHUS). J. M. Edmonds. (*7th Imp. revised.*)

GREEK MATHEMATICAL WORKS. Ivor Thomas. 2 Vols. (*3rd Imp.*)

HERODES. Cf. THEOPHRASTUS: CHARACTERS.

HERODOTUS. A. D. Godley. 4 Vols. (Vol. I. *4th Imp.*, Vols. II. and III. *5th Imp.*, Vol. IV. *3rd Imp.*)

HESIOD AND THE HOMERIC HYMNS. H. G. Evelyn White. (*7th Imp. revised and enlarged.*)

HIPPOCRATES and the FRAGMENTS OF HERACLEITUS. W. H. S. Jones and E. T. Withington. 4 Vols. (Vol. I. *4th Imp.*, Vols. II.–IV. *3rd Imp.*)

HOMER: ILIAD. A. T. Murray. 2 Vols. (*7th Imp.*)

HOMER: ODYSSEY. A. T. Murray. 2 Vols. (*8th Imp.*)

ISAEUS. E. W. Forster. (*3rd Imp.*)

ISOCRATES. George Norlin and LaRue Van Hook. 3 Vols. (*2nd Imp.*)

ST. JOHN DAMASCENE: BARLAAM AND IOASAPH. Rev. G. R. Woodward and Harold Mattingly. (*3rd Imp. revised.*)

JOSEPHUS. H. St. J. Thackeray and Ralph Marcus. 9 Vols. Vols. I.–VII. (Vol. V. *4th Imp.*, Vol. VI. *3rd Imp.*, Vols .I.–IV. and VII. *2nd Imp.*)

JULIAN. Wilmer Cave Wright. 3 Vols. (Vols. I. and II. *3rd Imp.*, Vol. III. *2nd Imp.*)

LUCIAN. A. M. Harmon. 8 Vols. Vols. I.–V. (Vols. I. and II. *4th Imp.*, Vol. III. *3rd Imp.*, Vols. IV. and V. *2nd Imp.*)

LYCOPHRON. Cf. CALLIMACHUS.

LYRA GRAECA. J. M. Edmonds. 3 Vols. (Vol. I. *5th Imp.* Vol. II *revised and enlarged*, and III. *4th Imp.*)

LYSIAS. W. R. M. Lamb. (*3rd Imp.*)

MANETHO. W. G. Waddell: PTOLEMY: TETRABIBLOS. F. E. Robbins. (*3rd Imp.*)

MARCUS AURELIUS. C. R. Haines. (*4th Imp. revised.*)

MENANDER. F. G. Allinson. (*3rd Imp. revised.*)

MINOR ATTIC ORATORS (ANTIPHON, ANDOCIDES, LYCURGUS, DEMADES, DINARCHUS, HYPEREIDES). K. J. Maidment and J. O. Burrt. 2 Vols. (Vol. I. *2nd Imp.*)

NONNOS: DIONYSIACA. W. H. D. Rouse. 3 Vols. (*2nd Imp.*)

OPPIAN, COLLUTHUS, TRYPHIODORUS. A. W. Mair. (*2nd Imp.*)

PAPYRI. NON-LITERARY SELECTIONS. A. S. Hunt and C. C. Edgar. 2 Vols. (*2nd Imp.*) LITERARY SELECTIONS. (Poetry). D. L. Page. (*3rd Imp.*)

PARTHENIUS. Cf. DAPHNIS AND CHLOE.
PAUSANIAS: DESCRIPTION OF GREECE. W. H. S. Jones. 5 Vols. and Companion Vol. arranged by R. E. Wycherley. (Vols. I. and III. 3rd Imp., Vols. II., IV. and V. 2nd Imp.)
PHILO. 10 Vols. Vols. I.–V.; F. H. Colson and Rev. G. H. Whitaker Vols. VI.–IX.; F. H. Colson. (Vols. I–II., V.–VII., 3rd Imp., Vol. IV. 4th Imp., Vols. III., VIII., and IX. 2nd Imp.)
PHILO: two supplementary Vols. (Translation only.) Ralph Marcus.
PHILOSTRATUS: THE LIFE OF APPOLLONIUS OF TYANA. F. C. Conybeare. 2 Vols. (Vol. I. 4th Imp., Vol. II. 3rd Imp.)
PHILOSTRATUS: IMAGINES; CALLISTRATUS: DESCRIPTIONS. A. Fairbanks. (2nd Imp.)
PHILOSTRATUS and EUNAPIUS: LIVES OF THE SOPHISTS. Wilmer Cave Wright. (2nd Imp.)
PINDAR. Sir J. E. Sandys. (8th Imp. revised.)
PLATO: CHARMIDES, ALCIBIADES, HIPPARCHUS, THE LOVERS, THEAGES, MINOS and EPINOMIS. W. R. M. Lamb. (2nd Imp.)
PLATO: CRATYLUS, PARMENIDES, GREATER HIPPIAS, LESSER HIPPIAS. H. N. Fowler. (4th Imp.)
PLATO: EUTHYPHRO, APOLOGY, CRITO, PHAEDO, PHAEDRUS. H. N. Fowler. (11th Imp.)
PLATO: LACHES, PROTAGORAS, MENO, EUTHYDEMUS. W. R. M. Lamb. (3rd Imp. revised.)
PLATO: LAWS. Rev. R. G. Bury. 2 Vols. (3rd Imp.)
PLATO: LYSIS, SYMPOSIUM GORGIAS. W. R. M. Lamb. (5th Imp. revised.)
PLATO: REPUBLIC. Paul Shorey. 2 Vols. (Vol. I. 5th Imp., Vol. II. 4th Imp.)
PLATO: STATESMAN, PHILEBUS. H. N. Fowler; ION. W. R. M. Lamb. (4th Imp.)
PLATO: THEAETETUS and SOPHIST. H. N. Fowler. (4th Imp.)
PLATO: TIMAEUS, CRITIAS, CLITOPHO, MENEXENUS, EPISTULAE. Rev. R. G. Bury. (3rd Imp.)
PLUTARCH: MORALIA. 14 Vols. Vols. I.–V. F. C. Babbitt. Vol. VI. W. C. Helmbold. Vol. VII. P. H. De Lacey and B. Einarson. Vol. X. H. N. Fowler. Vol. XII. H. Cherniss and W. C. Helmbold. (Vols. I.–VI. and X. 2nd Imp.)
PLUTARCH: THE PARALLEL LIVES. B. Perrin. 11 Vols. (Vols. I., II., VI., VII., and XI. 3rd Imp., Vols. III.–V. and VIII.–X. 2nd Imp.)
POLYBIUS. W. R. Paton. 6 Vols. (2nd Imp.)
PROCOPIUS: HISTORY OF THE WARS. H. B. Dewing. 7 Vols. (Vol. I. 3rd Imp., Vols. II.–VII. 2nd Imp.)
PTOLEMY: TETRABIBLOS. Cf. MANETHO.
QUINTUS SMYRNAEUS. A. S. Way. Verse trans. (3rd Imp.)
SEXTUS EMPIRICUS. Rev. R. G. Bury. 4 Vols. (Vol. I. 4th Imp., Vols. II. and III. 2nd Imp.)
SOPHOCLES. F. Storr. 2 Vols. (Vol. I. 10th Imp. Vol. II. 6th Imp.) Verse trans.

7

STRABO: GEOGRAPHY. Horace L. Jones. 8 Vols. (Vols. I., V., and VIII. 3rd *Imp.*, Vols. II., III., IV., VI., and VII. 2nd *Imp.*)

THEOPHRASTUS: CHARACTERS. J. M. Edmonds. HERODES, etc. A. D. Knox. (3rd *Imp.*)

THEOPHRASTUS: ENQUIRY INTO PLANTS. Sir Arthur Hort, Bart. 2 Vols. (2nd *Imp.*)

THUCYDIDES. C. F. Smith. 4 Vols. (Vol. I. 5th *Imp.*, Vols. II. and IV. 4th *Imp.*, Vol. III., 3rd *Imp. revised.*)

TRYPHIODOBUS. Cf. OPPIAN.

XENOPHON: CYROPAEDIA. Walter Miller. 2 Vols. (Vol. I. 4th *Imp.*, Vol. II. 3rd *Imp.*)

XENOPHON: HELLENICA, ANABASIS, APOLOGY, and SYMPOSIUM. C. L. Brownson and O. J. Todd. 3 Vols. (Vols. I. and III 3rd *Imp.*, Vol. II. 4th *Imp.*)

XENOPHON: MEMORABILIA and OECONOMICUS. E. C. Marchant (3rd *Imp.*)

XENOPHON: SCRIPTA MINORA. E. C. Marchant. (3rd *Imp.*)

---

## IN PREPARATION

---

### *Greek Authors*

ARISTOTLE: HISTORY OF ANIMALS. A. L. Peck.
PLOTINUS: A. H. Armstrong.

### *Latin Authors*

BABRIUS AND PHAEDRUS. Ben E. Perry.

---

### *DESCRIPTIVE PROSPECTUS ON APPLICATION*

---

London
Cambridge, Mass.

**WILLIAM HEINEMANN LTD
HARVARD UNIVERSITY PRESS**